Imperial Crossroads

Imperial Crossroads

The Great Powers and the Persian Gulf

EDITED BY
JEFFREY R. MACRIS AND SAUL KELLY

Naval Institute Press
Annapolis, Maryland

Naval Institute Press
291 Wood Road
Annapolis, MD 21402

Library of Congress Cataloging-in-Publication Data
Imperial crossroads : the great powers and the Persian Gulf / edited by Jeffrey R.
Macris and Saul Kelly.
    p. cm.
  Includes bibliographical references and index.
  ISBN 978-1-59114-489-2 (hardcover : alk. paper) 1. Persian Gulf Region—
Foreign relations. 2. Persian Gulf Region—Strategic aspects. 3. Persian
Gulf Region—History. 4. Great powers—History. I. Macris, Jeffrey R. II.
Kelly, Saul, 1957–
  DS326.I52 2012
  953—dc23

                              2012008457

∞ This paper meets the requirements of ANSI/NISO z39.48-1992
(Permanence of Paper).
Printed in the United States of America.

20 19 18 17 16 15 14 13 12   9 8 7 6 5 4 3 2 1
First printing

*The views expressed in this work reflect those of the individual authors, and not
necessarily those of the U.S. or UK governments, any branch of their military services,
or any academic institution affiliated with them.*

FOR OUR PARENTS

Contents

For centuries the world's great powers, along with their fleets, armies, and intelligence services, have been drawn to the Persian Gulf region. Lying at the junction of three great continents—Asia, Europe, and Africa—and sitting athwart the oceanic trade routes that link the cities of the world, the Gulf, like a magnet, has pulled superpowers into the shallow waters and adjacent lands of the six-hundred-mile-long appendage of the Indian Ocean. An observer at Hormuz at the mouth of the Gulf would alternately have watched pass in the fifteenth century the treasure ships of Chinese admiral Zheng He, in the sixteenth century the caravels of Portuguese admiral Afonso de Albuquerque, in the seventeenth century the merchant ships of the Dutch East India Company, in the eighteenth to the twentieth centuries the frigates and steamships of the British, and finally in the late twentieth century to today, the cruisers and aircraft carriers of the U.S. Fifth Fleet. Perhaps in the future the Americans may be supplanted by the Indians, or maybe the Chinese.

In the great powers' comings and goings since the 1400s, several consistent broad interests emerged. For the majority of this time, for example, the superpowers entered the Gulf region not to colonize, as the Europeans did in other places, but rather to further trade, which in the twentieth century increasingly included oil. They also sought a military presence in the Gulf to protect seaborne flanks to colonial possessions farther east, on the Indian subcontinent and beyond; India, in fact, has long cast a shadow over the Gulf, given its historic trade and cultural ties to the Gulf region, strong ties that continue today. In their geopolitical jockeying, furthermore, the great powers sought to deprive their rivals of access to the states bordering the Gulf region. In tending to these enduring interests inside the Strait of Hormuz, the great powers, throughout history, concentrated their trade, political, and military presence along the coasts and in the littorals. Not surprisingly, their navies have played a substantive role.

Imperial Crossroads is a collection of connected chapters, each of which investigates a different perspective in the broader subject of the great powers and their involvement with the states of the Persian Gulf. This volume concentrates on four Western nations—Portugal, Holland, Britain, and the United States—and concludes with a look at the possible future involvement of two rising Asian powers—China and India. This book emerged from the proceedings of the Gulf and the Globe conferences, a series of interdisciplinary gatherings of distinguished historians, political scientists, military officers, diplomats, and businessmen from around the world, the first of which took place in Annapolis, Maryland, in 2009, jointly sponsored by the U.S. Naval Academy's Center for Middle East and Islamic Studies, and the UK's Joint Services Command and Staff College's Corbett Centre for Maritime Policy Studies.

That the diminutive coastal states of Portugal and the Dutch Republic played a prominent role in the affairs of the Persian Gulf in the sixteenth and seventeenth centuries is remarkable. The states, after all, were physically small—together, both would fit into the American state of Pennsylvania—with populations to match their sizes. Both states shared a deep maritime heritage, however. Portugal's position alongside the Atlantic at the westernmost point of Europe, for example, made its people naturally turn toward the sea. Likewise, during the late European Middle Ages, Dutch merchants set off from their ports on the North Sea to trade with others in the Hanseatic League.

Prince Henry the Navigator launched the Portuguese into their leading role in the Age of Discovery with his founding in the early 1400s of a school that brought together shipbuilders, cartographers, and sailors. Shortly thereafter Portuguese sailors probed the western coast of Africa, sailing south of the legendary sea monsters of Cape Bojador, past which no European had dared to venture. In the 1480s the Portuguese rounded the Cape of Good Hope, and in 1498 Vasco da Gama arrived on the west coast of India. Taking advantage of the maneuverability of their seagoing ships and the long range of their cannon, the Portuguese dominated their lightly armed foes in Africa and Asia, and shattered the monopoly on trade with the East that for centuries had been the preserve of the Muslim empires of the Middle East. For the next century the Indian Ocean became a virtual Portuguese sea. But Portugal's preeminence in the Indian Ocean would be challenged by other Atlantic powers. By the mid-1600s the English, Dutch, and French all had East Indies trading companies vying for markets and ports in the region.

Rudi Matthee opens the book with an overview of the Portuguese involvement in the Gulf in the sixteenth to the seventeenth centuries. Matthee argues that the growing Portuguese trade empire brought Lisbon's military forces into the Gulf. Garnering an influence that far exceeded the small size of its European population, by virtue of its coastal fortification on the island of Hormuz, Portugal proved able to regulate, control, and profit from maritime traffic in and out of the Gulf. The Portuguese never colonized the Gulf with large numbers of settlers, however. Lisbon was able to maintain its preeminent position in the region by taking advantage of rivalries between local rulers, and siding with one in exchange for vassal status. Matthee discredits the commonly held contemporary Arab and Iranian view that Albuquerque's 1507 capture of Hormuz represented the start of an unbroken chain of Western imperialism in the Gulf. The Portuguese population in the Gulf, in fact, normally numbered just in the hundreds, and their reach hardly penetrated inland. The vast majority of people who lived in what we would now consider the modern Persian Gulf states never saw a Portuguese sailor or soldier.

The second chapter, by Virginia Lunsford, contends that after the departure of the Portuguese in the seventeenth and early eighteenth centuries the Dutch proved the preeminent European power in the Persian Gulf. Beginning in 1623 Holland's East India Company used its naval and military might to eject the Portuguese and suppress the growing English presence, thereby establishing a number of Dutch trade bases in the region. The most important of these was located in the Persian port of Bandar Abbas, near the Strait of Hormuz. Unlike Holland's colonial practices in the islands farther east, however, the Dutch did not attempt to subjugate the local Persian and Arab populations of the Gulf, developing instead a mutually beneficial commercial relationship with the Safavid shah's regime. In the first half of the 1700s, however, as stability within Persia deteriorated, the Dutch East India Company's fortunes in the region waned. By 1765 the company ended all operations in the Persian Gulf: the Dutch era there was over.

With the departure of the Dutch, Britain became the dominant great power in the Gulf region, and increasingly played a more expansive role in the commercial, political, and military affairs of the region. Commensurate with the decline of the Portuguese and Dutch, the fortunes of the English East India Company (EIC) rose. It was ships of the EIC, after all, that took the army of Persian shah Abbas I from the mainland to the Portuguese citadel on Hormuz Island in 1622. It was those same ships that engaged and defeated the Portuguese fleet and then blockaded the island. The eventual fall of Hormuz gave the English what they sought: a factory at Bandar Abbas and lucrative commercial links with Persia. In the second decade of the seventeenth century, furthermore, the English established trading factories at Shiraz, Isfahan, and Jask. With the departure of the Dutch in the 1760s, Britain emerged as the most prominent European great power in the Gulf, although its presence in the region at that time was limited.

The Gulf in the late 1700s and early 1800s, in fact, was characterized more by decentralized control and disorder than by British rule. The Ottomans, who after Suleiman the Magnificent's 1534 conquest of Baghdad had expanded their reach southward to include Hasa in the eastern lands of modern Saudi Arabia, had largely withdrawn by the late 1600s. Wahhabi zealots sprang out of central Arabia to spread their message of fierce Sunni monotheism. Across the Gulf in Persia, the mighty Safavid Empire disintegrated in the 1700s. From what is now the United Arab Emirates, Arab pirates attacked ships plying the waters to and from British India. Tribal fighting, furthermore, spilled out onto the seas, disrupting the lucrative pearling season, which in turn led to further brigandage.

Into these troubled waters and surrounding shores Britain increasingly deployed its diplomats and naval forces. Drawing upon Britain's superiority on the high seas, frigates and other warships sailed into the Gulf in the 1790s and early 1800s, sending redcoats ashore when needed to punish unrepentant Arabs. A British Resident—a diplomat in the employ of the British-Indian foreign service—supervised Agents throughout the Gulf. In the first half of the nineteenth century, furthermore, the British penned a series of peace treaties with the local Arab sheikhs. These treaties were designed to ensure tranquility in the Gulf, to cement Britain as the ultimate arbiter of security, and to prevent the encroachment there of other great powers. It was this last mission, denying the use of the Gulf to other rival powers, that the British aimed to fulfill when they concluded an agreement with the sultan of Oman in 1798 in response to Napoleon Bonaparte's occupation of Egypt. A chief aim of British policy in the nineteenth century, then, became preventing other great powers from drawing close to India.

In that vein, Britain's supremacy at sea was well known, and London knew that if India faced a seaborne threat from a great power rival in the 1800s, the Royal Navy and Indian navy would prevail. British leaders felt much less confident regarding military threats emanating from Central Asia, however. Czarist Russia throughout the 1700s and 1800s had pushed southward to what are now the Central Asian republics of Turkmenistan, Uzbekistan, Tajikistan, and Kyrgyzstan. How much farther would St. Petersburg's czars push? London feared they would reach all the way down to the rich lands of India. Thus, in the nineteenth century, the land approaches to India—particularly Persia and the mountains and passes of Afghanistan—took on a special significance in the Anglo-Russian struggle known as the "Great Game."

In the third chapter, Robert Johnson examines one of London's strategic dilemmas in the nineteenth century: how to establish security for its shipping lanes and territorial possessions in the Indian Ocean region. A chain of coastal stations linked Britain, the Mediterranean, and the Indian Ocean, and the vaunted Royal Navy could defend them. But the defense of India presented London with a problem: India's long land frontier was vulnerable to a land attack from expansionist Russia, whose growth in the 1800s took St. Petersburg deep into Central Asia. The British strategy that emerged involved the creation of compliant littoral states and "spheres of influence," using a combination of diplomatic power backed by the threat and periodic application of force. In the nineteenth century London viewed the strategic value of Persia as having a growing importance; Persia's position adjacent to British India also made it a target of Russian designs. Britain applied diplomatic pressure to diminish Russia's reach in Persia, ran an intelligence/influence network through its consulates there, took advantage of its ownership of the Imperial Bank of Persia, and in 1856 sent its military forces ashore on Persia's Gulf shore to compel the Persians to terminate attacks on Afghanistan.

British domination of the Persian Gulf marked most of the twentieth century. Following World War I, for example, the British installed a compliant monarch in Iraq, and directed cash to the new king in Arabia, Ibn Saud. Across the Gulf in Persia, British military officers helped to engineer the rise to power of Reza Khan, who would later declare himself shah. British warships plied the waters of the Gulf, and British warplanes flew from bases near Basra, Iraq, and Sharjah, near Dubai. British Political Residents and Political Agents—British-Indian foreign service officers—continued to ordain the foreign policies of the small emirates that ringed the Arab side of the Gulf: Kuwait, Bahrain, Qatar, Abu Dhabi, Dubai, and others. Later, in World War II, British troops invaded Baghdad to restore a friendly monarch, and a joint Anglo-Russian force invaded Iran and compelled Reza Shah to abdicate in favor of his more compliant son.

Following World War II, however, the British lost both the raison d'être for their political and military presence in the Gulf, plus the riches to pay for it: India—whose protection originally took the great power to the Gulf—gained its independence in 1947. In the decades that followed, London never quite reconciled its enduring national interests in the Gulf with its diminished postwar financial situation. Great Britain continued to deploy a naval contingent to the region's waters, kept aircraft and airborne forces ashore there, and reassured ruling sheikhs that Britain's defense commitments remained solid. But a string of financial crises in the 1960s led the ruling Labour government in 1968 to announce that within three years London would give up the bulk of its defense commitments "East of Suez," to include its paternalistic involvement in the Gulf emirates with which it had treaty relations. By the end of 1971, in other words, those Arab emirates on the western side of the Gulf that had prospered under British tutelage would be set free. In their surprise announcement, Labour leaders paid scant attention to the question of who would assume the enduring missions in the Gulf that the British had fulfilled for over a century: maintaining the free flow of trade in and around the Gulf (which increasingly involved the export of oil), maintaining interstate order, and keeping out other great powers.

Britain's twentieth-century influence is examined in several chapters. First, Saul Kelly offers a historian's retrospective of London's century and a half of patrimonial involvement in the Gulf. In the fourth chapter, he examines how the British established their dominant position in the Gulf, the challenges they faced in maintaining it, their eventual departure, and the consequences that this move elicited. Jeffrey R. Macris follows on with an analysis of the American reaction to London's announcement of its impending withdrawal from the Gulf. He argues that the Johnson administration, in the weeks and months immediately following the surprise British move, adopted a U.S. policy for the region that would endure for years. Increasingly mired in Vietnam, the White House sought to avoid entanglement in the affairs of the Gulf, to neither increase nor decrease the size of its Persian Gulf Middle East Force, and—lacking both the military wherewithal and the political will to do otherwise—to turn to Tehran and Riyadh to tend to American interests in the region. Lastly, Tore T. Petersen examines this American decision to deputize two regional "policemen" in the Gulf, Iran and Saudi Arabia. President Richard Nixon, he argues, deliberately broke up the long and successful partnership between the major Western oil companies and the Western powers, to increase oil prices so that rapidly increasing oil revenues could pay for the necessary military hardware in the Gulf. In that vein, Great Britain and the United States would tolerate no challengers in the Persian Gulf during the Nixon era. For all practical purposes, the net result, according to Petersen, was to make the Persian Gulf an Anglo-American lake.

Britain's overt departure from the Gulf in the early 1970s did not mean that London stopped trying to prolong its influence there as long as possible. Clive Jones examines the Dhofar rebellion in Oman in the 1970s. An antigovernment insurgency posed a dire threat to the British-allied Sultanate of Oman, whose defeat by Communist-funded rebels, it was believed, might pose a peril to the other conservative monarchies of the Gulf. Should the rebels prevail, London feared, radical antimonarchical movements elsewhere in the Gulf might gain momentum, threatening Western energy supplies and other interests. Despite the magnitude of the potential consequences of the uprising in Oman, very little has been written regarding the use of intelligence in the Dhofar counterinsurgency. Chapter 7 seeks to address this lacuna by exploring two key themes: how intelligence structures evolved across Oman during this period as a reaction to a Marxist-inspired insurgency in Dhofar, and secondly, how the nascent Omani intelligence service, supported by Britain, came to play an integral role in consolidating a dynastic order whose previous legitimacy had been overly dependent upon London's financial and military largesse.

Despite these successful travails to prop up the Westward-leaning regime in Oman, by the end of 1971 London had removed its military forces from inside the Strait of Hormuz and renounced its former security guarantees to Kuwait and the newly independent states of Bahrain, Qatar, and the United Arab Emirates. For two successive decades, no great power stood ready to assume those missions. As the West confronted one foreign policy challenge after another—the oil crisis of 1973–74, the fall of the shah, the Iran-Iraq War—Washington faced a challenging task: how to influence affairs in the Gulf with neither the military forces nor the national political will to do so. Frank L. Jones' chapter describes the evolution in U.S. strategic thinking toward the Persian Gulf as American leaders grappled with the insecurities of the great power vacuum in the region. On 23 January 1980, in his State of the Union Address, President Jimmy Carter warned that "an attempt by an outside force to gain control of the Persian Gulf region will be regarded as an assault on the vital interests of the United States of America, and such an assault will be repelled by any means necessary, including military force." The doctrine, however, according to Jones, was at the outset a bluff in that it relied on deterrence backed by a still-hollow military capability.

Jason H. Campbell's chapter continues the line of inquiry that Jones commenced with a look at America's gradual assumption of security duties in the Gulf in the aftermath of Britain's departure from the region. The year 1979 was a pivotal one in U.S.-Saudi security relations. The fall of Iran's shah in February left Washington with only one remaining regional pillar. The Soviet invasion of Afghanistan in December made it clear to American policy makers that strengthening Riyadh was more critical than ever. The succeeding decade, during which Ronald Reagan presided for eight years as the American president, saw a substantial across-the-board escalation of direct security assistance to Saudi Arabia and the region as a whole. This included unprecedented sales of U.S. military technology, the complete transformation of Saudi Arabia's bases into formidable defense facilities, and the evolution of the U.S. Central Command from a force-in-theory to one of the region's most influential entities.

Finally, this book's two concluding chapters examine Asia's two rising great powers, and the role that they have played in the past, and may play in the future, in the Gulf. In the second decade of the twenty-first century two great powers are rising in Asia—India and China, the two most populous nations on Earth. Through the centuries both of these Asian giants have shaped the states of the Gulf. Archaeologists excavating the Dilmun civilization in Bahrain, for example, have uncovered evidence of seaborne trade linking Mesopotamia with the peoples of the Indus Valley on the Indian subcontinent as far back as three thousand years ago—contact likely stretched back much further in time. More recently, Britain's colonial domination in India brought London to the Gulf, along with Indian soldiers, traders, and laborers. In commerce, India has also cast a long shadow over the Gulf: reflecting the Indian subcontinent's economic hegemony, through much of the twentieth century, into the 1960s, the Indian rupee was the Gulf's accepted currency. Today, the vast majority of laborers and tradesmen in the wealthy Arab states of the Gulf—its carpenters, plumbers, electricians, and ditch diggers—hail from India, Pakistan, and Bangladesh.

China, likewise, has long shaped the region, albeit to a lesser degree than India has. The land passage across Asia that linked China and the Middle East—the fabled Silk Road—for two millennia traversed the modern states of Iran and Iraq. Chinese merchants, as the name of the ancient superhighway implies, exported exquisite silk fabrics and porcelains, and received in exchange horses from Arabia, carpets from Persia, or other goods from Europe.

In the twenty-first century, as these two great powers continue to modernize, changes will be unleashed that will increase their involvement in the Gulf. As their economies demand more energy, it is natural that both nations will seek out long-term, stable energy supplies. As their manufacturing and exporting industries expand, Indian and Chinese merchants will seek access to more international markets including those of the Gulf. The region's central location athwart the seaborne and airborne routes that connect the continents will bring India and China's merchants to transshipment facilities like those in Dubai. Likewise, as Gulf states grow, fueled by petroleum receipts, the need for cheap and plentiful labor will draw thousands from both states.

James R. Holmes and Toshi Yoshihara's chapter evaluates India's desire to dominate the seas surrounding the Indian subcontinent and how this might impact the Gulf. In Holmes and Yoshihara's view, Indian officials and pundits today look to the Monroe Doctrine, the 1823 American policy statement that declared the Western Hemisphere off-limits to new European political or territorial aggrandizement, as a model for India's grand strategy. But the Monroe Doctrine took on increasingly interventionist overtones during the century after its inception. Each generation of Americans reinterpreted former president James Monroe's precepts according to its own view of the United States' needs, interests, and power. In the future, Indians may do the same, in Holmes and Yoshihara's view, as New Delhi pursues a great "blue water" sea power capability for the first time. This chapter also considers possible futures for India's naval posture in the Gulf, considering what sort of interactions it may bring about with leading Gulf states such as Iran, Saudi Arabia, and Iraq.

Ben Simpfendorfer pens the closing chapter on the future in the Persian Gulf of Asia's other great power, China. An economist, Simpfendorfer suggests that the Gulf and China have long been connected by spurs of the ancient Silk Road, and that in the future those ties will grow deeper. In the past two decades, he relates, Gulf traders have returned to China at the same time that the Asian great power gains a larger share of the global economy. This rapid economic growth, furthermore, has increased dependence of the Asian superpower on the oil exports of the Persian Gulf. Beijing's national interests in the Gulf, therefore, will continue to grow, as well as the nation's desire to protect those interests, perhaps with military force.

ACKNOWLEDGMENTS

The editors wish to thank Professor Richard Abels of the History Department, and Professor Brannon Wheeler, director of the Center for Middle East and Islamic Studies, both at the U.S. Naval Academy in Annapolis. Their encouragement and support made possible the first Gulf and the Globe Conference in Maryland, from which many of the following chapters emerged. From the beginning, these conferences and the volumes that have followed stemmed from the combined efforts of the scholars at the U.S. Naval Academy and that of the UK Joint Services Command and Staff College in Shrivenham, England. We thank Professor Geoffrey Till, director of the Corbett Centre for Maritime Policy Studies, King's College London, for his support, as well the British Academy for providing travel monies.

We also wish to thank the Naval Institute Press, particularly senior editor Adam Kane, production editor Emily Bakely, and copy editor Jehanne Moharram for their tireless efforts in support of this project.

ABBREVIATIONS

ARAMCO	Arabian-American Oil Company
AWACS	airborne warning and control system
BNA	British National Archives
BP	British Petroleum
bpd	barrels per day
C3	command, control, and communications
CASOC	California Arabian Standard Oil Company
CENTCOM	U.S. Central Command
CENTO	Central Treaty Organization
CG	Consolidated Guidance
CNA	Comprehensive Net Assessment
CNPC	China National Petroleum Company
COIN	counterinsurgency
CSAF	Commander, Sultan's Armed Forces (Oman)
DEFE	Defence (TNA collection, London)
DLF	Dhofar Liberation Front
EIC	English East India Company
FCO	Foreign and Commonwealth Office (British)
FO	Foreign Office (British)
FRUS	*Foreign Relations of the United States*
FYDP	Five-Year Defense Plan
G2Int	Sultan of Oman's Intelligence Service (renamed Omani Intelligence Service in the early 1970s)

GCC	Gulf Cooperation Council
HBZ	Hambantota Development Zone
HMG	Her Majesty's Government
humint	human intelligence
IOR	India Office Records (London)
IPC	Iraq Petroleum Company
IRG/NEA	Interdepartmental Regional Group/Office of Near Eastern Affairs (UK)
JCS	Joint Chiefs of Staff
JIC	Joint Intelligence Committee (UK)
LBJL	Lyndon Baines Johnson Library, Austin, Texas
MC	memorandum of conversation
MIDEASTFOR	Middle East Force (U.S.)
MODUK	Ministry of Defence, UK
MPS	maritime prepositioning ships
NAM	National Army Museum (London)
NATO	North Atlantic Treaty Organization
NDF	National Defense Council (Oman)
NLF	National Liberation Front (Aden)
NSC	National Security Council (U.S.)
OIS	Omani Intelligence Service
OPEC	Organization of the Petroleum Exporting Countries
ORD	Oman Research Department
OSD	Office of the Secretary of Defense
PD	Presidential Directive
PDRY	People's Democratic Republic of Yemen
PFLOAG	Popular Front for the Liberation of Oman and the Arabian Gulf
POL	Political Affairs and Relations (within National Archives, College Park, Maryland)
POWE	Ministry of Power (TNA collection, London)
PREM	Prime Minister's Office (TNA collection, London)
PRM	Presidential Review Memorandum
PRPG	Political Resident, Persian Gulf

RDF	rapid deployment force
RDJTF	Rapid Deployment Joint Task Force
RNNSC	Richard Nixon Presidential Materials Staff, National Security File
SAF	Sultan's Armed Forces (Oman)
SALT II	second Strategic Arms Limitation Treaty
SAS	Special Air Service (UK)
SIO	Sultan's Intelligence Officer (Oman)
SIS	Secret Intelligence Service (UK)
SOCAL	Standard Oil of California
SSBN	fleet ballistic-missile submarine
SSN	nuclear attack submarine
TNA	The National Archives (London)
TR	Theodore Roosevelt
UAE	United Arab Emirates
USNA2	U.S. National Archives II, College Park, Maryland
USSR	Union of Soviet Socialist Republics
VOC	Verenigde Oost-Indische Compagnie (Dutch East India Company)

Imperial Crossroads

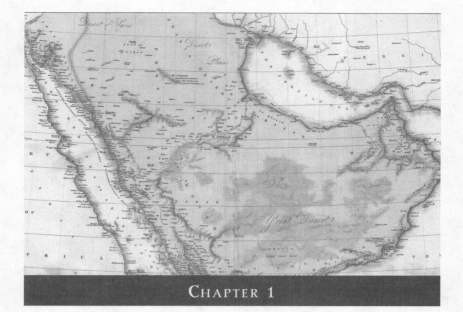

CHAPTER 1

The Portuguese Presence in
the Persian Gulf

An Overview

Rudi Matthee

The year 2007 marked the quincentennial of the entry of the Portuguese into the Persian Gulf.[1] The commemoration of the arrival of Admiral Afonso de Albuquerque and his men at Hormuz in 1507, which inaugurated a presence that would span fully two centuries, generated a great deal of academic interest in the form of two international conferences, both of which led to scholarly volumes offering a fresh view and much new information on the interaction between Portugal and Safavid Iran in the early modern period.[2] This overview will first sketch the contours of the Portuguese activities in the Persian Gulf and their interaction with the Safavids, the dynasty the Portuguese encountered when they entered the Persian Gulf, and next focus on three issues: 1) the objectives of the Portuguese; 2) the challenges they faced in interacting with other powers in the region, and their ways of dealing with those challenges; and 3) the extent to which they succeeded or failed in achieving their objectives in light of their loss of power and, ultimately, their retreat from the Persian Gulf in the late seventeenth century. This chapter will examine these questions with an eye to broader history, long-term patterns of outside interference, and interaction with regional powers—patterns that still resonate today.

General Observations

At the risk of invalidating the entire topic, it is important to offer two caveats at the outset. The first concerns the idea that the Portuguese controlled the Persian Gulf in the sixteenth century in a manner that betrays imperialist and proto-colonialist designs. The second relates to the notion that Iran in this period was a Persian Gulf state with both the intent and the ability to control the region. Both are staples of Iranian nationalism, often uncritically accepted and unthinkingly reproduced, not just by the general public but by many educated people as well, even some who specialize in the period and the region. Iranians tend to see the Portuguese presence in the Persian Gulf as the beginning of a long history of Western interference involving the Dutch, the English and, ultimately the Americans, designed to dominate their country and rob it of its riches. In this narrative Western imperialism goes back all the way to the early sixteenth century. The idea that Safavid Iran was a Persian Gulf power is built on anachronistic notions about nationalism having animated the elite of the Safavid state, and goes back to attempts by Iran's twentieth-century leaders to see their country become and be accepted as a Gulf power. It is important to dispel or at least complicate both myths—not to annoy Iranians, but in order to historicize the Portuguese presence in the Persian Gulf.

The Portuguese presence in the Persian Gulf was predicated on superior firepower, revolved around commercial interests, and had a territorial dimension. But the Portuguese never controlled the Gulf, certainly not territorially—aside from holding Hormuz and monitoring access to the entrance of the waterway, from the moment Albuquerque established real control over Hormuz in 1515 until a combined Anglo-Iranian naval operation ousted them from the island in 1622. They also held Bahrain until 1602; after losing Hormuz they decamped to Muscat and held that town until 1650; they had a trade factory in Kong on the Iranian littoral from 1630 onward, and over time they attacked several Gulf ports, but they did little to establish a permanent territorial presence. The Portuguese Empire was, in Sanjay Subrahmanyam's felicitous term, an empire "written on water."[3] The landed component of the Estado da Índia in particular was slight, built as it was around four Asian naval bases: Melaka (Malacca), Goa, Hormuz, and Aden. The idea that the Portuguese were engaged in imperialism is entirely anachronistic, if not in design, certainly in practice. In Hormuz they arguably exhibited quasi-imperialist forms of behavior. But like the English and Dutch after them, they never established any military presence or economic domination in the Iranian interior—such as they were able to do with various small and weak principalities in the East Indies. Like all foreigners from Christian lands, the Portuguese operated on Iran's mainland at the sufferance of the Safavid shah, as outsiders soliciting commercial rights, diplomatic concessions, and permission to operate mission posts. The only cards they were able to play—beyond holding on to Hormuz—were the use of their shipping facilities, and the offer of potential military assistance to the Safavids, who did not have a navy.

All this was in part a function of long distances, primitive logistics, and small numbers—the number of Portuguese sailors and soldiers in Hormuz never much exceeded five hundred![4] But the limited resource base provided by the Persian Gulf basin played a role as well. The Persian Gulf lay aside from the major Portuguese concerns, which concentrated on India, with its immensely productive hinterland, and the regions farther east, including the East Indies and China. The Persian Gulf's shores thus did not spawn settlements like Batavia (modern Jakarta), Macao, or Goa, ports that over time would turn into major cities. The reasons for this vary and range from brutal climatic conditions and an unyielding religious environment, to the fact that the region was mostly barren and rather unproductive. Hot, humid, and arid, the Persian Gulf until the advent of air-conditioning was one of the most inhospitable places on earth. Drinking water was a perennial problem in many places, including Hormuz. Converting the local population to Christianity proved to be an exercise in frustration. Most importantly, the region was economically of modest interest. It offered nothing like the East Indies with its coveted spices and especially nothing like India, the manufacturing powerhouse of the world until the Industrial Revolution. In the words of one modern historian, the Persian Gulf "was and remained on the periphery of Portugal's Asian empire, whose center was in India's west coast, and the Gulf only mattered if Indian security was menaced by a naval power emerging from the Strait of Hormuz, or if the economic viability of the Cape route was threatened."[5] This marginality is reflected in the issue of fortresses. Of the almost 250 Portuguese strongholds around the world, some 50 were located in India and Ceylon, eleven were constructed in the Far East, and only a handful were built in the Persian Gulf. Some ascribed to the Portuguese by tradition were actually not even erected by them. Only the fortresses of Hormuz, Bandar Abbas, and Qeshm are indisputably Portuguese in origin.[6]

As for Iran, it only became a Persian Gulf state in the twentieth century. Well into modern times the Gulf was oriented toward India in its ways and customs, in terms of the ethnic makeup of much of its population, its food, its commercial direction, and the coinage in circulation, which was different from the currency used in the interior. Iran's rulers were concerned about rival powers in the Persian Gulf, but their real interests and resource base continued to be located in the interior. Until the early seventeenth century Safavid relations with the Persian Gulf littoral were mostly tributary in nature. This only changed with the effort of Shah Abbas I (r. 1587–1629), the most forceful and forward thinking of the Safavid rulers, to establish full control over the coastal area. Yet even Shah Abbas I made no attempt to build a navy, so that well into the eighteenth century Iran's rulers lacked any enforcement mechanism for control over the waters of the Persian Gulf.

The corollary of these circumstances is that, even if the Portuguese played an important role in the Persian Gulf as a waterway, relations between Portugal and the littoral states were limited, intermittent, and of a peculiar nature. Surely there was contact, but far less than one would imagine thinking in modern terms. Iran's interior was separated from the coast by long stretches of desert and mountainous terrain. Distances were great, travel was exceedingly slow and perilous, and there was thus little coordination so that sequential action was difficult to achieve, leaving a huge gap between intent and achievement.

Objectives

The primary Portuguese objectives in the Persian Gulf can be summed up as commerce and Christianity. Their trade interests resulted from a well-known desire to circumvent the Ottoman Empire and to capture the Asian spice trade by going around the Cape of Good Hope. As the story goes, the Portuguese sought to establish a presence in the Red Sea, trying to weaken the Egyptian Mamluke rulers by way of blockading the Red Sea between 1502 and 1509. Shortly thereafter they were confronted with the Ottomans, who in 1516–17 took Syria and Egypt and subsequently managed to extend their power into the Red Sea as far as Aden. The Portuguese thus were forced to limit their regional aspirations and ended up focusing on the Persian Gulf as an extension of their Indian operations, turning Hormuz into a hub of their west Asian commercial activities. Unlike the English and the Dutch, however, who soon after their arrival acquired trading posts in the Safavid capital and various other towns in the interior, they never made any efforts to extend their commercial operations to the Iranian mainland.

The commercial dimension of the Portuguese initiative in west and south Asia tends to get the most attention in modern (English-language) scholarship, but in truth cannot be separated from the missionary urge—the desire to convert the peoples of the East and to fulfill a long-cherished dream of Christianity by "liberating" Jerusalem from Muslim overlordship. This urge colored much of their diplomatic interaction with Safavid rulers, beginning with the founder of the Safavid state, Shah Isma'il (r. 1501–24). The champion of this religiously inspired drive was King Manuel I (r. 1495–1521), who dreamed of crowning himself king of all of Christianity. The Portuguese were thoroughly traditional in this, inhabiting a universe that blended the profane and the sacred, a desire for profit and the lofty ideal of spearheading a divine mission. In their desire to spread the Christian faith in Asia the Portuguese differed from those who came after them, the English, and certainly from the ultimate pragmatists, the Dutch, who were mostly interested in running a profitable trade.

The religious dimension came in the form of missionary efforts in Hormuz, which were directed from Portugal's Indian headquarters in Goa. The first Christian men of the cloth to enter the Persian Gulf were the fathers of the Society of Jesus, who in the mid-sixteenth century arrived in Hormuz under the auspices of the so-called Padroado Régio, the administration of ecclesiastical affairs that regulated the Portuguese mission in Asia. Protected by the secular authorities, the Jesuits actively sought to convert the island's mostly Sunni population. Like all those who came after them, the followers of Ignatius of Loyola found it impossible to convert the local population in any significant numbers. Their brazen methods, which included attempts to have resident Jews expelled and mosques destroyed, created a great deal of friction with the people on the island, and only worsened the reputation for violence that Albuquerque had first established when, sailing up the Persian Gulf in 1507, he had pillaged and torched various port towns that refused to submit and become tributary to the Portuguese. It was Portuguese Augustinians, finally, who gained a foothold and established a lasting presence on the Safavid mainland at the turn of the seventeenth century.

Strategic objectives formed a third component of the Portuguese interaction with Iran. These revolved around a joint interest in containing and building up a joint alliance against rival powers, first the Mamlukes of Egypt and, after 1517, the Ottomans. The early reign of Shah Isma'il saw a series of exchanges between Iran and various European nations, including Portugal, whose rulers witnessed with excitement the rise of a new Muslim dispensation led by a charismatic ruler who was rumored to have Christian inclinations and who soon became involved in a deadly struggle against his neighbors to the west. The Iranians reciprocated, considering the Portuguese potential allies in their confrontation with the Turks, even if they soon came to realize that Western assistance would never go much beyond rhetorical statements of intent. Hence the exchange of envoys between the Portuguese and Shah Isma'il and the conclusion of a treaty between the two states *after* the Portuguese had seized Hormuz. The Safavids also requested armaments, including artillery, from the Portuguese, and on occasion requested the use of their shipping facilities. Most importantly, the Iranians used the Portuguese as a counterweight against other European nations and, eventually, the Omani Arabs.

Challenges

The Portuguese insinuated themselves into a fluid world in which multiple groups coexisted and operated alongside each other. Their success in finding a place in this universe initially owed much to the firepower of their naval forces and the violence they brought to bear on their adversaries and competitors. The supremacy thus gained translated into the ability to hand out so-called *cartazes*, safe-conducts for Asian ships, a practice they transferred to the Persian Gulf from India. Yet their staying power owed as much to their ability to adapt to the region's traditional divide-and-rule policies conducted by deeply divided and fiercely competitive local rulers, none of whom was strong enough to establish definitive supremacy. All were thus amenable to concluding (tributary) agreements with outside powers. The Safavids conformed to this pattern as well. In 1515, the year when the Portuguese returned to Hormuz to consolidate their control over the island, the Safavids, who had previously treated the kings of Hormuz as their vassals, concluded an agreement with the Portuguese whereby the latter would assist the Iranians in any naval operations against Bahrain and Qatif. Iran's rulers continued to request shipping facilities provided by the European maritime powers, and at times relied on the Portuguese—and later on the English and the Dutch—for military assistance against rebellious coastal principalities and their Arab neighbors. This is what allowed the Portuguese to maintain themselves in the region with a very small force, just as it allowed later colonial powers, especially the British, to establish a significant presence with little manpower from India to the Persian Gulf, from the early nineteenth century onward.[7]

Portuguese diplomatic interaction with the Safavids centered on shared concerns about the Ottomans, whose reach extended to the western Mediterranean in the sixteenth century and whose influence spread to the Persian Gulf as well with the establishment of nominal control over southern Iraq and Basra in 1546. This gave Istanbul an excellent opportunity to launch an eastward offensive in the direction of the Indian Ocean and to gain control over transit routes. Although scholars differ in their opinion about the extent to which this offensive was part of a purposeful and comprehensive strategy, the Ottoman foray into the Persian Gulf clearly contributed to a new surge in Luso-Iranian diplomatic relations.[8] And it temporarily led to armed conflict between the Ottomans and the Portuguese in the mid-sixteenth century. The actual military confrontation with the Ottomans was relatively brief, taking the form of Portuguese intervention in the affairs of Basra and a number of naval battles culminating in a failed Ottoman attempt to seize Hormuz in 1552. This violence rarely came at the expense of a continued flow of trade, though, and even with the Ottomans diplomacy usually prevailed, leading in 1565 to a truce between the two powers and ushering in a relative peace that would last until 1622.

As said, the Portuguese were successful in establishing missions on the mainland. Shah Abbas I received the Augustinian friars cordially, granting them the right to build convents and schools for Armenian children, and to engage in (circumscribed) proselytizing among his Christian subjects. This receptiveness bespeaks a kind of toleration vis-à-vis people of different faiths that would have been unthinkable in contemporary Europe—and that even took the form of including the Christian men of the cloth in disputations about religion and philosophy held at the royal court. But for the Iranians, political motives were at play as well. To Shah Abbas I and his successors, the Iberian friars were useful as emissaries in a complex diplomatic exchange designed to forge a grand anti-Ottoman alliance. This comes through very clearly in the journeys of the Portuguese Augustinian Antonio de Gouvea to Iran. This missionary-cum-diplomat, the founder of the Portuguese Augustinian mission in Isfahan, visited the Safavid capital three times between 1602 and 1613, combining his role as a representative of his order with that of political envoy representing the Portuguese crown.[9] The shah also used him and his entourage—and the Catholic missionaries in general—in his domestic divide-and-rule policy, both with regard to his own Muslim clergy and his Christian subjects, to keep them in check and sow discord in their ranks, skillfully manipulating the desire among some of Iran's Armenians to throw in their lot with the Church of Rome.[10]

De Gouvea's last trip to Iran in 1613, which followed the conclusion of a peace treaty between Iran and the Ottomans that lessened Iran's dependence on Western assistance, ended in disaster, prefiguring the conflict that would soon erupt over Hormuz. In 1615 Safavid troops took the Portuguese-held port of Gamrun (in English, Gombroon), across from Hormuz, as a first phase in the shah's plan to circumvent the land-based trade route through Ottoman territory by opening a maritime outlet for Iran's exports, particularly silk. In the same year the shah welcomed the English to his realm as a counterweight to the Portuguese, giving them commercial rights, including the right to establish a trading factory on Iranian soil. Several years later the powerful governor of Fars, Imam Quli Khan, put pressure on the English to assist him in moving against the Portuguese to oust them from Hormuz. Following this, the town of Gamrun, renamed Bandar Abbas after Shah Abbas I, became Iran's main Persian Gulf port.

Failure and Retreat

It is remarkable how much the Portuguese, hailing from a relatively backward, sparsely populated country on the promontory of Europe, achieved in Asia, including the Persian Gulf. For more than a century they managed to regulate, control, and profit from maritime traffic in and out of the Gulf via Hormuz, making use of the *cartaza* system. They were also successful in establishing a permanent mission on Iran's mainland. Yet they ultimately failed in most of their objectives in the Persian Gulf. They never monopolized the spice trade. They failed to cut off Turkish access to trade routes, in part because the Red Sea remained open to Ottoman commerce. Overland routes to Europe continued to function and even to flourish, and became more diverse—as exemplified by the development of the Russian Volga link.[11]

Contrary to Niels Steensgaard's claim that the fall of Hormuz marked a great turning point in the history of the Persian Gulf, it changed the structure of trade very little.[12] The loss of Hormuz was a financial blow to the Portuguese, though, which is one of the reasons why they never gave up dreaming of regaining the island. In the interim they remained very active in the Gulf. They turned to Basra, assisting the local ruler in resisting Safavid aggression in 1624. But Basra never became a success story for them. Muscat, the main port of Oman, became their next stronghold. The Portuguese retained the town as their headquarters until 1650, at which point the rising Omani Yariba state, a formidable thalassocratic power in the making, drove them out. This is also the time when Portugal became more aggressive, turning into a predatory naval power desperate to regain its former supremacy. Imam Quli Khan in 1624–25 and again in 1632 toyed with the idea of chasing the Portuguese from Muscat and approached the English and the Dutch for possible naval assistance with this endeavor, but, disappointed with the commercial agreements they had made with the Safavids, they proved reluctant to help him out. In the winter of 1629–30 the Portuguese sent a force to Qeshm and plundered the island. The Iranians thereupon switched from confrontation to accommodation, and began to use the Portuguese as a counterweight against the other maritime companies. Imam Quli Khan agreed with Admiral Ruy Freyre to allow the Portuguese to collect half the toll at Kong and to force all ships destined to go on to Basra and Qatif to first stop at that Iranian port. The Iranians also agreed to pay the Portuguese tribute for the island of Qeshm. As a result the Portuguese temporarily stopped harassing ships.

Their ouster from Oman in 1650 was part of a larger Portuguese retrenchment in the wider Indian Ocean basin at that time, which also included the loss of Malacca, Ceylon, and their remaining possessions on the Indian Malabar coast, all of which they had to cede to their main competitors, the Dutch. Even if these setbacks did not immediately cause the precipitous decline described in traditional historiography, they did contribute to a long-term loss of Portuguese influence and activity around the Indian Ocean.[13] This extended to the Persian Gulf. Supplanted by the more efficiently organized Dutch and English East India Companies, and now concentrating on Kong, the Portuguese in the second half of the seventeenth century engaged in a bitter naval conflict with the Omani Arabs involving mutual harassment of merchant vessels and several naval clashes. All this greatly diminished security in the Gulf, forcing the Portuguese to give up conducting direct trade links with its ports.

Just as they did elsewhere in Asia, the Portuguese nevertheless continued to play a role in the region. The Safavid authorities made various attempts to enlist their naval support against Omani depredations. This leverage allowed the

Portuguese to persist in their claim to the moiety of Kong's toll income following their long-standing agreement with Isfahan, which they managed to have reconfirmed in 1696. In most years Goa sent a squadron to the Gulf to collect Portugal's share of the port's revenue. The officials in Kong never offered anything near the full amount, but even the lump sum of 1,100 tomans the Portuguese typically garnered made the port their most profitable asset in Asia in the 1680s.[14]

In the decades that followed matters took a turn for the worse. Between 1695 and 1714, the Omanis repeatedly attacked and ravaged Kong, severely reducing its commercial significance. And in the chaos that preceded the dissolution of the Safavid state in 1722, the Portuguese ceased to play any role of commercial or diplomatic import in the Gulf.

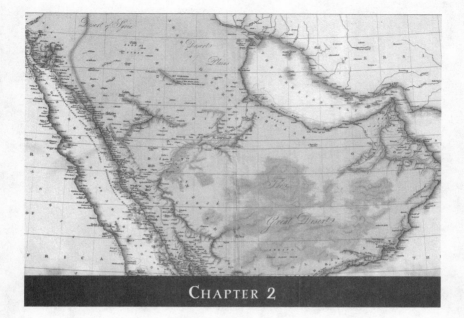

CHAPTER 2

The Dutch in the Persian Gulf

Virginia Lunsford

T he Persian Gulf has long been a distinctive region with its own rich identity and history. In the words of Lawrence Potter, the Gulf is "a world of its own, a geographically and culturally distinct region."[1] Western historiography, however, has typically treated the Gulf as just a Middle Eastern border zone, a strategic conduit, and an appendage to the modern nation-states that border its shores, not recognizing the Gulf's status as a separate civilizational unit. Fortunately, recent scholarly efforts such as this volume are addressing this misconception and treating the Persian Gulf as a special and separate place worthy of study. This new approach reflects how the "Khalijis"— the people of the Gulf—have traditionally viewed themselves.[2] To some extent, the early-modern Dutch saw the Persian Gulf in this way too, as a distinct geographical and cultural sphere that was, at the same time, a vital part of a greater Indian Ocean market.[3] During most of the seventeenth and eighteenth centuries, the Dutch were indisputably the most dominant European power in the Persian Gulf. While the Portuguese were the first Westerners to establish a presence there, and Britain later would become preeminent, the Dutch held sway for nearly 150 years, and to great effect. For it was the Dutch, in the form of the Dutch East India Company (Verenigde Oost-Indische Compagnie, or VOC), the most prominent of the early-modern trade companies, that brought about the integration of the Persian Gulf region into the new, emerging capitalist world system over which the Dutch exerted hegemonic supremacy.

The Dutch World System and the VOC

The role of the Dutch Republic in early-modern economic and world history is extraordinary. As Jonathan Israel has affirmed, "Except for Britain after around 1780, no one power in history ever achieved so great a preponderance over the processes of world trade as did the Dutch . . . from the end of the sixteenth down to the early eighteenth century."[4] Something unprecedented and momentous happened during the waning years of the sixteenth century: the birth of the modern "world system," that is, a worldwide, capitalistic economy centered in the West that represented a wholly new and different form of organization, and which became the foundation for today's thriving global economy.[5] Larger than any one political unit, the system was held together by economic links between different regions of the world. These economic links, in turn, were supported by political arrangements.[6]

The new system evolved as a result of the imperial connections forged by Portugal and Spain during the fifteenth and sixteenth centuries, as well as the vibrant trade links that existed at a local and regional level around the globe. What the Dutch accomplished—and no previous power had achieved this—was the incorporation of the disparate parts of this system into a new whole, and then, economic domination over it.[7] In other words, the Dutch, building on the connections initially developed by the Iberian states, created a network that linked all the world's major economic zones, often via intermediary depots. The Persian Gulf region was included in this integration. In turn, this network radiated out of the great commercial center of Amsterdam.[8] As Israel concludes, "Dutch supremacy in world trade . . . revolutionized the world economic order." The Dutch created, for the first time ever, "[a] fully fledged world entrepôt, not just linking but dominating the markets of all continents," and this event "was something totally outside human experience. The fact is that never before—or perhaps since—has the world witnessed such prodigious concentration of economic power at a single point."[9] The tiny Dutch Republic, then, was the first hegemonic power of the capitalist world economy, a prodigious and rare feat in world history subsequently achieved only by Great Britain and the United States.[10]

From its starting point in the late sixteenth century, Dutch success occurred quickly. Israel identifies 1590 as the initial point when Dutch dominance began to appear tangibly.[11] As C. R. Boxer affirms, "By 1648 the Dutch were indisputably the greatest trading nation in the world, with commercial outposts and fortified 'factories' scattered from Archangel to Recife and from New Amsterdam to Nagasaki."[12] The many reasons for this unprecedented surge in economic power are not within the scope of this essay to discuss.[13] Important factors, however, were policies and capital that encouraged the development of investment-funded, joint-stock companies.[14] The Netherlands was home to many such companies, and the biggest, richest, and most influential of them all was the Dutch East India Company. Founded in 1602, the VOC was an amalgam of several smaller, earlier ventures that were dedicated to opening commercial activity with Africa and Asia in competition with other Europeans. The Portuguese controlled the maritime trade between Europe and this part of the world, ruthlessly enforcing a monopoly that had collapsed only in 1594. Consequently, the States General, the central government of the Dutch Republic, conferred upon the new Dutch East India Company the monopoly in Dutch trade in all waters and territory east of the Cape of Good Hope and west of the Straits of Magellan. (Early-modern Europeans generally considered the entire littoral area of East

Africa and Asia as one region and called it the "East Indies.")[15] The States General's belief was that one, large, united company, rather than a collection of smaller enterprises, could compete much more robustly against the Portuguese, and this turned out to be the case.

Over the years, the VOC experienced tremendous success in the "Indies trade," earning copious riches for its directors and investors, and becoming the most dominant of the trade companies before it was formally dissolved in 1800.[16] Although other trade companies existed, the VOC was the most eminent and powerful of them all. One could fairly describe it as the first multinational corporation in the world, and the first company to issue stock to its investors. Its charter from the States General granted it extraordinary powers that were quasi-governmental in character, including the right to wage war, negotiate treaties with foreign governments, coin money, build forts, appoint its own administrators, and establish colonies.[17] Within its monopoly region, this granting of liberties transformed the VOC into a veritable sovereign power. Thus, in Asia, it assumed the character of an autonomous political entity, possessing its own government in Batavia, Indonesia (today's Jakarta), its own diplomatic corps, its own political and military allies, and its own military operations. Dutch colonial and commercial activities in the VOC's zone were completely undertaken and controlled by the company, not the Dutch government. The Dutch East India Company, then, was a state of sorts, even as it resembled no other existing state form.

The VOC's "state-like" character gave the company great power and flexibility, lending it tremendous latitude to conduct business in the way company administrators saw fit. For example, its possession of a military and its right to conduct its own foreign policy meant that it often pursued and achieved its aims through conquest.[18] It represented a true fusion of public and private interests: a joint-stock company funded by investors that was, at the same time, a quasi-sovereign political entity. In terms of its organizational character, its pricing, its access to capital, its means of moving goods, and its predictability in the market, the VOC represented a major institutional innovation over its commercial predecessor, the Portuguese Estado da Índia ("State of India," i.e., the network of Portuguese settlements, bases, and fortifications in the Indian Ocean coastal region).[19] By 1669, the VOC was the richest private company in world history, possessing a fleet of over 150 merchant ships and 40 warships, 50,000 employees (including some 17,000–18,000 men in Asia), and a private military of 10,000 soldiers.[20]

What were the business aims of the Dutch East India Company? The VOC's monopoly area encompassed the east coast of Africa, the Near and Far East, and everything in between, a vast swath of the globe that included the Persian Gulf. At is most fundamental level, the company's raison d'être was to gain control over the Spice Islands (part of today's Indonesia) in southeast Asia, and it spent its first two decades achieving this goal. As the company expanded, it imported a variety of Asian goods to Amsterdam, where these commodities were sold to the wider European market. Indeed, the VOC's success contributed to Amsterdam's ascension as the trading capital of the world. At the same time, the company intentionally sought to eradicate the Portuguese Estado da Índia.[21] This goal, in turn, served two purposes. First, removing the Portuguese from the scene certainly would enable the VOC to reap more profits through the elimination of a commercial rival. (This was the same reason why the VOC had a generally hostile relationship with England's East India Company, a peer company founded in 1600 with similar designs on the East Indies trade.) More important was Portugal's role in the Dutch Republic's struggle for national survival. Spain and the Netherlands were locked in the grinding Eighty Years' War (1568–1648), the cause of which was the Netherlands' rebellion from the Spanish Empire (and a conflict that the Dutch would eventually win). As a result of Spain's 1580 annexation of Portugal, Portugal became an official military adversary in the Dutch Republic's struggle for independence. The VOC's bellicose attacks against Portugal in the East, then, directly served the national interest. The Dutch perceived—correctly—that any Portuguese defeat in the Indies abetted the Dutch national cause.

Beyond these initial goals, though, company directors soon realized that there was much money to be made by the VOC's vigorous participation in intra-Asian commerce. Indeed, the intra-Asian trade solved a particularly thorny challenge the VOC faced. Europeans could offer few goods that Asian consumers wanted, except silver and gold. Therefore, Dutch traders had to pay for spices with precious metals, a resource that was in short supply in Europe (except for in Spain and Portugal, which had access to the vast reserves of silver in South America). The obvious solution, VOC leadership realized, was to start an intra-Asian trade network, the profits of which could be used to finance the spice trade with Europe. This trade minimized the need for precious metals from Europe because the VOC was able to acquire goods the company wanted (like spices) via the exchange of other regional commodities local consumers sought (such as the Japanese desire for Chinese silks). Already entrenched in southeast Asia and aware of the close commercial ties between that region and the Indian Ocean, the VOC concentrated its efforts in the 1610s and 1620s on expanding to India's west coast, and thereafter, the Persian Gulf. While this intra-Asian trade network initially posed its own financial challenges (it required the formation of a large capital fund in the Indies, which the VOC met by reinvesting a large share of its profits until

1630), it ultimately thrived. By the mid-seventeenth century, nearly half of the company's ships that left Europe remained in Asia for regional use.[22]

So the general cycle ran thus: ships departed from the Netherlands and sailed to Batavia, transporting supplies intended for redistribution to other VOC settlements in Asia. Silver and copper obtained from the trade with Japan were exchanged in India and China for silk, cotton, porcelain, and textiles. These products, in turn, were either traded within Asia for the highly desired spices or imported to Europe, where the VOC made top dollar due to its tight control of the market. In all of its dealings, the company sought to achieve monopoly status because of the potential for high profits. Thus it could be ruthless in the pursuit of this aim. It achieved its monopoly over the Indonesian archipelago, and the cloves, nutmeg, and mace grown there, through brutal military and naval action and the development of an oppressive colonial system.[23] As M. A. P. Meilink-Roelofsz comments, "The Dutch made more strenuous efforts than the Portuguese and Spaniards to extend their monopoly in Asia. Their efforts were concentrated on excluding all rivalry whatsoever, in order to be able to buy products there as cheaply as possible, by means of treaties or even violence if need be, and then to sell them for as high a price as possible."[24]

This zealous dedication to the monopolization of lucrative commodities, as well as its strong role in the intra-Asian trade, was the company's recipe for staggering financial success. Becoming a presence in the Persian Gulf fit this business model, for access to goods in the Gulf fulfilled all of the VOC's primary aims. Not only could the wares acquired there be brought back to Amsterdam and sold to the wider European market (the VOC was especially interested in Persian silk), but the VOC hoped to participate in, if not dominate, the vibrant trade in commodities such as wine, textiles, and foodstuffs that existed between the Gulf and its neighbors. In particular, Gulf societies had long been oriented toward the Indian Ocean, and busy trade routes linked Iran to the west coast of India.[25] As the VOC developed a network of "factories" (trading posts) in northern India (in Broach, Cambay, Ahmadabad, Agra, Burhanpur, and Surat), extending into the Persian Gulf was only logical. Moreover, the VOC's commercial relationship with the Persian Gulf region, and with the Iranians in particular, would help address the company's hunger for silver coinage, an important resource that the Iranians possessed. (The VOC had hoped to satisfy this need by doing business in the Red Sea. However, the VOC was thwarted there by the Yemenis, who controlled Mocha, a key commercial port along the eastern coast near Bab al Mandeb, in today's Yemen; and, even more problematic, general Ottoman resistance to European penetration of the Red Sea.)[26]

The VOC Trade with the Persian Gulf

Thus, the Persian Gulf became the focus. This would necessitate a direct confrontation with the Portuguese, who maintained major trading stations at Hormuz, Muscat, and Bahrain. Of course, the Dutch were not the only Europeans to entertain such plans. While the French were not yet contenders, the English had high hopes of penetrating the Persian Gulf market. To realize this shared goal and in order to eject the Portuguese as efficiently and completely as possible, the VOC and English East India Company (EIC) did something quite unexpected in light of their typically competitive and antagonistic relationship elsewhere: in 1620, they made an agreement to join forces for the purposes of militarily eradicating the Portuguese from the Persian Gulf and jointly financing the development of the Iranian silk trade; the VOC retained the majority share. Coincidentally, VOC and EIC designs on the Persian Gulf arose at the same time as a momentous political change, the rise of Safavid Iran. This development would shape profoundly the Dutch East India Company's activities in the Gulf for the next two centuries.[27]

Shah Abbas I of Iran (1568–1629) wished for the departure of the Portuguese. Why? The shah had imperial ambitions in the Persian Gulf region, with specific strategic and commercial plans. Part and parcel of these designs was his intention to expand the market for Iranian silk, and to that end, he wanted access to the European market.[28] The overland route to the Mediterranean ports was blocked by his perennial adversary, the Ottoman Empire. Meanwhile, the Portuguese stringently controlled access to the Persian Gulf from their bases, especially their strategic stronghold at Hormuz, the linchpin in their western Indian Ocean operations.[29] (Those traders whom the Portuguese admitted to the Gulf had to carry a Portuguese pass, although much interloping did occur.)[30] At the same time, the relationship between the shah and the Spanish-Portuguese crown had become strained due to broken promises on the part of the Iberians.[31] Shah Abbas I, then, sought an arrangement with a Western maritime power that could buy Iranian silk directly in Iranian ports, as well as provide naval support against the Portuguese, since the Iranians did not possess an adequate fleet for such confrontations. Already, the shah had achieved important victories against the Portuguese, driving them from Bahrain in 1602, and from Gamrun, a town on the mainland near Hormuz, in 1615. The conquest of Hormuz itself, however, required naval power, both because of its island location and because its importance within the Portuguese system had resulted in Portugal's permanent concentration of strong naval assets there.[32]

The Dutch East India Company possessed the kind of naval and military power the shah craved. As Sir Michael Howard has detailed in his history of Western warfare, the violent offenses of the early-modern trade companies led directly to greater wealth and power for Western states, so the European governments encouraged the companies' accretion and use of naval and military might.[33] The VOC was certainly no exception; the company's arsenal of ships, weaponry, and personnel was significant.[34] At its height, the company employed some 25 percent of the Dutch Republic's sailors and 33 percent of its soldiers, and it supplemented these forces with thousands of local Asian soldiers.[35] One contemporary estimate affirmed that the total number of VOC soldiers in the Indies approached ten thousand; moreover, the armies of Asian allies, often numbering in the thousands, increased the VOC forces even more.[36] The VOC paid for its high military and naval costs in various ways, from direct capital expenditure, to sponsoring privateers against rival European powers, to forging military alliances with local Asian powers, to using donations of money, cannon, and ships from the States General.[37] Throughout the East, typical military and naval means the company used to expel its competitors included blockading enemy harbors, attacking and besieging adversaries' forts and "factories," and utilizing violence to compel monopolies and advantageous commercial terms upon local rulers.[38] The Portuguese were frequent targets. As Tristan Mostert has commented, "VOC fleets actively looked for Portuguese fleets on their way to the Indies in order to attack them, the Company tried to oust the Portuguese from various regions, and drew up exclusive contracts with the various local rulers in order to exclude the Portuguese from the trade. This latter practice was very successful and very soon developed into something of a market strategy."[39]

Because its commercial "empire" was maritime in character, the company particularly stressed naval capability. In general, indigenous Asian craft could not compare to Western-style sailing ships; Western naval power, as the Portuguese had discovered in the early 1500s, was a great European advantage.[40] The company was fortunate to be based in the Netherlands, since the Dutch possessed the strongest and most innovative navy during most of the seventeenth century.[41] This meant that the company had access to excellent shipbuilders, shipyards, weaponry, naval stores, and naval techniques. Amassing such assets was vital if the company wished to enjoy security in the Indies, never mind offensive capacity, for protecting VOC trade routes and factories was not the responsibility of the Dutch Navy. In fact, the navy's only obligation to the company was to provide naval escorts in the North Sea for the last segment of the VOC merchant fleet's annual return voyage, and the company compensated the navy for this service.[42] The VOC used East Indiamen, and these ships served well as both hardy merchant vessels and strong, maneuverable warships.[43] To satisfy the company's evolving needs, the VOC also ordered vessels of various designs to be built in the Netherlands and the Indies.[44] Because of the number of ships the company maintained, as well as the existence of a centralized naval strategy dictated by company administrators in Batavia, the VOC arguably achieved maritime hegemony within the waters of the East Indies as early as 1650.[45] At sea, then, the VOC ruled supreme, vis-à-vis other Western colonial powers and local Asian powers.

In 1608, Shah Abbas I had sought Dutch military assistance, but the VOC was neither ready nor able to provide aid at that time. By 1620, however, things had changed. The shah's appeals for help occurred simultaneously with Dutch desires to consolidate the VOC's network in the Indian Ocean, so the VOC agreed to a military alliance and trade partnership with the EIC. Thus, in September 1621, the VOC sent a fleet of nine ships to attack the Portuguese bastion at Hormuz. While this Dutch fleet arrived too late to see action, the English fleet fought jointly with Iranian land forces, capturing Hormuz in May 1622. VOC merchant Huybert Visnich reached the Iranian port of Bandar Abbas (Portugal's erstwhile Gamrun) on 20 June 1623, and began the formal process of opening the company's trade with Iran.

VOC trade in the Persian Gulf began in 1623, then, when the company struck a deal with Shah Abbas I and hence was able to establish a number of factories and bases in Iran, the most important of which was located in Bandar Abbas, home to the VOC's Persian Directorate.[46] In addition to Bandar Abbas (1623–1765), the company also set up trading stations in Isfahan, Iran's capital (1623–1745), Kirman (1659–1758), and Bushire (1734–53), as well as rest houses in Shiraz and Lar, situated on the caravan route between Isfahan and Bandar Abbas. Additionally, in the mid-eighteenth century, the company operated a short-lived post on Kharg Island. Outside of the Safavid orbit, the company established bases in Muscat (controlled by Oman after 1650) and Basra (1645–1753). Although the Basra station was only intermittently maintained, it was important in its own right. Basra, located at the Gulf's northernmost end, was one of the Persian Gulf's principal port cities, and a key possession of the Ottomans. Over two centuries, Basra functioned as a commercial alternative to the Iranian ports, when the company and the shah were at odds. It also served as a relay station for the company's homeward-bound mail, since it stood at the end of one of the shortest land corridors between the Indian Ocean and the Mediterranean.[47] Basra and Muscat notwithstanding, however, VOC commercial policy in the Persian Gulf emphasized the Iranian trade above all.

VOC commercial expectations during the seventeenth and eighteenth centuries were predicated upon the contracts negotiated with Shah Abbas I in 1623 and Shah Abbas II in 1652.[48] The shahs viewed the VOC as a ready source of cash and a purchaser of raw silk, a commodity over which the shahs sometimes held a royal monopoly. Important provisions stipulated that the VOC enjoyed freedom of trade within Persia; was exempt from the payment of tolls, under certain conditions; had the right to export silver coinage; and was free from royal inspection. In return, the company agreed to three key provisions: first, to buy a set number of bales of raw silk from the shah each year, at a fixed price; second, to provide a specified quota of imported goods at fixed prices; and third, to pay for 25 percent of the silk in cash.[49]

Although its rate of growth never met VOC expectations, the company's trade with Iran ended up being highly remunerative. In fact, so successful were the company's first years that the profits in Iran were greater than those of any other company factory, except Batavia itself. Its success sparked VOC Governor-General Jan Pieterzoon Coen to exclaim in 1627, "God grant the Company a long and peaceful trade with Persia."[50] For over a century, this was the case, for the VOC's posts in Iran were the most lucrative company establishments on the mainland of Asia. In the early years, 1623–36, silk profits typically averaged between 30 and 40 percent. Later, even though silk earnings decreased, other products entered the mix, increasing profits more. During the period 1683–1740, when total company profits amounted to about 90.5 million guilders, approximately 20 million guilders of this (22 percent) was profit from the Iran trade. Despite intense competition from rival merchants, the company achieved market domination through competitive pricing of the goods the VOC traded. The upshot was that throughout the seventeenth century and much of the eighteenth century, the VOC was Iran's most important foreign trading partner.[51]

This commercial success came at the expense of the English. While the two companies had pledged mutual support when they first entered the Persian Gulf trade, such amity fell by the wayside, and ultimately, the Dutch ruled supreme until the mid-eighteenth century. The EIC had established factories at Shiraz, Isfahan, and Jask in 1617–18, and once the Portuguese had been ousted from Hormuz, the EIC expanded, adding a commercial headquarters at Bandar Abbas in 1622. However, the EIC's Gulf trade remained modest.[52] Despite the VOC and EIC's initial agreement in 1620, joint voyages had ceased by 1630, and competition between the two erstwhile allies thereafter became fierce. The VOC became especially aggressive during times of conflict. During the First Anglo-Dutch War (1652–54), for instance, the Dutch swept English ships from the Gulf, shut the English out, and displayed, English merchants reported, "an imperiousness 'almost past beliefe.'"[53] A major naval battle took place, too, near Bandar Abbas, with the Dutch emerging victorious. By 1763, political upheaval in Iran, as well as a decline in trade generally, forced the EIC to close the Bandar Abbas factory and transfer the headquarters to Basra, where a post had been located since 1723.

The Portuguese, of course, also suffered. When they lost Hormuz in 1622, their hegemonic hold on the Persian Gulf collapsed, and their power quickly eroded. Bandar Abbas—up to this point only a minor fishing village but now the location of the VOC's main factory in Iran—suddenly became the most important commercial port in the Persian Gulf and remained so until about 1750. In 1625, the Portuguese tried to retrench and oust their European opponents, fighting a combined Anglo-Dutch fleet at the Battle of Lar, probably the largest naval battle ever waged in the Gulf. The battle ended in a draw, indicating definitively that the Portuguese had lost control of the Gulf. As D. W. Davies observes, "With the fall of Ormuz [Hormuz], the power of Portugal in the Persian Gulf was really broken, despite a later attempt by them to recapture the city, and despite the fact that Muscat was still a Portuguese stronghold."[54] Although VOC forces declined to search actively for Portuguese ships in the Gulf, whenever their paths happened to cross, the company captured and confiscated the Portuguese vessels.[55] When Muscat fell to the Omanis in 1650, this signaled a fundamental change, for Portugal now had no territorial possessions in the Gulf. Clinging to their vestigial presence, the Portuguese were forced to base themselves in Bandar-e-Kong, a minor trade post located just north of Qeshm Island (and near to modern Bandar-e-Lengeh) that the Iranians had permitted them to establish in 1628. After 1653, they were mostly absent from the Gulf, save for erratic, annual visits to Kong. Their days of glory had ceased.

As Portuguese power in the Persian Gulf declined, the VOC became deeply entrenched in indigenous Indian Ocean commercial networks in which the Persian Gulf served as a key node. Vibrant trade routes had long linked Iran with ports on the west coast of India, particularly Surat.[56] Surat remained a very important node within the VOC system, and that of the EIC as well, for that matter, for both companies maintained busy factories there. This Gujarati port connected the VOC's Indian Ocean trade network to Iran, Mocha (in the Red Sea), and the centers of the Mughal Empire. Many Indian and Armenian merchants were involved in the India-Iran trade, and they continued to compete with the VOC. Thus, despite Westerners' best efforts, no one company or outfit—including the VOC—was able to achieve trade or shipping monopolies in Iran.[57] Moreover, the work of the VOC and EIC was not limited to the import and export of their own companies' trade goods. In fact, both companies were heavily involved in the independent carrying trade, hauling non-company freight between India and Iran.[58] Additionally, because of the increase in piracy in the Arabian Sea, especially during the later seventeenth century, VOC and EIC ships performed escort duties for Indian commercial traffic in the region, since the Indians lacked an adequate navy.[59]

With so much competition, then, why did the VOC come to dominate the Persian Gulf? What did the Dutch offer, compared to the English and the Gujarati traders? As Israel reveals, the sheer volume and variety of goods the VOC provided was simply bigger and better: "[The] Dutch trade network in Asia . . . furnished a much wider range of commodities than did that of any actual or potential rival."[60] The principal commodities the VOC imported into Iran were copper, sugar, textiles, and spices such as cloves, cardamom, tamarind, pepper, and cinnamon. Other key goods included candied and plain ginger, coffee, tea, dyeing agents such as madder and indigo, drugs like benzoin and sarsaparilla, tin, pewter, steel, steel products such as gun barrels and coats of mail, sandalwood, sappan wood, Dutch fabrics, tobacco, porcelain, camphor, and Japanese lacquerwork. Certain commodities were in greater demand than others. For instance, Iran was one of the major Asian markets for sugar. To meet this appetite, the VOC imported sugar from its factories in Taiwan, Bengal, and Java. Likewise, Indian textiles were very popular in Iran, particularly in Isfahan, and especially those fabrics manufactured from inferior-grade cotton and intended for mass consumption. (The VOC did not garner as much profit from the textile trade as it would have liked, however, for here, in particular, it was competing against ultra-aggressive Indian and Armenian merchants who had access to sophisticated credit and capital investment.) Finally, since the shah's contract stipulated that a percentage of VOC purchases in Iran must be paid in cash, silver was a highly valued import as well.[61]

In comparison, the export trade from Iran was smaller. The chief export items were raw silk and Iranian silver coinage (much of which was smuggled out against Iranian wishes). The export trade in precious metals became particularly important to the VOC. Beginning in the 1640s, the factory at Bandar Abbas was a major supplier of silver. In 1650 alone, for instance, more than 1 million guilders' worth of silver coins were procured in that factory, mainly for the trade with Surat. Although the silver supply declined from 1660 to 1690, VOC exports again rose beginning in 1690, and in the long run, from 1650 to 1700, 500,000 guilders' worth of gold and silver were exported per year, and at times, more than 1 million guilders' worth.[62] As Om Prakash has affirmed, "At the turn of the century, Iran had become the single largest Asian source of precious metals for the Company."[63] Additional export products included goat hair, dried fruits and nuts, Shiraz wine, and rhubarb. Rose water and foa (a red dyestuff) were also exported, but at a negligible rate in comparison to the other products.[64]

The profitability and vibrancy of the VOC-Iran trade belied its erratic history, the source of which was the haphazard implementation of the contracts the VOC had forged with the Iranians. These trade agreements were a frequent source of frustration to the Dutch. (No less vexing to company leadership was the rampant corruption that afflicted VOC Gulf personnel.)[65] While the company's military capability gave it the means to dominate many of its other trade "partners" and dictate the monopolistic terms the company desired, this was not the case with the Iranians. (Likewise, the VOC's 1630 attempt to corner the market in all Iranian raw silk also failed.)[66] Iran was a large, strong state with its own sizeable military. VOC trading privileges with the Iranians, then, were the result of negotiation, not conquest, and were granted at the whim of the shah. Within the Iranian system of governance, the shah was the fount of all power and authority, so the company had no alternative but to deal with him. Meanwhile, the shah had the company over a barrel, for he could always procure the goods the VOC sold via the land route from India, or from other traders plying the maritime route. The Dutch really had no choice but to accept his terms.

From the VOC perspective, the shah could seem exasperatingly arbitrary.[67] After all, he and his officials did not always adhere to the contracts they had made with the company. Moreover, business transactions in Iran necessitated a constant stream of gifts and inducements (which Iranian culture viewed as "service fees").[68] Everything was mutable, and everything had its price. Such practices were at odds with the VOC's expectations and normal operating procedure. As Meilink-Roelofsz notes, "The Company was always careful to observe the legal forms." For the VOC, contracts were understood to be ironclad and binding, and in other parts of its domain the company would simply wage war if a contract was violated.[69] Floor explains that "[the] Dutch wanted a clear agreement, based in law, which would be respected by all parties."[70] Since that option was not possible in Iran, the company was forced to accept what the VOC considered an inconsistent and maddening way of doing business.

This meant that relations between the Iranians and the VOC were often tempestuous, and sometimes downright acrimonious. While the Iranians complained about the company's periodic cash-flow problems, the VOC grumbled about the sometimes meager quantity and poor quality of the shah's silk supply. The company also chafed at the contractually fixed prices that did not reflect changing market conditions.[71] Occasionally, violence erupted. In 1641 and 1668, the governor of Bandar Abbas and his men beat the VOC director when the latter did not concede points in discussions. In 1645, 1685, and 1712, outright armed conflict broke out, and the Dutch went so far as to use military force, blockading Safavid ports, seizing Iranian vessels, and attacking the fortress at Qeshm Island, near Bandar Abbas.[72] Even during times of tension, though, business usually continued. Willem Floor points out: "The fact that the VOC traded at Bandar Abbas, offering an array of best-selling goods, plus the fact that the roads connecting Bandar Abbas with Isfahan were better than in the case of . . . other ports, ensured that it maintained a certain baseline of trade."[73] And eventually, all strains were resolved, typically after more negotiation and the presentation of gifts to the Iranians. In the long run, a harmonious rapport with the Iranians and other Gulf merchants was a high priority for the VOC, and so company personnel went to great lengths to maintain sociability.[74]

For the shah's part, the VOC presence in the seventeenth- and eighteenth-century Persian Gulf existed because he found the company's efficient commercial network and wide array of products to be convenient. For him, the VOC was simply the quickest and most dependable way to import Asian spices and Indian textiles, and to export Iranian silk. Due to the VOC's market position, it could supply the shah with large amounts of cash, and do so quickly, predictably, and reliably. While he found the VOC's military and naval clout to be useful, he was not intimidated by it, nor did he appear to care about Dutch power generally. The Dutch were just tolerated foreigners, and that was all. The shah and the Iranian elite were not interested in or even aware of Iran's newfound participation in the Dutch "world system." As Willem Floor observes, "[The] power elite had no direct experience with the outside world. At best, they had heard about Europe and the European naval forces in the Persian Gulf, but they had no frame of reference to understand its [the outside world's] true import. True, the Safavid court knew very well that the Dutch were the stronger power in the Persian Gulf, when compared with England. . . . However, it had no real idea about the strategic political and military situation in the Indian Ocean, or in Europe."[75]

The End of the Dutch Era

The VOC posts in Iran were on the westernmost fringes of the company's "empire," and far removed from the company's center of gravity, Batavia. They lay, in the words of Kerry Ward, "marginally and practically outside the orbit of Batavia's political control, by virtue of . . . [the Persian posts'] direct trade and correspondence links with Europe."[76] This had consequences in terms of the company's ability to respond to conditions in the Persian Gulf efficiently and coherently. By the second decade of the eighteenth century, much of the kingdom of Iran was either in a state of rebellion or unstable due to marauding by tribal groups and invasion from insurgent Afghan forces; the Afghans seized power in 1722. There was nothing much the company could do to improve the prospects of its beleaguered factories and posts. The Afghan overthrow not only devastated Iranian commerce, but profoundly disturbed the trade of western India as well.[77] The entire Indo-Iranian network was upset. Although the Safavids retook control of the state in 1730, great damage had been done, for the VOC had been unable to transact any business with Iran during this period, instead shifting its focus to Basra in 1724.[78]

With the return of Safavid rule in 1730, trade resumed, but the previous commercial arrangements were in shambles, and the Iranian authorities made frequent arbitrary demands that were often expensive and onerous. Sometimes, these demands were for naval and military aid, which the VOC was reluctant to fulfill.[79] Political and social turmoil resumed after the death of Shah Nadir Shah in 1747. To mitigate the upheaval's effect on business, the VOC tried a different strategy, opening a new factory at Kharg Island (near Bushire) in 1753, and closing the posts in Basra, Bushire, and Bandar Abbas (1765). The rationale for the Kharg Island location was that it would be free of meddling and demands by local officials. However, the factory never thrived due to attacks by indigenous pirates, squabbling local factions, and ineffective trade policies. The company closed the Kharg Island post in 1765.[80]

So concluded 143 years of continuous Dutch presence in the Persian Gulf. Despite years of high profitability, the fall of the Safavid dynasty in 1722 represented a sea change. Due to losses of capital and ships, lack of access to Iranian precious metals, higher personnel costs, decreased sales, and a decline in exports, it simply became too costly for the VOC to do business in Iran after 1765, and the company departed.[81] Despite subsequent invitations from the governors of Hormuz, Bandar Abbas, Bushire, and Basra, the VOC never returned. Although one to two Dutch ships annually sailed to the Gulf to trade, these vessels were privately owned, not company ships. The VOC had decided that the Persian Gulf was too unstable, risky, and thus unprofitable. Instead, the company simply sold its goods to private traders in Surat, who in turn marketed them in the Gulf.[82]

As it turns out, the VOC's problems in Iran were not isolated and reflected an overall decline in the company's fortunes. In general, the VOC faced daunting challenges. From 1730 to 1750, its intra-Asian trade steadily decreased, instigated by changes in the political and economic landscape throughout Asia (and changes that the VOC could do little to alter). In the long run, this phenomenon weakened the VOC posts in Surat, the Malabar Coast, and Bengal. The company increasingly had to confine its operations to the belt it physically controlled, from Sri Lanka through the Indonesian archipelago. The volume of intra-Asian trade and its profitability therefore shrank.[83] At the same time, the EIC's influence expanded. By 1765, Britain had become the leading European power in India, and its East India Company evolved from a mere trading company into a territorial power. This transformation, in turn, seriously affected the EIC's Persian Gulf operations.[84] Despite the expense of operating in the Gulf and the unimpressive trade returns, the English remained for several reasons. First, their post in Basra was integral to the overland dispatch route to Europe, the key line of communication between India and London. Second, the English were still heavily involved in the local carrying trade, and served as key transporters of Muslim pilgrims to Mecca. Third, the company's "Bombay Marine," its local naval escort force, was heavily committed to protecting the commerce of the Armenian and Indian merchants on India's west coast, and these merchants did extensive business in the Persian Gulf. Finally, the English did not want to withdraw and leave the Gulf to the French, who were steadily building influence in Muscat.[85] Britain's star was now ascending; it would become the prevailing European power in the Persian Gulf by the end of the 1700s, and achieve true supremacy in the nineteenth century.

The Dutch—via their great trade company, the Verenigde Oost-Indische Compagnie—were unquestionably the dominant power in the Persian Gulf during most of the seventeenth and eighteenth centuries. When the VOC brought the Persian Gulf into its Indian Ocean network, it pulled the Khalijis—the people of the Gulf—into a greater, capitalistic, world economic system, the first history had ever known. During the years spanning 1590 to 1740, the Dutch Republic—with its copious array of shipping, commercial, financial, and industrial facilities—was a vibrant emporium that possessed the capability to marshal force and political pressure to pursue its economic objectives, and could regulate and influence the production, processing, and global distribution of myriad commodities.[86] The Dutch were the first hegemons over a vast, globally extensive, interconnected network of commercial enterprise that both radiated out of and led to Amsterdam. In its own ways, the VOC's Persian Directorate was an important part of that overall system.

The eighteenth-century decline and eventual demise of the company in the Persian Gulf mirrored changes in the Dutch-centered world economic system as a whole. Although Dutch dominance lasted until about 1740, for various and complex reasons, power thereafter began to shift, and shift rapidly.[87] The VOC—and, by extension, its posts in the Persian Gulf—could not help but be caught up in this process. Even as the company was experiencing the pains of global systematic contraction, its local Persian Gulf trade withered. As conditions changed and Dutch influence receded, it would be Britain and eventually the United States that would become the dominant powers, both globally and within the Persian Gulf. Perhaps it is fitting then that, long after Dutch commercial influence had waned, it was a Dutchman, A. Holz, who was the first capitalist pioneer to drill for oil in Iran, in the mid-nineteenth century.[88] Like the great Dutch trade company that had preceded him, Holz initiated an important step that would forever transform the fate and fortunes of the Persian Gulf and its people.

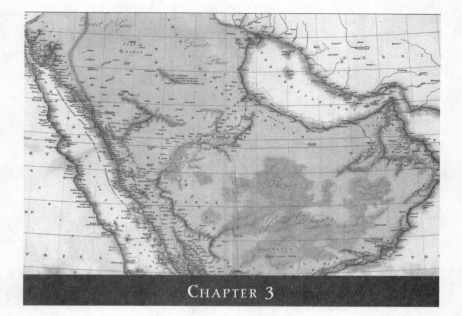

CHAPTER 3

The Great Game and Power Projection

Robert Johnson

Were it not for our possession of India, we would think but little of Persia.

—ROBERT CECIL, 3rd Marquess of Salisbury,
British prime minister and foreign secretary

In the nineteenth century, the relative decline of the Persian Safavid Empire compared with the ascendancy of the West, the eclipse of Central Asian trade by maritime commerce, and the existence of small neighboring powers presented British strategists with a dilemma: how to protect Britain's largest and most valuable possession, India, against landward threats when its primary arm for defense was the Royal Navy. It was relatively easy to secure maritime trade at sea and to deter attacks on its colonies with a large fleet, but there were greater challenges to Britain's efforts to eradicate slavery and piracy in the Persian Gulf, to act in support of amphibious expeditionary warfare against Persia, or to deter the great powers from applying pressure on the British Empire, because there was always the risk that Britain could be drawn into costly occupations or unnecessary conflicts, or forced to fight in the interior of Asia where its naval power could not be brought to bear.

Britain's preference was to project influence by other means—through diplomacy, consulates, financial services, infrastructural communications (railways, roads, and telegraph), and commercial concessions. However, specific crises sometimes forced Britain to demonstrate its power to Persia and Arab states, and to rival great powers like France, Russia, and Germany. There were amphibious operations against Persia in 1856–57, and there was a show of force in the Persian Gulf in 1903. In short, the methods of maintaining British interests were furthered by four approaches. First was diplomacy, using a system of residencies and consulates with allies amongst the local elites, supported by an intelligence network. This was augmented by agreements or the settlement of differences with other European powers and, in the case of Persia, with a specific Anglo-Russian convention. Second, there were spheres of influence, often through building relationships with local elites, financial services, building infrastructure, and military training teams. The contest for local support and the intrigue of the chief rival, Russia, was subsequently referred to as "The Great Game."[1] Third, buffer states were also required and Persia became the outwork in the landward defenses of India. The Ottoman Empire also served this function throughout the nineteenth century, acting as a bulwark to Russian annexations. Local rulers, including the shah of Persia and the amir of Afghanistan, were granted direct financial reward or military aid. Fourth, periodic military and naval interventions were used, such as the operations against piracy in the Gulf and against

Persia in the mid-nineteenth century, and these became, in the twentieth century, periods of military occupation (as in post-1914 Iraq, and the Gulf states).

All these were cemented by the notion of prestige, which was important in diplomacy but also acted as a means of deterrence. It was an idea that had to be reinforced constantly: Britain had to assert its power and demonstrate that it was both capable and willing to exercise force. In the second half of the nineteenth century, British policy toward Persia had sometimes lacked consistency as strategic considerations in Europe and India came first. However, despite growing pressure from Russian intrigue and commercial rivalry, by the beginning of the twentieth century Britain had reasserted its exclusive control of the Persian Gulf, ringed the region with compliant or allied states, and rationalized its relationship with Persia.

"The Great Game": Persia and the Russian Threat in the Mid-Nineteenth Century

The Russian threat to British India was the driving force behind the competitive intrigues known as the "Great Game" or the "Tournament of Shadows," but even though an actual invasion of India was favored by only a handful of Russian officers and political figures in the Asiatic section of the Russian foreign ministry, both sides played the game earnestly enough. As far as many British statesmen and soldiers were concerned, each of the states on the periphery of India had to be considered part of the defense scheme—and that included Persia and Afghanistan. Today, it is generally thought that Russia was carrying out *maskirovka*: applying pressure in one strategic location to effect change elsewhere. The Russian newspaper *Golos* summed it up at the time: "The Indian Question is a simple one: Russia does not think of conquering India, but reserves to herself the power of restraining outbreaks of Russophobism among British statesmen, by possible diversions on the side of India."[2] In particular Russian sensitivities about the Black Sea and the Straits of Constantinople, worsened by their experiences in the Crimean War (1854–56), meant they needed to challenge the British somewhere, and the absence of a comparable fleet meant that they had to take advantage of a continental front: Persia, Afghanistan, and the Indian border provided that opportunity.

For the British, two locations stood out as particularly important—Persia's northern Khorasan province and Herat, the westernmost city of Afghanistan. Herat had once been part of the Persian Empire, and in 1836 the shah tried to reassert his control of the city by force. To British alarm, Russian troops accompanied his army.[3] When a Persian attempt was made to storm the city in June 1837, the British broke off diplomatic relations with Tehran. George Eden, the Earl of Auckland and the British governor general in India (1836–42), then ordered two steamers with troops to land at Karrack (Kharg) Island in the headwaters of the Gulf, which the Persians interpreted as a full-scale invasion. Consequently, an ultimatum delivered by Britain was accepted and the siege of Herat was abandoned.[4] Nevertheless, the British were so concerned by this Russian-inspired intrigue, they moved to invade Afghanistan, precipitating the First Afghan War (1838–42).

The historian Garry Alder believed that the British obsession with Herat as the "Key to India" was wholly misguided.[5] British officers at Tehran had argued that if Herat fell to a hostile Persia, Russia, its "ally," would have secured for itself a base within Afghanistan from which to harass the Indian border. Dost Mohammed, the Afghan ruler in Kabul, remarked: "If the Persians once take Herat, all is open to them as far as Balkh, and neither Kandahar nor Kabul is secure."[6] The city was variously styled the "Gate of India" and the "Garden and Granary of Central Asia," and even those who did not think it was likely to open up Afghanistan to occupation believed it would provide a means for Russia to dominate Persia. The debate about the city's value continued throughout the nineteenth century, but one viceroy of India, Lord Charles Canning, reflecting on the fact that any Russian attack would have to cross five hundred miles of barren terrain inhabited by hostile Afghans, mused: "If Herat be the key to India, that is, if a power once in possession of it can command an entrance into India, our tenure of this great empire is indeed a feeble one." He summed up the solution to the problem succinctly: "The country of Afghanistan rather than the fort of Herat is our first defense."[7]

Nevertheless, those who saw Herat as the vulnerable bastion on India's glacis regarded every Russian advance across Central Asia and every annexation that followed as evidence of the growing magnitude of the czarist threat. The contemporary British liberal press took a more charitable view, and suggested that the destruction of the uncivilized khanates and the steady advance of Christian Russia would, eventually, ensure greater stability. However, the historian Edward Ingram has argued that Edward Law, the first Earl of Ellenborough and the governor general of India (1842–44) who advocated a proactive policy in Persia and Afghanistan, showed "the truer perception of the needs of a continental state," which Britain now was through its possession of India.[8] Ellenborough was especially worried about the complacency of the government in London as it was far removed from the concerns of Central Asia and the Indian frontier. The British government believed that naval power was sufficient to protect its imperial possessions, since, apart from India and Canada, the British Empire was still no more than an assemblage of littorals and had at its disposal a vast fleet. However, there was growing concern in many quarters about Russia's grasping policy and her broader ambitions with regard to Asia.[9] Ellenborough felt that, although Russia was still too distant to be an immediate threat, it was vital to seize advantages while there was still time.

The problem of the instability in buffer states was highlighted by a new period of unrest in Persia that flared up after the death of the shah in 1848. The new shah, Nasr-ud-din, took two years to crush the revolt in Mashhad and had to contend with three revolts by the movement known as the Babis. In 1852, the Babis came close to success in their attempt to assassinate the shah, and the regime reacted with savage reprisals. As predicted, the instability offered an opportunity for Russia to extend its influence in Tehran still further. It was against this background that the Herati ruler, Sa'id Mohammad, permitted Persian troops to enter Herat to crush discontent there. Fearing Russia was behind the move, the British protested to the shah. As a result a convention was negotiated in January 1853 where Persia agreed not to send troops into Herat unless it was invaded by a foreign enemy, clearly intending this to mean Russia. No permanent occupation was to be tolerated, and Persia was not to intrigue within the city. For its part, Britain pledged to keep foreign interests out. The convention was never ratified by the British government, largely because the British had clearly set out their wishes by the diplomatic exercise and the Persians were under no illusion about these intentions.

Yet within two years, Britain and Russia were at war in the Baltic and Crimea, and Herat would once again take on a new significance. At the outbreak of the conflict, Britain had insisted the shah remain neutral. However, soon after, the British Foreign Office representative took offence at an alleged slight at the Persian court and withdrew his negotiating party. This actually deprived Britain of a presence at a crucial moment in the diplomatic contest. In the absence of firsthand information, rumors grew that the shah would conclude a treaty with the Russians in order to regain lost possessions in the Caucasus, or perhaps elsewhere. As a precaution, Britain dispatched a warship to the Persian Gulf to send a clear warning. However, it was not the Caucasus that was the target of the shah's ambitions, it was Herat, and plans to take the city were already well advanced. In Herat itself in September 1855 events played into the shah's hands. Mohammad Yousaf, a member of the former Afghan royal family, led a revolt, killed the governor, and seized power. Meanwhile, Dost Mohammad of Kabul had launched an attack of his own on Kandahar as a first step in consolidating his rule in Afghanistan, and was thus in no position to resist any Persian attack.

The shah intended to exploit this unrest in Afghanistan, and immediately advanced on Herat. The city fell to the Persians on 25 October 1856. In London there was considerable anxiety that the Russians would open a consulate in Herat prior to the development of espionage aimed at the subversion of Afghanistan, Persia, and perhaps India.[10] The idea of sending a British-Indian column across Afghanistan was rejected because of the recent memory of the difficulties of the First Afghan War and the possibility that this would simply offer an opportunity for the Russians to fight on Persia's behalf. Instead, the British would make use of their naval strength and make an amphibious expedition to Bushire in the Persian Gulf. When their ultimatum to Tehran was rejected, the British declared war on 1 November 1856.

The Anglo-Persian War of 1856–1857

This short war was an amphibious operation with limited objectives.[11] The Royal Navy first took Karrack Island as a forward operating base and a landing was made in Hallila Bay, twelve miles south of Bushire, on 7 December 1856. It took two days to assemble all the troops, horses, guns, and stores, but from then on rapid progress was made and the land force, led by Major General Foster Stalker, reached the old Dutch fort at Reshire soon after. There, the Persians were entrenched but this provided scant protection from British naval guns. Stalker's force stormed the fort and local Dashti and Tungastani tribal irregulars were quickly overwhelmed.

At Bushire two hours of naval bombardment compelled the Persians to capitulate. The captured town was placed under martial law. The British declared that the traffic in slaves was to cease immediately, and all black captive men, women, and children were released. Coal stocks were brought in, while grain and cattle were procured from the region. However, while possession of the port was relatively easy, penetration of the interior would be more difficult. Moreover, the shah felt that the loss of Bushire, on the very periphery of his empire, was a manageable problem. Diverting forces from the south and central regions, he began to concentrate an army that could eject the British expeditionary force.

British reinforcements arrived at Bushire on 27 January 1857 under General Sir James Outram.[12] He quickly organized his force into two divisions, one led by General Stalker, the other by Sir Henry Havelock, a veteran of the Afghan and Sikh Wars. He also sent a reconnaissance to Mohammerah where reports had been received that the Persians were fortifying themselves. However, his scouts discovered a large Persian army assembling at Burazjoon, forty-six miles inland from Bushire. To seize the initiative, Outram decided to take the war to the enemy, and make a bold offensive thrust against the Burazjoon force.[13] Taking the Persians by surprise, the British destroyed stores and ammunition that had been concentrated there, and when the Persian general, Shujah ul-Mulk, tried to harass the British withdrawal at the village of Khoos-ab, the Persians were overmatched by the firepower and determination of the British force. The Persian formation collapsed leaving seven hundred dead, while the British had lost sixteen men. Outram's army slogged back through deteriorating weather to Bushire, completing the battle and a march of forty-four miles in just fifty hours.

The Persians were not yet ready to seek terms. At Mohammerah, they had constructed strong field fortifications. Earth had been packed into walls some twenty feet high and eighteen feet deep, upon which were mounted artillery. The arcs of these guns were designed to cover not just the landward approaches but also the entrance to the Shatt al-Arab. The garrison, 13,000 strong with thirty guns, was commanded by Prince Khauler Mirza, and he was confident of being able to check the British. Outram decided on an amphibious attack. He packed 4,886 men into steamers and transports with fighting sloops in a fire-support role, and after a three-hour bombardment, the Persian bastions had been silenced. Landings were made and the infantry began systematically working through date groves, but the Persians retreated in disorder, leaving seventeen guns and most of their camp equipment behind. Outram kept up the pressure, sending a flotilla of three steamers, each with one hundred infantrymen on board, upriver in pursuit. Near Ahwaz, they encountered about seven thousand Persian troops, but Captain James Rennie, the British naval commander, decided to put his three hundred men ashore, deploying them to give the impression they were far more numerous. His ships' guns were ranged against the Persian position and, as his small land force advanced toward Ahwaz, the Persian formation broke up, bringing all resistance to an end.

Peace was restored by the Treaty of Paris on 4 March 1857 and Persia agreed to withdraw all its forces and its territorial claims from Afghanistan. Britain got effective control of Persian foreign policy and agreed to withdraw its occupying troops.[14] From the British perspective, the short campaign had been a great success. For a small cost, the British had used their naval guns to project their power against a littoral state, made amphibious landings, and destroyed the resistance of far greater numbers of entrenched forces. Perhaps more importantly, it persuaded the Persians that Britain's wishes had to be taken seriously. Russia, it seemed, had been defeated by Britain in the Crimea, and Persia too had suffered reverses. With its prestige enhanced, Britain had no difficulty in persuading the Persians to accept a telegraph line across the country in 1862, linking India and London. In 1873, the British invited the shah to visit England, and there can be little doubt that this too was an attempt to remind him of British power. However, the shah maintained links with Russia to counterbalance British influence, while being careful not to make an alignment obvious either way. For their part, the British established a listening post at their consulate in Mashhad in 1874 to collect intelligence on Russian movements in Central Asia.

Persia in British Policy, 1877–1907

In the 1870s, Russia appeared to be advancing everywhere. It had taken territory from China in East Asia, seized khanates in Central Asia, captured the great Uzbek city of Khiva in 1873, and on 19 May 1877 a Russian force seized the village of Kizil Arvat on the Persian border, in modern day Turkmenistan. British concerns were highlighted when Ronald Thomson, the British chargé d'affaires in Tehran, obtained a report that detailed Russian plans for Persia and Afghanistan. The document was drawn up by Dmitri Miliutin, the Russian war minister, and it began with a condemnation of Britain, the "Despot of the Seas," and called for an "advance towards the enemy" that would show "the patience of Russia is exhausted," and "that she is ready to retaliate and to stretch her hand towards India."[15]

In July 1877, as the Russians fought the Ottomans in the Balkans, the British cabinet decided that any Russian attack on Constantinople would constitute a casus belli. When the Russians broke through and reached the outskirts of the city, the Royal Navy moved to within striking distance. As anticipated, the Russians prepared for war in the Southwest Asian theater. Miliutin aimed to keep Persia neutral, in case the British retaliated and contemplated an attack through Persia into the Caucasus,[16] but he ordered that the Russian army should prepare a force of 20,000 men to move to the Afghan border.[17] British intelligence sources suggested that the Russians were about to seize the Akhal Oasis on the Persian border, perhaps prior to a move on Herat. Eager to augment their salaries, Persian officials were actually preparing to support with supplies a Russian advance through Trans-Caspia, the region to the east of the Caspian Sea that approximately coincides with present-day Turkmenistan.[18] Thomson urged the Persian government to stop the Russians, and, despite some protests, they agreed to lodge a complaint.[19] Britain's willingness to fight and Russia's diplomatic isolation in Europe persuaded St. Petersburg not to make further advances in either the Balkans or Central Asia. However, the viceroy of India, Robert Bulwer-Lytton, first Earl of Lytton, was anxious about the vulnerability of Afghanistan and launched the Second Afghan War (1878–81) to control the buffer zone more firmly.

This British military action was noted in Tehran. In early 1879, the shah requested an alliance in return for British military support against Russia, but, eager to avoid long-term commitments, Britain refused, instead demanding that as a "friendly power" Persia should not offer any assistance to the czar's forces or help them to annex territory en route to the Afghan border. The Persians, disappointed that the British would not commit themselves to defend Tehran as they had Constantinople, took the view that cooperation with Russia was still the only guarantee of survival. The British cabinet considered that, in the interests of India's security, Herat might, in fact, be given to Persia.[20] When this proposal was made to the shah, he was also informed that Britain would insist on closer military and commercial ties after all, but they would also demand that the Persians assert their historic claims to the Central Asian city of Merv against the Russians, who seemed poised to annex it. However, just at the moment when the shah approved, a Liberal government came to power in Britain and withdrew the alliance proposal.

This hasty change of British policy had been the result of a lack of useful intelligence on Russia and its true intentions toward India, Afghanistan, and Persia. The need for a screen of agents or consuls across Persia and Afghanistan to assess actual Russian capabilities was obvious. General Sir Archibald Alison, the quartermaster general of the Intelligence Division in London, noted: "Early and reliable information with regard to Russian or other military movements near the Northern Border of Persia therefore appears to be the most important, and this information can only be satisfactorily obtained on the spot."[21] He argued that the monitoring of Russian troop movements was the surest way to gauge Russian plans in Central Asia. The Intelligence Division recommended a permanent consulate at Astarabad, near the southeastern shore of the Caspian Sea, as well as the one at Mashhad: "If we were kept accurately informed about the state of affairs in those regions the government would be at once able to dispel the discreditable state of alarm into which this country is periodically thrown. . . . If knowledge is power, ignorance is weakness, and this weakness we constantly show by the undignified fear displayed at every report or threat of Russian movements."[22] The Liberal government at home was unmoved and informed the government of India that, in their view, the movements of Russia in Central Asia simply did not merit anxiety about an invasion of India.[23]

The fear of czarist advances toward India and Persia was soon revived. In January 1881 the last stronghold of the Central Asian Turcomen was annexed by Russia.[24] By 1885 agents working for the British, operating out of Mashhad, were able to report that the Russians had augmented their strength in Turkestan (today's Central Asia) to a total of 50,000 men and 145 guns.[25] An intelligence

assessment showed that a Russian attack on Herat with this strength would suc-
cessfully tie up the entire Indian army, leaving only the Royal Navy and about
36,000 troops in the United Kingdom as a counteroffensive force.[26] As a solution
to the dilemma, Captain James Wolfe Murray, an intelligence officer, examined
the possibilities of a British attack through the Caucasus via Persia or Turkey to
save India. An offensive here, providing Turkish or Persian cooperation could be
secured, would sever the Russian lines of communication to Trans-Caspia and
force the czar's troops to make the far more difficult journey from Orenburg to
Turkestan. However, he concluded that secrecy was almost impossible to maintain in the region. This would mean "it would be almost useless to undertake the
operations without having a force most fully equipped for an immediate advance
upon landing [in the Persian Gulf]."[27] To achieve surprise, he considered the
transmission of false telegraph messages that might tie up Russian forces for some
time. Others felt there ought to be a permanent British presence in Persia with a
more extensive espionage screen of local agents.

The British consulate at Mashhad was clearly designed to resist Russian
covert operations and diplomatic intrigue in the Persian province of Khorasan.
Although the first efforts exposed the inexperience of the personnel, the aim was
to deny the growth of Russian influence, to counter Russian propaganda, and,
if necessary, to spread disinformation in northern Persia. The consulate had a
responsibility for a long frontier some five hundred miles in length, but Mashhad
was selected because it lay close to the Russian lines of communication between
Krasnovodsk and the rest of Trans-Caspia.

Throughout the 1880s there were frequent border incidents that kept the
intelligence agents on the frontiers busy and the politicians in the capitals anxious for news.[28] The British Foreign Office believed that building railways might
offer the chance for Persia to develop and be less susceptible to the commercial temptations or political pressure offered by Russia. A railway link down to
the Persian Gulf would, it was reasoned, tie Persia more closely to the maritime
trade of Britain and India. The head of the Intelligence Branch at Simla, the
summer capital of British India, Colonel Mark Sever Bell, concurred enthusi-
astically with this assessment.[29] He went to visit Sir Henry Drummond Wolff,
the minister at Tehran, and suggested that a line might link Quetta, the forward
base of the Indian army, with Seistan in Persia.[30] Lord Salisbury, the prime minister, was nevertheless lukewarm, and after further inquiries the Foreign Office
realized that the volume of Russian trade and the development of Russian roads
and railways in Persia had been exaggerated, and that the costs for the British
would not merit the project.[31] The Intelligence Division in London believed
that any British-backed railway in Persia would provoke the Russians into

actually building a rival line toward northern Afghanistan.[32] But Drummond Wolff continued to take the view that the Russian railway project was inevitable. Moreover, when built, he argued, it would raise the prestige of Russia in the eyes of the Persians. Only the construction of a British railway, partly funded by Baron Reuters, offered the opportunity of a strategic balance of power.[33]

The December 1888 edition of the Indian Intelligence Branch report noted that Russian agents were "active in Persia."[34] Major General Sir Henry Brackenbury, the director of Military Intelligence in London, thought this alarmist, but the Russians were indeed pressing the shah for an answer on their railway schemes and Wolff was anxious that Britain was losing its influence over northern Persia, perhaps even the whole country.[35] The Intelligence Division, in fact, believed Persia was already a lost cause. Brackenbury didn't think "the advance of a single line of railway to a remote corner of Persia would make our influence in that country equal to that of Russia," which virtually "controlled" Persia anyway. Britain fell back on the idea of developing Baluchistan as a base of operations while winning over the local tribesmen there.[36] Salisbury urged Wolff to block the Russian railway schemes and ensure that any concessions to the Russians in the north were balanced by concessions to the British south of Tehran.[37] In the end, Evgenii Karlovich Butzow, a new Russian minister to Persia, concluded an agreement with the Persians and the British to ban all railway development for ten years, much to everyone's relief. Sir Edward Morier, the British ambassador in St. Petersburg, revealed that the Russians had been just as fearful of a British railway into the heart of Persia, and concluded, with some feeling: "We are quit of the question."[38]

The continued decay of Persian central authority fuelled the rivalry between British and Russian officials. When, in 1898, Tehran decided to sell off customs revenue to raise capital for the near-bankrupt Persian government, it provided an opening for foreign interference.[39] Joseph Rabino, the manager of the British-owned Imperial Bank of Persia, pointed out that a proposed road from the Persian Gulf to Tehran had been abandoned as the £80,000 allocated from British sources had been insufficient. By contrast, Russia had spent £250,000 on a road from the Caspian Sea town of Resht to Tehran.[40] General Vladimir Kosogovsky, commander of the Russian-officered Persian Cossack Brigade, claimed that the British were "predatory" when it came to obtaining concessions from the shah, while his own side was "inactive." However, the Commercial Bank of St. Petersburg was eager to loan money to Persia in return for control of all Persia's customs revenues to manage debt repayments. This would mean, in effect, the whole country, including southern Persia, would fall under Russian influence. Henry Mortimer Durand, the British foreign minister of the government of

India, tried to block it, and suggested a joint Anglo-Russian loan.[41] The Russians rejected the idea and continued to penetrate Persia commercially: mine concessions were obtained, and port taxes at Enzeli on the Caspian were payable to the Russian government.

There was considerable resentment in Persia of British commercial power and the Royal Navy presence in the Persian Gulf.[42] In 1888, the Karun River, a tributary to the Shatt al-Arab, was opened to international navigation, largely to Britain's advantage, and in 1891 a tobacco concession was granted to a British company. However, the latter events proved to be the trigger for nationalistic anti-British rioting. In this environment, and promoting their loan offers aggressively, the Russians put forward monopolistic terms that included the total exclusion of the British in any national fiscal arrangements. The Iranian historian Firuz Kazemzadeh noted that the British saw loans in a commercial sense (asking themselves whether the Persians could repay any amount), but the Russians subordinated economic interests to political ones: they simply intended to gain a monopoly of influence over Persia.[43] As far as commerce was concerned, that could be developed after they had secured control.

In January 1900, when a large part of the British army was committed to the war in South Africa, Count Mikhail Nicholayevich Muraviev, the Russian minister of foreign affairs, urged the czar to authorize a more determined effort to penetrate Persia economically and to block British influence there. Above all, he wanted to push Russian influence farther south in the future. Consequently, he did everything he could to encourage Russian commerce in the region, including the development of trans-Caspian shipping, and postal and telegraphic links.[44] Others at the Russian court advised caution and stressed the far greater importance of reaching the Bosphorus rather than the Persian Gulf. The final decision rested with the czar, who, according to General Aleksei Nicholayevich Kuropatkin, "had grandiose plans in his head: to take Manchuria for Russia, to move toward the annexation of Korea to Russia. He dreams of taking under his orb Tibet too. He wants to take Persia, to seize not only the Bosphorus but the Dardanelles as well."[45] Yet pragmatism prevailed in St. Petersburg and there was, in the end, no dash for the Persian Gulf.

Lord George Nathaniel Curzon, the viceroy of India (1899–1905), was deeply alarmed by Russian intrigues and demands to open diplomatic relations with Afghanistan, which suggested a desire to interfere in India. He believed that Persia was in such a state of decay that it could not be revived, and that it was particularly vulnerable to Russian imperialism. As a solution, he proposed the country should be considered as a set of zones with consulates in every quarter, high-profile visits to the Gulf by the Royal Navy, and urgent improvements to the telegraph system so as to provide early warning of a Russian coup de main. Ever critical of the snail's pace of British officialdom, he was soon frustrated by the British government's focus on the South African War.[46] His memorandum on Persia and the Gulf got little reaction from London and his reminders in 1901 were ignored. Curzon privately warned: "One day the crash will come, and then my despatches will be published and in my grave I shall be justified. Not that I care for that. But I long to see prescience, some width of view, some ability to forecast the evil of tomorrow, instead of bungling over the evil of today."[47]

Lord Salisbury, the British prime minister, wrote to Curzon that any schemes for Persia could not be put into effect because of their cost. He stated: "We must cut our coat according to our cloth. It is obvious that our fighting power in the Persian Gulf must be confined to the sea coast. In the rest of Persia we could only fight at the cost of efforts which would swallow up twice or thrice as much income tax as the Transvaal."[48] Reminders were sent to the Persians that customs in southern ports must not be handed over to any foreign power, but Curzon grew more belligerent. He advocated reciprocal moves to any aggression, including the landing of troops along the southern coast if the Russians seized the northern provinces. By the early 1900s, the Russians also began to believe that the disintegration of Persia into satellite zones was the best policy, avoiding any firm boundary that might give the British reason to block future development or expansion in the region. It appeared to Curzon that Persia could no longer serve as an effective buffer state, and it seemed to be on the brink of a colonial partition.

Curzon had therefore looked to increase British connections with the rulers of the Gulf principalities and authorized the British Resident in Bushire to conclude a secret alliance with the sheikh of Kuwait in 1899. This move seemed all the more important when the Russian cruiser *Askold* made a high-profile visit to the Persian Gulf in 1902, a move that had greatly impressed the local populations. With a deliberate exaggeration designed to shame the British government into action, Curzon asked:

> Are we prepared to surrender control of the Persian Gulf and divide that of the Indian Ocean? Are we prepared to make the construction of the Euphrates Valley Railroad or some kindred scheme an impossibility for England and an ultimate certainty for Russia? Is Baghdad to become a new Russian capital in the south? Lastly, are we content to see a naval squadron battering Bombay?[49]

Curzon had argued that Russia intended to take all of Persia and therefore any agreement with the czarist regime to limit their expansion would, ultimately, fail. Curzon was confident, however, that if a consistent line was taken by the British government, any Russian schemes could be thwarted. If the Russians ever managed to reach the Gulf they could not actually threaten India and the trade routes unless they established a naval base in the Persian Gulf, and this could only happen, he posited, if the British government showed inadequate resolve.[50] He urged that the British should grant a loan to the Persian shah similar to that of Russia, but felt that Persia might have to be coerced into greater compliance. The conclusion of the South African War in 1902 and Curzon's promptings eventually paid off. The *Askold* visit finally persuaded the Foreign Office that Russia may indeed have intended to establish a naval base in the Gulf. In a House of Lords speech in the summer of 1903, Lord Lansdowne, the foreign secretary, warned Russia that any attempt to establish such a base would be "resisted with all means at [Britain's] disposal."[51] The same year, the British loan to Persia was made available, and the British government acquiesced to Curzon's demand for a high-profile tour of the Persian Gulf, but, anxious about Curzon's intentions, they warned that no commitments were to be made.

Curzon's Persian Gulf tour was a success. His party on board the SS *Hardinge* was accompanied by four British warships and was clearly designed to demonstrate Britain's naval supremacy in the region. Curzon also hoped to get a clearer picture of the strategic possibilities the Persian Gulf might offer. At Muscat the British Resident had prepared the ground, and Curzon got an enthusiastic reception, complete with an artillery salute. Although an 1891 treaty had established Muscat as an independent partner with Britain, the sultan of Muscat made references to Britain's new paramountcy in the region, and his own intention to uphold it.[52] The second stop was to convene a durbar, a ceremonial gathering under the British Raj, at Sharjah for the Trucial Coast sheikhs. After awarding them swords, rifles, and gold watches, Curzon reminded his guests that Britain had brought the local violence to an end, ensured their independence, and expected that British supremacy would be maintained.[53] The tour then continued to Bushire, Bahrain, and finally to Kuwait. The Kuwaitis had no port facilities or wheeled transport, so Curzon's party had to land on a beach and bring its own carriage, but the reception was probably the most exuberant of all the states, with a guard of honor firing joyously into the air. The sheikh himself presented Curzon with a sword of honor, professed his admiration for Britain, and stated that he considered himself part of the military system of the British Empire. The British government was somewhat embarrassed by the exuberance of the Arabs at Curzon's receptions, but the visit had been an undeniable success: local rulers felt that British power was manifest, not least in the form of welcome prosperity and the protection of the ships of the British fleet. Moreover, Russia believed that Lansdowne's declaration in the House of Lords was not empty rhetoric, and the Royal Navy had gained valuable information about the hydrography of the Persian Gulf waters in preparation for future operations there.

The Anglo-Russian Convention of 1907

The defeat of the czar's armies and fleets in the Russo-Japanese War (1904–5) and the subsequent revolution in Russia in 1905 marked a turning point in Anglo-Russian relations. The external defeat of its land and naval forces combined with widespread internal unrest graphically demonstrated Russia's weaknesses. Financially too, it was evident that Russia lagged far behind the Western powers, and, despite its size, it lacked the industrial capacity of Britain and Germany. The logic of Britain's Entente Cordiale with France in 1904 was now, as Lansdowne had predicted, to settle their differences with France's ally Russia. Just two years later, on 31 August 1907, the British government concluded the Anglo-Russian Convention.[54]

The terms of the convention provided for two spheres of influence in Persia, the north to Russia and the south to Britain with a neutral strip between. The Persian regime, now seen as decrepit and on the verge of collapse, was not consulted about the arrangement. Farther east, both countries guaranteed the territorial integrity of Afghanistan and Tibet, and Russia also obtained Britain's approval for the eventual Russian occupation of the Bosphorus, provided other leading powers agreed.

Russia's sincerity in the convention of 1907 may not have been questioned in London, but in India the old suspicions remained, and with good reason. Russian intrigues in Persia did not abate. The Russians seemed just as active in trying to extend their influence throughout the country, with the effect that the Persian state was destabilized further as rival factions sought foreign backing. However, it was the arrival of German consuls in the region and their blatant attempts to win over the Muslim world to further their own territorial ambitions that tended to draw the British and Russians into some semblance of cooperation.

What alarmed the British the most was Germany's rapid naval building program, which seemed deliberately designed to threaten the British Empire. In Persia and the Ottoman Empire, German agents were sent on thinly disguised "archaeological expeditions" to gather intelligence and visit the oil fields, and a number of German banks and businesses appeared offering low rates of interest to undercut the British-owned Imperial Bank of Persia. The much-vaunted idea of a railway from Berlin to Baghdad also raised the possibility that commerce would be drawn away from the coasts, on which Britain depended, to the interior, where the continental powers like Germany and Russia would be favored. Such a railway might also provide a strategic route for the deployment of German troops deep within the Middle East, or even the establishment of a Gulf port.

The government in London now seemed reluctant to do anything similar lest it jeopardize the Anglo-Russian Convention. The government of India therefore sent Major Percy Cox, an officer in the Indian army and in the political service and former Resident of Muscat, to southern Persia to monitor German intrigue and to befriend the local Persian elites by extending the informal networks that already existed. It was to prove a prescient decision, as Cox, schooled in the art of the Great Game, would go on to thwart German espionage in the Gulf during World War I and assist in the establishment of the modern state of Iraq.

Conclusions

For the British, prestige and informal controls or influences could reduce the need for physical and costly occupations, although the policy came with risks. Given the impossibility of occupying every littoral of the British Empire, or extending security zones for its possessions deep into the interior of Asia, the British "soft power" policy was the pragmatic and cost-effective solution. British interests in the region were essentially the promotion and protection of trade, the security of India, and the exclusion of rivals from the Persian Gulf. Britain had the advantage of "force multipliers," namely local agents, the personnel of the Indian army (who provided all the local security for Britain's residencies, consulates, and commerce), and the ships of the Indian navy. Britain also had the strategic advantage in the nineteenth century that its enemies had no comparable fleets, which gave it considerable power and reach.

However, Britain nonetheless faced a number of challenges. There were asymmetrical problems that were difficult to resolve, particularly intrigue by Russia, unstable buffer states, and unreliable allies. There were also broader strategic weaknesses to confront. The British government had to take a global strategic view, and regarded the Persian Gulf as relatively unimportant compared with the Mediterranean or the Channel, but the government of India saw things differently, and regarded the Persian Gulf and Persia itself as important elements in the security of the subcontinent, and this conflict meant that policies with regard to Persia appeared to be inconsistent. The fact was that the British Empire was not as strong in land forces and simply could not afford to occupy Persia or the Arab littoral sheikhdoms. The consistent aspect of British policy was that it needed Turkey, Persia, and Afghanistan as bulwarks for its security, but the challenge was that they were weak and Britain found itself trying to shore up failing states. A settlement of differences with Russia alleviated the pressure in 1907, but this fundamental dilemma was never quite resolved.

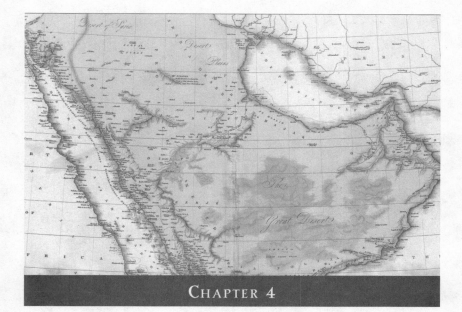

CHAPTER 4

The Gamekeeper versus the Mercenary Spirit

The Pax Britannica in the Gulf

Saul Kelly

T he Portuguese experience in the sixteenth century demonstrates the importance of maritime power in securing paramountcy in the Gulf. Apart from Portugal the only other modern state that succeeded in imposing "hegemony upon the waters" was another maritime nation, Great Britain.[1] Whereas Portuguese domination in the Gulf was part of a grand plan to capture the trade of the Indies by seizing its traditional outlets, British control of the Gulf was achieved "in a more haphazard fashion."[2] As J. B. Kelly pointed out over forty years ago now, in his study *Britain and the Persian Gulf*:

> Whereas the Portuguese came to the Gulf as soldiers and conquerors, to impose their will upon the Gulf states, the English came initially as merchant adventurers, seeking trade and fortune. Two centuries were to elapse before the attainment of territorial dominion in India compelled them to obtain and hold command of the Gulf. By the second quarter of the nineteenth century their position there was unassailable, and from that time forward the guardianship of the Gulf rested in British hands.[3]

This chapter will seek to address the questions that arise from this quotation: First, how did the British establish their guardianship of the Gulf, what did it comprise, and how did it work? Second, what were the challenges to it? And third, how did it end? But there is a fourth question that must be addressed as well: Why is the British experience, like the Portuguese before it, still relevant to our task of understanding the dynamics of security in the Gulf? It is the main contention of this chapter that by studying the example of Britain in the Gulf, we begin to understand how a hegemonic power has operated there in the past, and how the demise of its power, like the Portuguese, creates an anarchy that the major littoral states avail themselves of in their contest for primacy over the Gulf. It is no accident of history, in my view, that Britain's departure from the Gulf in 1971, in particular the manner of her going, resulted in a power vacuum that the larger littoral states tried and failed to fill. Since 1971 we have seen three major wars and the downfall of two regimes, the tottering of others, and the reassertion of authority by outside powers, and especially by the United States. The genie of insecurity is out of the bottle in the Gulf. Can it be put back or is that an impossible task? What does the British experience tell us?

How Did the British Establish Their Guardianship of the Gulf, What Did It Comprise, and How Did It Work?

There is a symmetry between the British exit from and entrance to the Gulf, and this lies in the mercenary spirit. The English East India Company (EIC) established trading factories at Shiraz, Isfahan, and Jask in the second decade of the seventeenth century in order to foster trade with Persia. It was ships of the EIC that took Shah Abbas I's army from the mainland to the Portuguese citadel on Hormuz Island in 1622. It was those same ships that engaged and defeated the Portuguese fleet and then blockaded the island. The eventual fall of Hormuz gave the English what they sought: a factory at Bandar Abbas and lucrative commercial links with Persia.[4] It was the same mercenary spirit that presided over Britain's retreat from the Gulf in 1971, as we shall see.

For the British, as for the Portuguese, the Dutch, and the French, Hormuz, along with Muscat and later Aden, represented the keys to command of the Arabian Sea and control of the maritime trade of Arabia, Persia, and India. It was the British authorities in India that secured all these keys by the nineteenth century. The paramountcy, or Pax Britannica, that Britain eventually established in the Gulf and around the shores of Arabia had its start in the agreement concluded with the Al Bu Said Sultan of Oman in 1798 in response to Napoleon Bonaparte's occupation of Egypt.[5] It continued in the nineteenth century with the trucial system and the special treaty relationship with Bahrain and the seven sheikhdoms of the Trucial Coast. The trucial system rested on a duty by Britain not only to maintain the maritime peace of the Gulf against outbreaks of piracy and maritime warfare, but also to protect the independence and territorial integrity of the sheikhdoms that had signed the truce.[6] It fitted in with the eastern Arabian tradition of protection-seeking.[7] It was only upon this reciprocal basis that the British managed to conclude the restrictive agreements with the sheikhdoms over the slave trade, the arms trade, foreign relations, and oil concessions. Britain's duty was made explicit in the case of Bahrain (1861) because the latter's frontiers were defined by the sea and could be defended by naval power.[8] A similar commitment was made to Qatar over its maritime frontiers in 1916, but not its land frontiers, which were then undetermined.[9] For a similar reason no such commitment was made to the Trucial sheikhdoms. There was the added consideration that it would have transgressed the abiding principle of British Gulf policy not to become involved in the internal affairs of the Arabian Peninsula. There was no doubt, however, that Britain was obliged, by the trucial system and the subsequent agreements, to defend the sheikhdoms against external aggression.[10]

Kuwait was the only sheikhdom whose internationally agreed land frontiers Britain was obliged, under the November 1914 agreement, to defend.
Although, as a result of the oil boom, Kuwait achieved independence in 1961,
there remained a stipulation in the instrument abrogating the 1899 and 1914
protectorate agreements for Britain to extend a friendly helping hand if necessary.[11] This soon came to pass when the Iraqi dictator, Brigadier Abdul Karim
Qassim, made aggressive noises toward Kuwait in 1961 and was only silenced
after Britain deployed a joint force to the territory in Operation Vantage, the
success of which should have been borne in mind by policy makers in Arabia
and the West in 1990.[12]

Challenges to British Guardianship of the Gulf

The ending of the British protectorate over Kuwait in 1961 marked the start
of the unravelling of the treaty relationship binding Britain to the minor
Gulf states, which culminated in Britain's withdrawal from the Gulf in 1971.
Moreover the states "system," which regulated relations between states and had
guaranteed law and order in the Gulf for over one hundred years, was swept away
and not really replaced by the establishment of the Gulf Cooperation Council
(GCC) in 1981.[13] The precarious peace of the Gulf, and the security of shipping
transiting its waters, relied on the self-interest of the larger littoral powers, Iraq,
Iran, and Saudi Arabia, and their various great-power backers, the Soviet Union
and the United States, to keep a tight rein on their rivalry. That they patently
failed to do so soon became apparent after 1971.

What Were the Various Challenges Posed to the Pax Britannica
in the Gulf by Iraq, Iran, and Saudi Arabia?

Iraq. Iraq's very narrow coastline (a few dozen kilometers) and lack of maritime power has, historically, deprived her of the ability to establish a political
supremacy in the Gulf. Even when the Turks, following the opening of the Suez
Canal in 1869, projected naval power into the Gulf and established control over
Hasa and a loose suzerainty over Kuwait and Qatar, they did not pose any real
threat to the British position in the Gulf. With the British seizure of Iraq from
the Turks during World War I, the establishment of the mandate, and the drawing of the new country's frontiers by the British, the Iraqis had little opportunity
to intervene in the Gulf. It was Britain again who thwarted the attempts in the
late 1930s and in 1961 by a now independent Iraq to press its claim to Kuwait.
That successive Iraqi regimes should do so was due to the dictates of geography.

Kuwait had the best harbor in the upper Gulf and Iraq's only real outlet was the Shatt al-Arab. Even here Iraq's control, under the 1937 treaty with Iran, was increasingly challenged by Iran until it was renounced in 1969. Alarmed by this, and by the Iranian seizure of Abu Musa and the Tunbs in 1971, Iraq's response was to revive her claim on Kuwait and to seek Soviet support. The Soviet Union showed a growing interest in the Gulf after Britain's announcement in 1968 of her intention to withdraw.[14]

Iran. In contrast to Iraq, Iran has a long coastline stretching from Khuzestan in the west to Mekran and Baluchistan in the east. But from the late seventeenth century to the early twentieth century successive shahs had no sustained control over it. This was due in part to the administrative weaknesses of Persian government, but also to the fact that Persia's rulers did not have the sea power to patrol Gulf waters. This did not prevent them from advancing dubious territorial claims to the delta of the Shatt al-Arab, Kuwait, Bahrain and other islands, the Trucial sheikhdoms, Oman, Mekran, Baluchistan, and Seistan—wherever, in fact, a Persian foot had trod. Frustrated by the gap between their insistence on their inalienable rights to these territories and their inability to secure them, successive Iranian governments did their best to thwart Britain in her suppression of piracy, the slave and arms trades, the survey of Gulf waters, the laying of telegraph cables, the installation of aids to navigation, and the setting up of a quarantine system. The pinprick policy followed by the Qajar and then the Pahlevi dynasties was, after the aggressive expansion of the Saudi emirate of Nejd, the largest source of disruption and disorder in the Gulf. And it is to the Saudis that we must now turn.[15]

Saudi Arabia. Even that great Western propagandist for the Saudis, Harry St. John Philby, father of the more infamous Kim, admitted that Wahhabism, as harnessed by the Al-Saud clan of Nejd, was driven by "constant aggression at the expense of those who did not share the great idea."[16] After conquering most of central and eastern Arabia by 1800, the Wahhabis took the al-Buraimi oasis, the key to inner Oman and the adjacent Gulf sheikhdoms. Winning over the Qawasim, the strongest pirate tribe on the Arabian shore, they launched a seaborne jihad against Indian and European shipping that took two British punitive expeditions (in 1809–10 and 1819–20) to put down before the Qawasim and other seafaring tribes were forced to sign a treaty agreeing to end piracy. It became a governing principle of British policy to watch and prevent the growth of Wahhabi influence over the Gulf sheikhdoms in case it undermined the maritime truce. By guaranteeing the sheikhdoms' independence, Britain set herself in opposition to the expansion of Wahhabi dominion in eastern Arabia beyond Nejd and Hasa. For some eighty-three years after the expulsion of the Wahhabis from al-Buraimi in 1869, they made no attempt to venture there again, nor were they in a position to do so. It was not until after the establishment of the Kingdom of Saudi Arabia in 1932 that Abdul Aziz ibn Saud felt able to direct Saudi eyes again toward the Gulf sheikhdoms. His award of an oil concession to Standard Oil of California (SOCAL) in 1933 raised the question of the eastern boundaries of the new Saudi kingdom and he was quick to lay claim to large tracts of Qatar, Abu Dhabi, and Oman. The British Foreign Office, in line with the prevailing spirit of appeasement in British foreign policy at the time, was prepared to give away part of the sheikhdom of Abu Dhabi in the hope of winning over Ibn Saud as an ally in the Middle East, and especially in Palestine. The Foreign Office was only prevented from doing so by the British Government of India, and its representative department in Whitehall, the India Office, on the grounds of principle and policy.

However, the spirit of appeasement lingered on in the Foreign Office and, after inheriting responsibility for the Gulf from the India Office after the demise of British power in India in 1947, it manifested itself in the mistaken British response to a renewed frontier claim made by the Saudis in 1949. The latter now demanded four-fifths of the sheikhdom of Abu Dhabi, where Petroleum Concessions Limited (a subsidiary of British-run Iraq Petroleum Company, IPC) had the concession to prospect for oil. In order to placate the Saudis, and particularly the foreign minister, Emir Faisal ibn Abdul Aziz, the Foreign Office in August 1951 accepted the Saudi proposal for a ban on all oil-prospecting activities while a commission determined the frontiers. This was tantamount to admitting that California Arabian Standard Oil Company (CASOC) and Saudi Arabia had concessionary and territorial rights in the area, which in the minds of British officials they did not, and that IPC's rights were invalid. The Foreign Office compounded this error by also agreeing to Faisal's demand that the British-officered Trucial Oman Levies (later Scouts) should not operate in the disputed areas. In turn the Saudis agreed not to engage in activities that might prejudice the work of the frontier commission. Whereas the British honored their side of the standstill agreements, the Saudis engaged in wholesale bribery of tribal leaders in and around the al-Buraimi oasis in order to have them declare their allegiance to Saudi Arabia. It culminated in the illegal, in the minds of the British, Saudi occupation of the al-Buraimi oasis in August 1952. The Foreign Office then acceded to a Saudi and American request that the sultan of Oman, who governed three villages in the oasis, should not eject the interlopers by force and disband his tribal levies. This allowed the Saudi force to remain in al-Buraimi for nearly two years and to continue its subversive activities. By staying in the oasis the Saudis hoped to bolster their claim to the western areas of Abu Dhabi and to penetrate inner Oman. The final mistake by the Foreign Office, in July 1954, was to agree to the continuance of the limitations on British activities under the 1951 agreement, while the dispute went to arbitration by an international tribunal, in exchange for the withdrawal of the Saudi occupying force from al-Buraimi. This simply allowed another smaller Saudi force, intended along with a comparable British unit to police the oasis, to continue Saudi subversive activities at al-Buraimi. It was only when the Saudis tried to ensure a sympathetic finding by the international tribunal sitting in Geneva through bribery that even the Foreign Office decided it had had enough. It not only ended the arbitration but led to the ejection of the Saudi force from al-Buraimi by the Trucial Oman Scouts in October 1955, much to the disquiet of the Saudis, ARAMCO (Arabian-American Oil Company), and the U.S. government. After the Suez Crisis in 1956, and the severing of diplomatic relations by the Saudis, the Foreign Office returned to its former defensive and apologetic approach to such an extent that by 1970 it was prepared, as will be seen, to facilitate Saudi claims on Abu Dhabi territory in order to ease Britain's passage out of the Gulf.[17]

End of British Guardianship in the Gulf

The Pax Britannica in the Gulf had been maintained for one hundred and fifty years, and it was swept away in ten, from Kuwaiti independence in 1961 to the final British withdrawal in 1971. The latter had been announced by Harold Wilson's Labour government in 1968 and carried out by Edward Heath's Conservative government three years later. An end to the formal British presence in the Gulf had to come in the postcolonial age, and the treaty system needed revision. But it was in the manner of Britain's going from the Gulf that it managed to betray all that it had stood for and achieved during its long guardianship of the Gulf. Britain simply abandoned the small Gulf sheikhdoms to their fate. There was no attempt to reformulate the treaty system in order to retain its implicit defense obligations, thus providing for a continued British military presence that would have maintained stability in an area that had become increasingly vital to not just British but Western interests. It was argued at the time by politicians, diplomats, and their apologists in the media, and has been repeated since by some historians, that the British government could no longer afford the £12–14 million cost of continuing a military presence in the Gulf because of the parlous state of Britain's finances and her military commitments elsewhere, especially in Northern Ireland. Twelve to 14 million pounds sterling seems cheap given that it was the cost of protecting hundreds of millions of pounds' worth of Gulf oil for Britain and the West. Moreover, the sheikhs of Abu Dhabi and Dubai offered to pay it in full, since they, like the sheikh of Bahrain and the sultan of Oman, did not want to see Britain leave the Gulf. The boorish reply of the British defense secretary, Denis Healey, spoke volumes about his lack of strategic vision, his engrained political prejudices, and the rank hypocrisy of the British government. He proclaimed that he was not "a sort of white slaver for Arab sheikhs," and that "it would be a very great mistake if we allowed ourselves to become mercenaries for people who like to have British troops around."[18] Strangely enough he did not object to the West German government contributing to the cost of maintaining the British army on the Rhine, nor did it prevent him, and his successors, from selling large quantities of sophisticated military equipment to Iran and Saudi Arabia, the two local powers, whose conduct and ambitions had for one hundred and fifty years posed the main threat to Gulf security. It was no excuse that other powers, principally the United States, were engaged in such a lucrative trade, for no other power had carried the responsibility for maintaining the peace of the Gulf, nor had they, like Britain, suppressed maritime warfare, piracy, and the slave and arms trades. Any chance that the mistakes of the Labour government would be rectified by their Conservative successors was dashed when the Heath government tried to pressurize the sheikh of Abu Dhabi into surrendering a large chunk of his oil-rich territory to Saudi Arabia, and then connived at the Iranian seizure of Abu Musa and the Tunbs. In its unseemly scramble to get out of the Gulf by 1971, Britain had reverted to the same mercenary spirit that had marked its entry three hundred and fifty years before.

Lessons from the Pax Britannica in the Gulf: Gamekeepers and Poachers

What lessons can be drawn from the British experience in the Gulf?

First, if a great maritime power is drawn into the Gulf, for mercenary or other motives, and it is to stay there to guarantee its interests, it eventually has to deal with the threats to the stability of the area posed by warfare or piracy. The use of force to coerce reluctant actors will be necessary, and diplomatic tools will have to be employed to build alliances that will work in keeping the peace in the Gulf. Such a system, and its infrastructure, must be guaranteed in the last resort by the paramount maritime power.

Second, the British position in the Gulf had always been based on the lower Gulf, on the trucial system and the long relationship with Oman, and not on Britain's relations with Iraq, Iran, and Saudi Arabia, or even Kuwait. The major Gulf states had always resented Britain's role in the Gulf, had attempted to negate it, and had welcomed Britain's exit.

Third, withdrawal from the Gulf was yet another step in Europe's withdrawal from Asia and Africa after World War II. It has been represented, usually by way of excuse, as the inevitable response to the rise of Afro-Asian nationalism, though increasingly historical research reveals it to have been due to the collapse of the Europeans' will to defend their interests in the wider world. This failure of will led Britain and Europe increasingly to consign the defense of these interests in the Middle East and elsewhere to the United States, which had always been as much a rival as an ally in these areas. Eschewing Britain's former gamekeeper role, the U.S. government pursued a pointless "twin-pillars" policy in the 1970s of handing over the security of the Gulf to two of the main poachers, Iran and Saudi Arabia. The collapse of the Iranian pillar, with the fall of the shah in 1979, raised serious questions about the stability of the remaining Saudi one and, indeed, the continued viability of U.S. policy. It took the third poacher, or the thief of Baghdad, Saddam Hussein, to reveal, in three large-scale and bloody wars, the consequences of the collapse of the states system in the Gulf following Britain's withdrawal, and the dangers of appeasing local aggressors.

Since the Iranian Revolution in 1979 there has been a renewal of the religious division in the Gulf, between Sunni Arabia and Shia Iran, and this has reached fever pitch since 2003 and the events in Iraq. It is symbolized by the February 2006 Sunni Arab bombing of the Askariya shrine at Samarra, one of the holiest Shia sites (where lie the tombs of the Tenth and the Eleventh Imams and where lies a shrine to the Twelfth or Hidden Imam, Muhammad al-Mahdi). In the long history of Sunni-Shia antagonism it bears comparison with the Wahhabi devastation of Karbala in 1801 and desecration of the shrine of Husain, the grandson of the Prophet. It is a factor that outside powers in the Gulf will increasingly have to bear in mind, especially as it intersects with, and is complicated by, a general rise in tension between the Islamic world and the rest of the world.

And finally, since 1987 the United States has played the reluctant policeman in the Gulf. With the bitter experience of Iraq and Afghanistan in mind, there may well be a waning appetite for continuing such a role. But in reappraising the role of the United States, U.S. opinion formers and policy makers need to keep in mind what happened when, in a similar mood in the early 1970s, at the end of the Vietnam War and in consequence of Britain's withdrawal from the Gulf, they handed over the security of this most vital waterway to the two main poachers in the area. To continue this metaphor, the Gulf needs gamekeepers, headed by the United States, as much today as in the past, assisted by those powers who have a vital economic and financial stake in the area, whether European, South Asian, or East Asian. We cannot afford, in this globalized world, to allow the destabilization of one of the key areas on the planet. Let the gamekeeper rather than the mercenary spirit inform our attitudes and policies toward the challenges in this area.

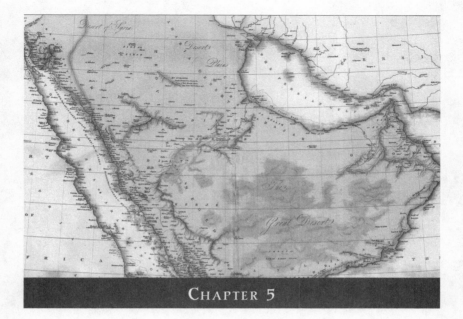

CHAPTER 5

Why Didn't America Replace the British in the Persian Gulf?

Jeffrey R. Macris

T he years 1968–71 proved momentous in the history of the Persian Gulf, for during those years Great Britain's century-and-a-half-long stewardship of the region ended, and several independent states emerged. Washington officials—who received entreaties from leaders both in London and the Arab emirates during this time to assume Britain's existing security obligations and military basing rights—declined the opportunity to expand their modest military and diplomatic presence in the Gulf. Emirs and sheikhs dangled in front of the Americans the keys to British bases along the Arab western side of the Gulf, and proffered cold cash to lure and keep them there. Why did the Americans decline, choosing instead to deputize two local surrogates? How did American leaders interact with their British partners? How did the existence of the U.S. Navy's Middle East Force influence America's thinking toward Gulf affairs? These questions serve as the focus of this chapter.

American Policy toward the Gulf Emerges Quickly in 1968

Although cooperation generally marked the strategic Anglo-American security relationship during the Cold War, the Labour government's decision to withdraw from the Persian Gulf virtually without prior notice met with fierce condemnation from Washington. In a testy rebuke not seen in the Anglo-American dialogue since the Suez Crisis, on 6 January 1968 U.S. Secretary of State Dean Rusk sent a scathing letter to London concerning rumors that London was about to make such a move. If true, he believed, British withdrawal from east of Suez represented a fundamental sea change for the Western alliance, and shouldn't be undertaken unilaterally. To announce this in a surprise fashion, as rumors suggested, represented a grave breach of faith. In Rusk's letter to his British counterpart, the U.S. secretary of state complained:

> I am deeply disturbed by information which has just reached me to the effect that HMG [Her Majesty's Government] may be considering accelerating its withdrawal from the Persian Gulf. As you know, we attach very high importance to the maintenance of the British position in the Persian Gulf for the indefinite future. We welcomed the repositioning of some of your forces there from Aden last year as an earnest [sign] of your determination to continue to play the essential stabilizing role in the Gulf which has been so

helpful to us all for so long. While economies can no doubt be made, I would earnestly hope that before we meet next week HMG will not have taken any irrevocable decisions. In our view, [the] fixing of [a] specific timetable at this early stage would be likely to feed instability in the region and increase your own problems in arranging [an] eventual orderly departure.[1]

The British diplomats confirmed the veracity of the rumors, and Foreign Office officials confided that even they, too, were caught off guard by the Labour Party decision. They explained that a financial crisis that caused the government in November 1967 to devalue the pound put "intense pressures" on them to reduce government expenditures,[2] especially defense spending overseas.[3] Not only would the British yield their special role in the Persian Gulf, they related to their American counterparts, but they would do the same thing in the greater Far East. The British explained that the two theaters were intertwined: "The decision to leave the Persian Gulf was dictated primarily by the fact that there would be no [aircraft] carriers or bases available to support or relieve the Persian Gulf after March 1971 when British forces would have been withdrawn from the Far East."[4]

America's Enduring Persian Gulf Policies Come Quickly during the Johnson Administration

The British announcement of withdrawal forced Lyndon B. Johnson's administration to cobble together on short notice an ad hoc policy toward the Persian Gulf that—although completed without the in-depth study that they almost certainly would have preferred—would nevertheless endure for years. This policy formation process took place in the shadow of an enormous foreign policy crisis in Washington: the January–February 1968 North Vietnamese Tet Offensive, which increasingly dominated the foreign policy and administrative functions of the U.S. government.

The private reaction of many Arab leaders in the small emirates was swift: they condemned the British move, and requested from Washington that America assume the role as security guarantor in the region. Afraid of the hostile designs of their larger neighbors, they wanted American protection. Kuwait and Bahrain, for example, both sought a larger U.S. Navy flotilla in the region.[5] The Kuwaitis and others asked to purchase arms.[6]

Although the philosophic rationale for U.S. policy toward the Persian Gulf would not become apparent until Henry Kissinger's stewardship of foreign policy several years later—the Nixon Doctrine—six key themes emerged in the

Johnson administration's last year in office that would endure for years as key tenets of the superpower's policy in the Gulf.

Do not replace the British as security guarantor in the Persian Gulf. The first and most conspicuous component of U.S. policy toward the Persian Gulf in early 1968 surrounded the steadfast and unflinching refusal of senior Washington officials to consider replacing the British as security guarantors in the region. This policy became apparent within days of Britain's January 1968 surprise announcement of its impending withdrawal, when a U.S. State Department spokesman announced, "We have no plans to move in where the British forces pull out."[7] With the U.S. military stretched thin with Vietnam and other Cold War commitments, the superpower simply could not—and would not—take on any new obligations in the late 1960s. As the *New York Times* summarized:

> Apparently taking into account the strong current of opinion in this country against making new security commitments abroad, Mr. Rusk was understood to have said that the United States was not going "to sideslip" into assuming British defense commitments east of Suez.[8]

Keep the British engaged. Related to this reticence to get involved in security commitments to the region came a second facet of America's initial policy toward the Gulf: keeping the British engaged in the region as long as possible. As notes from a February 1968 U.S. interdepartmental working group stated:

> Our policy should be directed along the lines of encouraging the British to maintain as much of their present special role in the Gulf as they can, as long as possible, including their role as principal arms supplier to various Gulf states.[9]

These two bulwarks of American policy to the region—refusing to enlarge security commitments there, coupled with an attempt to prolong British involvement—did not reflect a *break* of American policies as much as it did a *renewal* of America's long-standing attitude toward the region. In his decision earlier in the decade to refuse funding improvements to the Indian Ocean military base on Diego Garcia, for example, Secretary of Defense Robert McNamara cited both of these two policy goals. If America expanded the scope of her military involvement in the region, McNamara feared, in British minds the illusion may take root and grow that the United States stood ready to take over London's security commitments, prompting Britain's premature departure.[10]

The desire to steer clear of military commitments in the region led Washington officials early in 1968 to decide to forswear arms dealing with new clients in the Gulf. American officials correctly predicted that Arabs in the former British-controlled lands would soon turn to the United States for protection. As U.S. Assistant Secretary of Defense for International Security Affairs Paul Warnke concluded:

> We can anticipate that the small states and sheikhdoms of the Gulf will rather naturally look to us to take the place of the British, and that it is easier to avoid this temptation at the outset than it would be later to attempt to extricate ourselves.[11]

This drive to remain clear of foreign entanglements would prove very powerful, and would challenge even America's Cold War commitment to fight Communism. The esteemed Paul Nitze, foreign policy adviser to several presidents, remarked that the United States must steadfastly work against becoming too deeply involved in the Persian Gulf region through arms sales to the new Arab emirates: "Even in the event that they turn to non-Western sources for arms, it is preferable that we not become involved in an effort to make the sales ourselves."[12]

The Kuwaitis were the first to ask for arms. When in April 1968 the Kuwaitis requested from the Americans the right to purchase sixty troop carrier vehicles, for example, the Johnson administration reacted strongly and vociferously against the request: "I believe we should sell no arms to these states," said one mid-level official, a view approved in April 1968 by Warnke.[13] Although this prohibition on U.S. arms sales in the Gulf would fade away in the early 1970s—in part as the magnitude of potential profits became clear—in early 1968, U.S. officials curtly replied "no" to all other requests except those from Washington's tested allies in Tehran and Riyadh. In addition to preventing unspoken and undesired American defense commitments from developing with the small Arab emirates, Washington officials believed, this refusal would also likely cause the Arabs to turn back toward the British, which would reinforce the goal of prolonging British involvement there.

Brief attempt to promote defensive alliances. If American leaders refused to replace the British, who then would defend Western interests there, including continued access to oil? In what one might dub the third component of America's immediate policy toward the Gulf after Britain's announcement—one that did not endure for long—Washington expressed an early interest in encouraging the development of mutual security pacts. Within days of Britain's surprise withdrawal announcement, in that vein, presidential special assistant Walt Rostow suggested that in the future the United States might rely on "security groupings of nations in the region" to fill the vacuum in the Persian Gulf.[14]

The United States, in other words, might foster a NATO (North Atlantic Treaty Organization)-like concept of collective security for the Persian Gulf, using the shell of the existing Central Treaty Organization (CENTO), perhaps with some type of an enlarged role for the United States. In a February 1968 meeting with the British ambassador to Washington, Rostow ruminated whether "under an effective secretary-general CENTO could not be of greater value than in the recent past."[15] As time passed Rostow became more intrigued with his idea, which appeared at first blush to solve the American security dilemma of how to maintain order in a region possessing vital American interests, while at the same time doing so in a manner that would not involve substantial numbers of U.S. troops.

Rostow, however, soon discovered that any move by the United States to increase its influence in the region would evince wrath from all over the globe, with the strongest criticism originating from the Arab world itself. In a press interview that garnered wide attention around the world, Rostow discussed in public his views concerning a multinational regional security pact, one that might include American leadership, or even the use of American military trainers to assist Arab states. The reaction to it, however, proved hostile, ranging from "naive" according to London officials,[16] to "sinister" from Moscow representatives,[17] to outright condemnation from some nations in the Arab world, whose leaders proclaimed publicly (though some clearly did not believe it privately) that Gulf residents did not wish to evict one colonial occupier only to have a second follow in its footsteps.

Build up the "Twin Pillars." If American planners soon realized that such a NATO- or CENTO-like security alliance to maintain order would never get off the ground in the Gulf, upon whose shoulders would rest the role of regional security guarantor? In what one might call the fourth component of America's initial defense strategy in the Persian Gulf following Britain's 1968 announcement of its impending withdrawal, the United States effectively deputized two of the region's dominant powers, Iran and Saudi Arabia, as the policemen in the region. The idea of relying on local, indigenous forces to provide security for Uncle Sam at a minimal price, without the need to commit U.S. forces to the region, proved alluring to Washington officials. The policy appeared to rest upon a firm foundation, for American leaders thought they knew well their two primary Gulf allies. As Warnke summed up:

> We already have a fairly high degree of interest in and close relations with Saudi Arabia (i.e., King Faisal and ARAMCO), and with Iran, to whom we have just agreed to sell during the next five years $600 million worth of

additional arms. Aside from that, we think that the people of the area can manage their lives better without additional interference from us than they can with it.[18]

In essence, top Johnson administration officials in 1968—recognizing that they possessed neither the military wherewithal nor the political will to replace the British—had concluded that they had no alternative but to rely on surrogates to accomplish the mission that the British had done for over a century. Of the two surrogates, the real enforcer would be the nation with the stronger military, Iran, and its westward-looking leader the shah. As Warnke concluded in June 1968:

> In effect, we are placing our money on a modern Persian Emperor to keep open the Persian Gulf; and I advocate that we sell arms to no one else on the Gulf [in addition to Iran] except Saudi Arabia. . . .While it is quite possible that Iran's "peacekeeping" in the Persian Gulf may become from time-to-time a rather messy operation, I doubt that a large role by the United States would be any more effective—or less messy. I think that we are already sufficiently immersed in Arab affairs with respect to those states immediately surrounding Israel."[19]

It is thus worth noting that the U.S. decision to rely on Iran and Saudi Arabia to tend to U.S. interests in the Persian Gulf began during the Johnson administration, within weeks and months of the January 1968 British announcement of their impending withdrawal. As previously suggested, some historians attribute this policy to the Nixon administration. It is correct, however, to associate the rise of the term "Twin Pillars" with the Nixon administration, and especially with National Security Adviser (and later secretary of state) Henry Kissinger, who fleshed out the Persian Gulf policy and gave to it a philosophic underpinning. But the policy itself, however, originated in early 1968 as the Johnson administration struggled to react to Britain's surprise announcement of its impending withdrawal.

Keep the U.S. Navy's Middle East Force. One of the most difficult decisions with which United States defense and diplomatic officials had to grapple in the immediate aftermath of Britain's announcement surrounded the future of the U.S. Navy's Middle East Force, a small handful of ships that had sailed from Bahrain since the end of the 1940s. Although the force for twenty years had proved a symbol of American resolve with respect to the superpower's growing oil interests in the region, particularly in Saudi Arabia, the flotilla had in reality been little more than a diplomatic showpiece with almost no military punch. The flagship of the force, after all, was normally a submarine tender or a converted amphibious transport ship, possessing only small guns, and sporting a white paint job.[20] (White naval vessels, like Teddy Roosevelt's Great White Fleet, or hospital ships of today, typically reflect a lack of offensive firepower. In this case, the white paint was intended to keep the ship cool in the hostile heat of the Gulf. The association of white paint with a lack of offensive punch, however, proved fitting.)

The real military force, of course, and the ultimate arbiter of security in the region for almost 150 years, had remained the British; so when the British announced their withdrawal in January 1968, U.S. political and military leaders had to confront the question of what to do with the Navy's Middle East Force. Should they expand it, and give it a real military capability, with an eye to shaping Gulf politics in a way that only the British theretofore had possessed? Should they abandon it, noting that the British protective umbrella under which the U.S. Navy had sailed in the Gulf had disappeared, and that any U.S. force would be vulnerable? Or finally, should the United States pursue a middle course between withdrawal and augmentation, and perhaps keep the Middle East Force in the same size and shape as before? These questions proved explosive, both in Washington and in the capitals of the Gulf, for they essentially involved the larger political issue of what type of security structure would emerge in the aftermath of British withdrawal.

For their part, U.S. Navy officers saw the departure of the British from the Gulf as an opportunity to play an expanded role in a vital part of the world, and they set about on an ultimately unsuccessful campaign within Washington to enlarge the Navy's presence in the Gulf. Navy leaders proved especially desirous of HMS Jufair, the naval base in Bahrain. Less than two months after the British announcement of withdrawal, U.S. Navy officials—cognizant of the fact that neither the Pentagon nor the State Department had assented to the plan—responded affirmatively to a British question of whether or not the U.S. Navy sought HMS Jufair. British embassy officials in Washington documented these conversations, a dialogue that reveals both the strength of the Navy's desire to stake a claim on the Gulf facilities, as well as their realization that they were probably acting in advance of high-level, civilian political decisions:

> [U.S.] Rear Admiral [James W.] O'Grady (head of the Politico-Military Policy Division in the Department of the Navy) . . . said that the Americans intended, if we [the British] ran down our naval presence and showed that we were going to leave entirely, to ask the Bahraini authorities for permission to take over the facilities at HMS Jufair. He went on to state that the U.S. naval authorities foresaw the need for a naval force in the Persian Gulf

in the context of keeping the peace between Iran and the Arab countries of the area; he described Iraq as also a very uncertain factor.

We should prefer these views not to be quoted back to the Americans; there has incidentally been no reflection of them whatsoever at desk level in the State Department, and [U.S. Navy officials were] very concerned to underline that U.S. Navy thinking was not even Department of Defense policy.[21]

Navy officials were correct in their assumption that they were too far ahead of the politicians, because there existed substantial sentiment on Capitol Hill against opening up or enlarging any new American bases overseas. Senator William Stuart Symington of Missouri, for example, chaired an ad hoc subcommittee of the Senate Foreign Relations Committee looking into U.S. military affairs overseas. His particular goal, as the British surmised, was to prevent the Pentagon from "establishing foreign policy commitments over which the Congress later finds difficulty in imposing control."[22] Such concerns grew in the 1960s as a result of the U.S. entry into the Vietnam War; some believed that the United States stumbled into that conflict after the Gulf of Tonkin incident, based upon tacit agreements that the executive branch in Washington had provided to the South Vietnamese. Symington proved particularly interested in ensuring that the executive branch—and the military, over which the president possessed day-to-day control—did not enter into any type of agreement that might ensnare the nation in a future military engagement. The U.S. takeover of the Bahrain base represented just such a scenario. According to the British, the senator was on the "warpath" against any such extension of U.S. commitments overseas.[23]

Negative feelings toward keeping the U.S. Navy in the Gulf went beyond Capitol Hill all the way to Tehran. Like Senator Symington, the shah didn't want to see the U.S. Navy operating from a U.S. base in Bahrain, but the Persian monarch went one step further: he did not want the Americans in the Gulf at all. In public pronouncements the Iranian regime proclaimed that when the British departed the region, the era of outside interference in the Persian Gulf region must end. After that, only local powers, of which of course Iran dominated, would control the region. Despite the assistance since World War II that the Americans had provided to the Iranians in training and equipping their military, the shah appeared committed to drive the American military from the region. The London *Times* captured the flavor of Iranian thinking in April 1970:

The official Iranian attitude is one of outright hostility to the intervention of the great powers in the affairs of the Gulf after 1971 and of insisting that the responsibility for the security of the area must be with the littoral powers.[24]

American diplomats took seriously the shah's objections to the Navy flotilla, and worked assiduously to court his favor. The United States, after all, was placing in his hands the protection of American interests, and Washington needed to keep him happy. In attempting to get the shah to accede to a continued American naval presence in the Gulf, one Iranian sensitivity that American diplomats emphasized was the need to keep the Russians out of the Gulf. If the United States were to withdraw, they told the Iranians, the Russians might speed up their march into the Gulf, and deepen their growing presence in neighboring Iraq. In one exchange between an American diplomat and the shah of Iran:

> American ambassador [Douglas] MacArthur [said to the shah] that he quite understood that the Iranians did not want the Soviet Union to take any U.S. or UK action as a pretext for entering the Gulf. But [according to MacArthur] the Russians obviously intend to continue their presence in the Indian Ocean or the Gulf whether we [the Americans and Iranians] like it or not. From 1905 to 1968 no Russian vessel had entered the Gulf; but there had been five ship visits in the last two years. Moreover, there was the Iraqi base now under construction at the head of the Gulf.[25]

Notwithstanding the opposition from Tehran and Capitol Hill, by autumn 1968 the State Department and the Pentagon had concluded that the United States' interests would best be served by continuing to keep its naval force intact in Bahrain, with neither a sizeable increase nor decrease. The White House proposed formalizing a basing agreement with the Bahrainis, with the pledge that they would not expand the base or the scope of the naval presence there. This proposed policy of "non-change" in naval affairs, however, the fifth theme in America's policy toward the Gulf, got stuck in the U.S. bureaucracy for almost two years, and did not gain final approval until the Nixon administration. Desirous to keep some type of Western presence on the island, the British warned the Americans of the hazards of this delay, mentioning that "others had eyes on our facilities in Bahrain, including even the Iranians."[26]

Several Arabs privately welcomed the United States' decision to keep its naval flotilla in the region. Although subdued in public, in private the Bahraini ruler, for example, welcomed the news "positively."[27] The U.S. ambassador to Kuwait, furthermore, said that such positive sentiments existed up the coast:

> On various occasions when the subject of the future of MIDEASTFOR [Middle East Force] came up in my discussions with senior Kuwaiti officials they have reacted affirmatively to the idea of a continuing U.S. naval presence in the Gulf. Shaykh Jaber Ali strongly urged that it remain and be marginally strengthened. He claimed that this represents views of both the

governments of Kuwait and Bahrain. . . . However, despite these affirmative private statements, I suspect that Kuwait's public position would be cool to negative. I do not think they could logically maintain a public posture of advocating British departure and America remaining.[28]

Even the Saudis gave a quiet nod to the U.S. decision to keep its Middle East Force in Bahrain. Ambassador Nicholas Thacher in Jeddah explained that the decision stemmed from King Faisal's feeling threatened by "communist and radical encirclement."[29] Just as Bahrain and Kuwait's leaders felt constrained against publicly embracing such a plan, the ambassador explained, King Faisal would never endorse publicly a move to keep Western military personnel and hardware in the region, fearing a possible future backlash "should radical Arabs at some time in the future zero in on U.S. naval presence as a convenient 'imperialistic' political target in the post-British era."[30]

With the Arabs quietly welcoming the move, the big concern in Washington surrounded the shah's possible adverse reaction to the United States' decision to keep its naval force in the Gulf after British withdrawal. Toward that end, in the autumn of 1970 Ambassador MacArthur informed the shah of the American intention to stay. In his presentation he aimed to disarm most of the shah's possible objections, emphasizing as well that a continued U.S. presence would thwart Russian designs on the region. Denying the shah's notion that the United States wanted to become the policeman in the Gulf, the U.S. diplomat reminded the Iranian monarch that the naval force would spend the majority of its time outside the Strait of Hormuz.[31] The shah "made no rejoinder"[32] to the Americans' announcement that they would keep their flotilla in the region, suggesting that although he didn't necessarily approve of the decision, he would make no effort to fight it. With the shah's tacit consent, then, the U.S. Navy received the green light to keep intact its Middle East Force after the British withdrew.

Restrain the Soviets. The need to keep a watchful eye on the Soviets served as a sixth and final hallmark of the U.S. policy in the Gulf in the immediate aftermath of Great Britain's announcement of its impending withdrawal. This really marked a *continuation* of policies pursued during the Cold War rather than a shift, in that U.S. support for Iran as a check on the Soviet Union's southward advance had remained consistent since World War II.

Specifically, Washington officials in 1968 feared that Communist designs would spread through the Persian Gulf with the departure of the British. The Americans had good reason to fear this. In Yemen earlier in the decade, for example, Russian-supplied Egypt helped to stir up such opposition to the British that they fled from Aden in 1967.[33] Shortly thereafter both the Chinese and the

Russians involved themselves in the People's Democratic Republic of Yemen, the Communist state that emerged from the wreckage of south Arabia. Communist South Yemen, furthermore, served as a base for rebel attacks on two stalwart Western allies in the region, Saudi Arabia and Oman, giving rise to concerns in London and Washington about the repercussions of any further Communist moves into the Gulf.

Farther north on the Arabian Peninsula, furthermore, the Soviets increasingly courted post-revolutionary Iraq, a process that had started very quickly after the 1958 revolution that ousted the British-backed monarchy. Just a year after that revolution, for example, the new Iraqi regime signed commercial agreements with Moscow.[34] The following year the Communist Party gained legal sanction again after being banned for six years.[35] Although the fortunes of the Communists in Iraq would ebb and flow throughout the 1960s as they battled with the rival Ba'athists, after a 1968 coup that brought Saddam Hussein to the second most powerful position in the state, Iraq tilted further toward Moscow. The Iraqis that year purchased patrol boats from the Soviets, for example, and began hosting Soviet warships to port calls at Umm Qasr.[36] Observing this growing Russian presence in the Gulf, a London *Times* reporter went so far in 1968 as to ponder whether Pax Britannica in the Gulf might give way to Pax Sovietica.[37]

Washington officials clearly did not want to see a Pax Sovietica emerge from the vacuum that would follow the British departure, but they possessed very few options to prevent it. The U.S. military was stretched to the breaking point in the late 1960s and early 1970s, as the Vietnam War continued. There existed outright hostility on Capitol Hill, furthermore, to the Navy's desire to keep its Middle East Force in Bahrain after British withdrawal. There simply was no way that Congress would approve any increase in military expenditures aimed at beefing up the American military presence in the Gulf.

The conflict in Vietnam also robbed the U.S. military forces of prepositioning equipment that might have facilitated fighting a war in any distant locale like the Persian Gulf. A U.S. strategic preposition program launched in the early 1960s, for example, fell victim to Vietnam-era competing needs.[38] No strategic preposition program, in other words, emerged in the 1960s or early 1970s that would have strengthened the U.S. forces in these far-off lands.

Conclusion

The years 1968–71 were very important in the history of the Persian Gulf, for they marked the transition from Great Britain's paternalistic control of the Arab states along the western shore of the Gulf, and the emergence of independent states. The British decision to withdraw, however, led to calls from London and from the small Arab emirates for Washington to assume the same duties that the British had fulfilled in previous decades, entreaties that the United States declined. As it was increasingly mired in the conflict in Southeast Asia, there existed virtually no support in Washington for the superpower to increase its diplomatic commitments or military involvement in the Gulf. Instead, very quickly after the Labour Party's surprise announcement of London's impending withdrawal from the Gulf, during the waning months of the Johnson administration, the broad outlines of American policy for the next several years became clear: the United States must not replace the British as security guarantors in the Persian Gulf; the Americans should try to keep the British engaged; Washington should build up the Twin Pillars of Iran and Saudi Arabia; the Navy should keep the Middle East Force in its same size and shape as it had been in recent years; and the United States should attempt to restrain Soviet influence in the region. Within several years of Britain's military withdrawal in 1971, however, as the Gulf increasingly devolved into conflict and chaos, American leaders lamented their 1968 decision to forgo planting a foothold in the Gulf. As one foreign policy disaster followed another in the 1970s and 1980s, and as Washington tried desperately to deploy military power to the Gulf, they found that the Arab doors that in 1968 were wide open had been slammed shut.

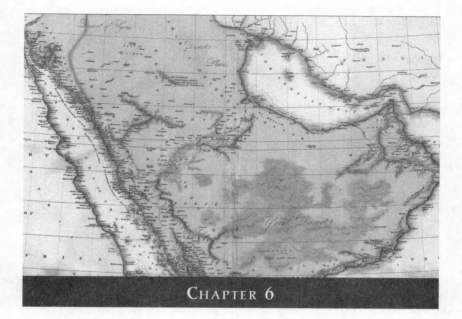

Richard Nixon, Great Britain, and the Anglo-American Strategy of Turning the Persian Gulf into an Allied Lake

Tore T. Petersen

W hen Harold Wilson's Labour government announced the withdrawal of its military forces from the Persian Gulf on 16 January 1968, U.S. president Lyndon Johnson protested bitterly: "Our own capability and political will could be gravely weakened if we have to man all the ramparts alone."[1] Declining to fill the vacuum after the British, the United States encouraged greater cooperation between the regional powers, most importantly Iran and Saudi Arabia, to safeguard Gulf stability and to prevent a local arms race. Richard Nixon would to a large extent follow Johnson's policies toward the Persian Gulf and the Arabian Peninsula, but with a bold new twist of his own. Iran, in particular, and Saudi Arabia were expected to fill the vacuum in the Gulf. To enable these two countries to pay for all the military equipment required in their new role, Nixon deliberately broke up the long and successful partnership between the major Western oil companies and the Western powers, to increase oil prices so that rapidly increasing oil revenues could pay for the necessary military hardware in the Gulf. The president proclaimed the Nixon Doctrine to give ideological cover for the American retrenchment; the United States would honor its treaty obligations, provide nuclear cover to its allies, and economic and military assistance in lieu of American troops.

But Iran and Saudi Arabia were simply too inexperienced and lacked the infrastructure to service the sophisticated military machinery they imported, being forced to rely on large numbers of Americans to run their armed forces. While the Nixon Doctrine's intended effect was to decrease the demands on American military personnel the reality was different, hugely increasing the American commitment, thus turning the doctrine on its head.[2] Even after withdrawal, Britain controlled the military and financial life in the lower Gulf, conducting a sustained multinational anti-guerrilla campaign in the Dhofar region of Oman between 1972 and 1975. It is ironic that even after withdrawal the British increased their commitments, particularly in the lower Gulf.

It is important not to confuse the rhetoric of withdrawal with reality; Great Britain and the United States would tolerate no challengers in the Persian Gulf during the Nixon era. In addition to containing Communist guerrillas in Dhofar, Britain effectively blocked an attempt by Iraq to invade Kuwait in 1973, while the United States, Britain, Iran, and Israel supported a Kurdish rebellion in Iraq from 1972 to 1975 in an effort to destabilize revolutionary Iraq. For all practical purposes, the net result, in this period, was to make the Persian Gulf an Anglo-American lake.[3]

Unfortunately, the Persian Gulf in the Nixon era has received comparatively little scholarly attention.[4] Stephen Ambrose finds Nixon's Middle East policy to be almost totally lacking, claiming: "America had no real policy in the Middle East."[5] Significantly, as many authors do, Ambrose equates the Middle East with the Arab–Israeli conflict. William B. Quandt claims: "During 1972 U.S. Middle East policy consisted of little more than open support for Israel." Nixon's most recent biographer, Robert Dallek, agrees, as does Burton I. Kaufman.[6] Nixon, of course, was fully aware that American interests in the Middle East went beyond the Arab–Israeli conflict.[7]

Nixon wished for and encouraged the resurrection of the "special relationship" between the United States and Great Britain.[8] While maintaining cordial relations with Wilson, the president was elated when Edward Heath was elected prime minister in June 1970.[9] But as Henry Kissinger, Nixon's secretary of state, laments in his memoirs, there were no takers in London: "Of all British political leaders, Heath was the most indifferent to the American connection and perhaps even to Americans individually." Heath, being the chief whip of the Conservative party during the Suez crisis, dragged it up from time to time, claiming that many problems between the United States and Europe had their roots in the crisis. Kissinger, too, thought that the crisis had been to the long-term detriment of Anglo-American relations, which for many British leaders had stimulated "a long-festering resentment and fostered a sense of impotence that accelerated their withdrawal from overseas commitments and added to American burdens."[10]

Paradoxically, the Suez crisis, having been an overwhelming demonstration of American power and concomitant humiliation of Great Britain, left the Americans in the long run with less power in the Middle East, and Britain with greater freedom of action in the region. While basking in the successful afterglow of the Suez crisis, Dwight Eisenhower's administration was confronted with rapidly growing anti-Americanism in Europe. President Eisenhower, in contrast to George W. Bush, realized that the United States would have difficulties in going it alone, that the United States needed allies and simply could not perform another Suez if it wanted to keep its friends. In fact, the United States refrained from military interventions in the Middle East after the invasion of Lebanon in 1958 to the first Gulf war in 1991, a point not lost on American allies or adversaries. For Britain, then, Suez became a useful bludgeon to beat the Americans in times of Anglo-American discord, as well as liberating Britain from the American embrace in the Middle East, and possibly also elsewhere. Thereafter the United Kingdom had little fear of American sanctions or pressures to act unilaterally in the region.[11]

But too much should not be made of Heath's alleged indifference to the "special relationship," despite Alan Dobson's claim that the years 1970 to 1974 "were rather barren for Anglo-American relations," and David Reynolds' belief that Nixon's overtures for closer Anglo-American relations were coldly rebuffed by Heath.[12] Meeting Heath on 3 October 1970, Nixon made a strong pitch for close Anglo-American relations: "The 'special relationship' was essentially a matter of personal relationship." He continued, "[The] United States knew very well that they were a great Power, whose authority and responsibility extended throughout the world. But this was a lonely position, and, perhaps, not a very healthy one. That explained why they had welcomed the new British Government's intention to reinstate a presence East of Suez. It was the political and diplomatic aspect of this presence which mattered more than its military content." Heath responded in kind, welcoming the president's invitation and "valued very highly the prospect of a close personal relationship of the kind which the President had described."[13]

Whatever the nature of the personal relationship, in the Persian Gulf and the Arabian Peninsula Anglo-American policies were closely aligned and thereby, whether by design or not, mutually reinforcing. While the Conservatives had protested loudly against Labour's decision to withdraw from the Gulf, the Heath government concluded that Britain had but little choice to withdraw given the lack of local support for a continued British presence. The Tories differed from Labour, however, in being intent on retaining as much influence as possible. For this purpose, the assistance of Iran and Saudi Arabia was deemed essential, dovetailing nicely with American priorities. What they did have in common, as Britain withdrew from fixed positions and the United States resisted resuming any, was a wish to upgrade their respective clients to allies. For the United Kingdom this meant transforming its relationship with Oman. One of the Tories' first acts in office after winning the election was deposing the old conservative sultan on 23 July 1970, allegedly because of his lackluster conduct of the anti-guerrilla campaign in the Dhofar province and refusal to modernize his country. The Heath government wanted to upgrade relations with Oman from being a British client to an informal alliance, but in the process British officers were in charge of military operations in Dhofar and commanded the Sultan's Armed Forces (SAF); British civil servants ran the Omani administration and evicted foreign companies for the benefit of British firms, making Oman an exclusively British enclave. In short, Britain reverted to an old-fashioned imperialism to facilitate the transition to modernity. In spite of the importance of British policy in the lower Gulf, the area has drawn relatively little attention from historians.[14]

The British did not bother to inform or consult the United States of the impending coup in Oman. United States Assistant Secretary of State Joseph Sisco advised Secretary of State William Rogers on 29 July 1970: "We learned of the coup through wire service reports on July 26." Still, Sisco foresaw no difficulties in recognizing the new regime in Oman.[15] Wm. Roger Louis downplays the British role in the coup, explaining that "the British had assisted in the overthrow of Oman's ruler, the Sultan bin Taimur."[16] Withdrawing from the Persian Gulf was meant to lessen British involvement, but the coup in Oman had the direct opposite result: it increased the British presence in the lower Gulf. But there were also real benefits, as the British ambassador to Oman, Donald Hawley, observed in his annual report for 1971: "We continue to enjoy a special position in Oman. I had free and easy access to the Sultan, the Prime Minister and Ministers whenever I wanted and dealings took place in an atmosphere of goodwill and friendliness. It was pleasant, let me say after a year or two in Baghdad, to have a Prime Minister who will come to dinner."[17]

The Heath government urged the small sheikhdoms of Qatar, Bahrain, Abu Dhabi, Dubai, Sharjah, Ajman, Umm al-Qawain, Ras al-Khaimah, and Fujairah to federate into the United Arab Emirates (UAE) and, in addition, Britain sought to settle the numerous border claims and counterclaims that emerged as a result of the decision to leave the Gulf. One of the most difficult was that the shah of Iran laid claim to three small islands in the Strait of Hormuz: Abu Musa Island from the sheikhdom of Sharjah and the Tunbs Islands from the sheikhdom of Ras al-Khaimah. King Faisal of Saudi Arabia revived his dormant claim to the al-Buraimi oasis in the British protected territories of Abu Dhabi, Muscat, and Oman. The dispute over the al-Buraimi oasis was the most difficult issue in Anglo-Saudi relations, since Saudi Arabia, with the aid and assistance of the Arabian American Oil Company (ARAMCO) had occupied the oasis in August 1952. The British reoccupation and eviction of Saudi forces in October 1955 was for then–Crown Prince (and later King) Faisal a terrible loss of face and prestige from which he constantly demanded redress from Britain all the way until the British withdrawal from the Gulf.[18] To settle their problems in the Gulf, the British sought the assistance of Iran and Saudi Arabia. But as foreign minister Alec Douglas-Home explained to Rogers: "The problem was elaborate and difficult because of the incompetence of the Arabs, because King Faisal was old and neither he nor the Shah had effective advisers who could exercise pressure on the Rulers." The whole point of the exercise was to establish an indirect British presence "so that we could exercise the maximum political influence with the minimum military presence." Rogers was in full agreement.[19] While publicly committed to a reversal of Labour's withdrawal decision, this was largely a play to the gallery. Heath informed the cabinet on 22 July 1970 that Britain's long-term objective was directed to "the establishment of a situation in which British interests would be safeguarded [to be] understood in the context of our long-term objective, which was to reduce our commitments and our expenditure in the area, and to bring a state of affairs in which the Gulf rulers, within the framework of an effective federation, could fend for themselves."[20]

In the summer of 1969, the president proclaimed the Nixon Doctrine: the United States would honor its treaty obligations, provide nuclear cover to its allies, and economic and military assistance in lieu of American troops. Ostentatiously, the doctrine was intended to cover the American withdrawal from Vietnam, but it also had global implications. Reducing American commitments, the Nixon Doctrine called for close American allies to substitute for the United States. In the Persian Gulf, Nixon believed that Iran, and to a lesser degree Saudi Arabia, fitted the job description as regional policemen.[21] Nixon himself was very clear that his doctrine was not a cover for an American retreat: "The Nixon doctrine rather than being a device to get rid of America's world role is one which is devised to make possible for us to play a role—and play it better, more effectively than if we continued the policy of the past in which we assume such a dominant position."[22]

The *shahanshah*, or king of kings, presided over Iran.[23] Having long chafed under restricting American tutelage, the shah came into his own during the Nixon administration. Eisenhower had denied him the weapons he thought he needed, while John F. Kennedy had forced reforms on him; the shah had felt liberated by Johnson, since Iran was one of the few Third World countries supporting the American effort in Vietnam and Israel. The grandiosity of the shah's title and pretensions hid rather humble origins. His father, the first Reza Pahlevi, was a Cossack sergeant before ascending the throne. Iran, for all the rhetoric of making it a major military and industrial power, was essentially a Third World country.[24] Luckily for the monarch on the peacock throne his ambitions largely overlapped with President Nixon's policies in the Middle East as enunciated by the doctrine carrying the president's name. The Americans were well pleased with the *shahanshah*. Kissinger would later observe: "Whatever the failings of the Shah, wrestling perhaps with forces beyond any man's control, he was for us that rarest of leaders, an unconditional ally, and one whose understanding of the world situation enhanced our own."[25]

Despite public appearances to the contrary, the United States in particular but also Britain consistently supported the shah when he squeezed the oil companies for increased revenues. The *New York Times* reported on 24 July 1971:

> Iran's military power on land, in the air, and on the sea, is being built up in the Middle East under a billion-dollar defense program quietly underwritten by the United States and Britain in preparation for the British withdrawal from the Persian Gulf later this year. . . . Acting with British-American blessings, the Iranian Shah, Mohammed Reza Pahlevi, has accepted responsibility of the Persian Gulf after Britain removes her protection and armed forces from Bahrain, Qatar, and the seven Trucial States.[26]

In October 1971, the *shahanshah* commemorated his newfound grandeur by celebrating the 2,500th anniversary of the Persian empire at Persepolis, erecting a grand tent city to receive visiting dignitaries from all around the world.[27] Ironically, everything manmade for the celebrations had to be imported from abroad, even the flower arrangements. The tents were from Saint Fréres, the plates from Limoges, the glasses from Baccarat, and the food from Maxim's restaurant in Paris.[28] The shah opened the ceremonies in front of the tomb of Cyrus the Great: "O Cyrus, great King, King of Kings, Achaemenian King, King of the land of Iran. . . . I, the Shahanshah of Iran, offer thee salutations: from myself and from my nation. . . . Rest in peace, for we are awake, and we will always stay awake."[29] But the grand show had its detractors, as *Newsweek* magazine reported: "Serious critics found it staggering that the Shah would spend $11 million of his country's money on food and liquor for some of the wealthiest people in the world when poverty and starvation still exist in Iran."[30] Furthermore: "And at home, much of Iran's populace still remains impoverished and ignorant. 'When you take off into the hills,' laments one economist, 'you are virtually back in biblical times.'" While much of Iran's progress in that decade could be credited to the tireless efforts of the shah, progress came at a price: "His one-man show has created a procrastinating and timid bureaucracy whose incompetence is matched only by its corruption."[31] All of this amply illustrates the shah's lack of ability to act independently of the West in general and the United States in particular.

Despite the weakness of Iran, and the shah's constant need, despite all his accomplishments, for reassurance, he was for the United States an almost ideal ally as Hal Saunders on the National Security Council (NSC) staff observed:

> Iran's strength, vitality, bold leadership, and willingness to assume regional responsibility are a classic example of what the United States under the Nixon Doctrine values highly in an ally. . . . The U.S.-Iranian partnership

is a crucial pillar of the global structure of peace the U.S. is seeking to build. Your [Nixon's] trips to Peking and Moscow exemplify your effort to develop a secure balance among the great powers. Great-power restraint—which we are seeking to build into the system—devolves more responsibility onto regional powers. The U.S. is counting on Iran to make a major contribution to regional and Third World stability, in the Persian Gulf and indeed in the Middle East and the whole non-aligned world.[32]

Oil was of lesser importance in American relations with Iran. After Nixon's Tehran visit in May 1972, the American–Iranian communiqué grandiloquently stated that the American president and Mrs. Nixon were summoned by "His Imperial Majesty Shahanshah Arya Mehr and Her Imperial Majesty the Shahbanou of Iran" and "were received with exceptional friendliness and warmth by their imperial majesties and by the government and people of Iran." Significantly, after a tour d'horizon of the world, nothing less would suffice; the lofty personages deemed it below their dignity to discuss oil politics, testifying to the unimportance of oil in American relations with Iran.[33]

The British, too, sought to capitalize on the shah's newfound status and international prestige, pandering to the Iranian monarch's vanity by inviting him and his wife to a visit of state in London in June 1972: "They came as guests of Her Majesty the Queen at Windsor for the Royal Ascot races, and spent two days in London when the Shah had most useful discussions with the Prime Minister and, separately, with Lord Carrington in the Ministry of Defence, supplemented by an impressive briefing on our latest weapons, which has since prompted orders for the Imperial Iranian forces."[34] Prime Minister Edward Heath took the occasion to do a little stroking of his own, namely that the fact that Iran was a point of stability in a volatile region was due to the credit of His Imperial Majesty. "[The] 2500th Anniversary celebrations at Persepolis in October last year were a reminder to the world of the splendour and historical significance of Iran. Long-founded 'establishments' not often connected in [the] public mind with progressiveness [are a] tribute to the Pahlavi dynasty, and particularly to the Shahanshah himself, for spearheading all that is progressive in Iran today."[35] By July Iran had placed orders of £100 million for military equipment, with a potential of more to come.[36]

Apart from pressuring the British and harassing the Americans to support their anti-Anglo ventures, Saudi Arabia did not have much of a foreign policy, while at the same time King Faisal carefully tendered his phobias, regaling his visitors with the twin evils in the world: Zionism and Communism.[37] Still, for Kissinger, Faisal was "that subtlest of diplomats."[38] In reality, as the Nixon

administration well understood, Saudi Arabia slumbered in its traditional leth-
argy: "Given Saudi military deficiencies and dependence on foreign (especially
U.S.) advisory and contract support, we do not want to encourage them to play
the role of 'policeman' in the Peninsula."[39] Passivity was the standard operating procedure of Saudi foreign policy; while supplying troops to Jordan in 1970,
Faisal made sure they stayed out of the fighting. In addition, Britain's hope for
Saudi assistance in settling their Persian Gulf problems failed to materialize. In
fact, given the increasing activities of Iran and Iraq, Saudi Arabia was strangely
absent in trying to map the future of the Gulf. Faisal's policy was quite simple,
according to the UK ambassador to Jeddah, Willie Morris: "The British are able,
if they put their minds to it, to produce solutions satisfactory to Saudi Arabia
and they owe it to him [Faisal] to do so."[40]

It was al-Buraimi, always al-Buraimi, that was the stumbling block in Anglo-
Saudi relations. For Faisal, his claim to al-Buraimi had priority over everything
else. And when Britain failed to deliver the solution Anglo-Saudi relations
deteriorated. After completing the withdrawal from the Gulf, the British simply washed their hands of al-Buraimi as the Foreign and Commonwealth Office
explained in an internal memorandum:

> We had spent fifty years trying to solve the dispute without success. We now
> had no responsibility for it and we did not wish to do anything to encourage
> King Faisal in the view that we were still involved. Furthermore, we did not
> regard the dispute as a serious threat to stability in the area. Even if it was
> solved it would be doubtful whether any great benefits would accrue to the
> UAE although the atmosphere would certainly clear.[41]

The penalty was, as always when Faisal wanted to punish Britain, loss of arms
contracts. Britain lost its exclusive hold over and supply of the Saudi National
Guard, where Britain had held sway since resuming diplomatic relations with
Saudi Arabia in January 1963.[42] Losing its foothold in Saudi Arabia was not
without its advantages for Britain, for there was no longer any great urgency to
placate the king's phobias and follies. With many areas of tension behind them,
the British, in the long term, could concentrate on getting as large a slice of
the lucrative Saudi arms market as possible without worrying about burdensome
problems like al-Buraimi or having any responsibility for Saudi security, particularly the royal house, as Britain's relationship with the National Guard previously implied. Faisal, fearing the winds of revolutionary Arab nationalism and
the susceptibility of his military officers to it, staffed the National Guard with his
loyal Bedouin in order to protect his throne if the regular army revolted.[43]

"What interest does the U.S., as a nation, have in the maintenance of the oil companies in their present forms in the producing countries?" Saunders questioned in February 1973. "A cruder way of putting this is: How would it affect that national interest—in contrast to the companies' interests—if they [the companies] were reduced to distributing oil after buying it from the producers on a contract basis? . . . There are some who would argue that takeover of the companies is only a matter of time and that there is no point in investing a lot of the President's prestige in fighting that problem."[44] The oil bureaucrats in the State Department discovered to their chagrin early in the Nixon administration that it was inconvenient, at best, that the oil companies acted at cross purposes or independently of established U.S. policy.[45] Not only that, for the State Department the oil company approach was outdated: "Our experience has been that their political acumen suits them ideally for the world of the late nineteenth century."[46] Oil policy was, initially, the one area of significant Anglo-American discord, but the British soon accommodated themselves to the price increases, benefiting from increasing arms sales and Saudi and Iranian assistance in suppressing the rebellion in Oman.[47]

From an oil policy perspective, the 1960s had been strangely tranquil, compared to the turbulent 1950s, when Great Britain and the United States were often at loggerheads over the control of oil, and to the oil crisis, 1969 to 1979, when oil prices shot up from $1.20 per barrel to $41 per barrel. The United States and Britain seemingly held the upper hand because of the producer countries' dependence on a global market for their oil. The Anglo-American oil companies and their governments easily brushed off attempts by the oil-producing nations in the Middle East to use oil as a political weapon after the Six-Day War in 1967. When the Middle Eastern oil producers embargoed oil as a punishment for Britain and the United States supporting Israel, the embargo collapsed within months. The United States cranked up its own domestic production, which with increased Venezuelan production made up the shortfall of Middle East oil production. This, combined with the loss of revenue for the oil producers, forced the termination of the embargo. But the very success in containing the oil producers also led Anglo-American policy makers to view questions of oil with less urgency than their predecessors.[48]

Historians have long suspected that the Nixon administration wanted to put relations with big oil on a new footing. And now with most of the records declassified many of their assumptions have been confirmed, but perhaps not the scale and scope of the Nixonian attempt to restructure the world of oil.[49] Richard Thornton argues that Nixon and Kissinger engineered oil price increases not only to support increased Saudi and Iranian defense spending, but also to reduce economic growth in Japan and Western Europe by siphoning off surplus to the oil producers, while at the same time the United States would only be marginally affected, thus increasing the American competitive position against its allies. "The Western allies as the primary importers of Middle East petroleum would help underwrite the cost of strengthening the defenses of the region, even if they were reluctant to devote additional spending to their own defenses." Furthermore, before the February 1971 Tehran agreement, the United States government, while claiming to support the oil companies, "purposefully and deftly maneuvered the oil companies into new structural relationships with each other and with the oil-producing countries and a new regime of higher petroleum prices based upon assured supply."[50] This ties in nicely with Alan Matusow's belief that the United States was practically engaged in economic warfare against its allies: "In 1971, the climactic year of his economic management, Nixon abandoned the postwar liberal ideal of a harmonious trade world in favor of a nationalist conception of U.S. interests. Western Europe and Japan were now considered not so much trading partners but rivals to be subdued."[51] For Francisco Para it is a source of wonderment that the oil crisis happened at all: "Why did the United States and Britain, as home countries to the major oil companies, not react anywhere adequately in defense of the companies when unilateral action was taken against them by the host governments?"[52] In agreement with Thornton, Bennett H. Wall claims that the West was more concerned about the security of supply than the price of oil, and goes on to describe how the West passively accepted to be challenged by the Arab producers.[53] Kissinger explains the lack of American counteractions this way: "Never before had nations so weak militarily—and in some cases politically—been able to impose such strains on the international system. A century earlier the consuming nations would have responded by seizing the oil fields. From time to time, as will be seen, the United States threatened to do just that but never received any support from the other democracies."[54] What Kissinger omits is that the United States never took any concrete actions to implement its threats. The United States protested verbally, but never once put forward credible threats to prevent further price increases.

In the early fall of 1973 Saudi Arabian oil production was in excess of its revenue requirements: to increase production further required the fulfillment of Saudi demands. Hisham Nazir, minister of state and president of the Central Planning Organization, explained those demands to the State Department on 28 September 1973: "U.S. cooperation in Saudi efforts to industrialize and diversify the economy to replace a non-renewable asset." Furthermore: "U.S. policy initiatives to improve the political atmosphere in the Middle East," which for the Saudis translated into breaking the strong American ties with Israel.[55] When John Love, special assistant to the president for energy matters and former governor of Colorado, met Nazir on the same date, the governor was extremely open about "the current oil supply picture in the U.S.," which was very tight. Nazir repeated his warning that the United States had to change its policies in the Middle East. Love opined: "The U.S. wanted to achieve relative self-sufficiency again for its energy requirements but this will probably not be possible for the next 10 to 15 years."[56]

As seen from the sampling of the documents above, everything was in place in late summer/early fall 1973 for the Saudis to use the oil weapon if they deemed it necessary to do so. There was Saudi "overproduction," that is the Saudis could cut back production with little cost to themselves; ARAMCO (the Arabian American Oil Company that operated on the Saudi oil fields) was in practice reduced to a Saudi subsidiary after the prolonged and sustained assaults on the oil companies, dating back to Libya driving a wedge between the majors and the independents in the fall of 1969. The United States made no attempt to hide its vulnerability on the energy sector, sending numerous signals that it no longer supported big oil and repeatedly stressing to Saudi interlocutors that the United States had an almost unquenchable thirst for oil. In case Saudi Arabia did not get the message, Nixon's oil expert, James Akins, practically begged the oil producers to increase oil prices in an article in *Foreign Affairs* in April 1973.[57] Anthony Sampson comments on Akins' infamous article: "Akins' warnings were prophetic, but some of his critics insisted that they were self-fulfilling: The State Department was virtually advising the Arabs to put up prices, and advertising the West's weakness."[58] It is simply inconceivable, given Faisal's extreme passivity and heavy reliance on the United States, that Saudi Arabia had instituted the oil embargo without at least implicit clearance from the Nixon administration. For Saudi Arabia the oil embargo was necessary to burnish its Arab credentials, as the Saudi contribution to the Yom Kippur War was decidedly limited, consisting of a brigade on the Syrian front that went into action one day prior to the cease-fire, suffering a grand total of two dead and four wounded.[59]

Most interestingly, when seemingly challenged by Middle Eastern oil producers the United States took no measures whatsoever, apart from the mildest verbal slapping of the Saudi and Iranian wrists, to counteract the alleged threat from Arab oil producers; nobody could have any fear of U.S. penalties. On the contrary, for pushing the West into a recession and laying down what appeared to be a clear challenge to American power, Iran and Saudi Arabia were rewarded by the United States setting up joint commissions to deepen its cooperation with its alleged adversaries in the Middle East. To show the extent of American displeasure, Kissinger participated in a seminar in the Saudi Central Planning Organization in Riyadh on 15 December 1973. Nazir introduced his prominent guest in the following way: "We would like to quiz Dr. Kissinger as he quizzed his students when he was a professor." Kissinger left no chance to praise his host after Nazir's presentation: "There are very few countries that have the possibility that yours does. Most countries I visit have a problem of finding resources to meet their ambitions; you may have the problem of finding ambitions to meet your resources." Kissinger continued by practically begging the Saudis to expand their cooperation with the Americans: "Should we set up a mechanism now [for cooperative arrangements?]" Nazir explained that Saudi Arabia never found it difficult to work with U.S. private companies, but now had other needs: "That is, technology that the U.S. government is particularly involved in which is not in the private market yet." For Kissinger this offered no problems: "We are extremely sympathetic. If you make your specific request, we will circumvent the normal procedures of bureaucratic response. We could set up means of rapid decision in Mr. Sisco's bureau."[60]

The answer from the United States to Iran for increasing oil prices was, as we have seen, the establishment of joint commissions to further enhance American cooperation with the shah. Kissinger wanted a joint commission that "would encompass political, defense, cultural, scientific, and technological cooperation." To show the importance he attached to the venture, Kissinger "decided to act as U.S. co-chairman." The purpose of the whole exercise was that "the two governments have decided that it would be timely and mutually advantageous to deepen and broaden the bonds of friendship between the United States and Iran."[61] As long as he ran U.S. foreign policy, Kissinger thought the American alliance with Iran was nothing but a success story, having an ally pursuing parallel politics with the United States while at the same time paying its own way.[62]

Britain, too, "punished" the Saudis by dangling the bait of expanded industrial cooperation to Faisal, or in the king's words, "joint industrial ventures in Saudi Arabia."[63] Douglas-Home explained to the British embassy in Jeddah on 27 December 1973 that the United Kingdom foresaw extensive future cooperation with Saudi Arabia: "We have already informed them that HMG are ready to reach an understanding with the Saudi Arabian government for long-term cooperation in shipping, refining, marketing, and the supply of oil to the mutual benefit of both countries and to continue discussions on industrial cooperation."[64]

Under the umbrella of the joint commissions, thousands of American civil servants and employees from the private sector took part in multi-dollar development schemes in the areas of defense, economic and agricultural development, technology transfer, and nuclear energy. But mostly, the joint commissions "acted as arms salesmen supreme."[65] Britain too joined in the arms bonanza.[66] Selling large quantities of military hardware hardly constitutes a policy, nor is it an effective substitute for policy. For Britain, trying to maintain its empire on the cheap left it in the long run with less influence in the region. Nixon and Kissinger's attempt at managing the Arabian Peninsula and the Persian Gulf, by relying on Iran and Saudi Arabia, ended in dismal failure.

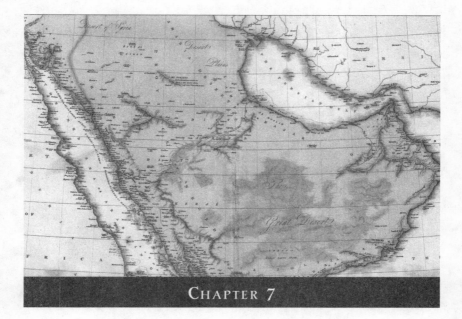

CHAPTER 7

A Guiding Hand or Controlling Grasp?

Britain, Intelligence, and the War in Oman, 1970–1976

Clive Jones

I t has become almost a historical axiom to view the British military with-drawal from the Gulf in 1971 as marking the final denouement of London's influence across the region. Unable to withstand a range of social and polit-ical forces that subsequently sapped its power and willingness to defend its economic and strategic interests across the Middle East, Britain evacuated its Aden base in November 1967 with an indecent haste that marked, according to Wm. Roger Louis, "the end of the Great Game in Western Asia."[1]

Yet the seemingly irresistible tide of progressive forces that appeared set to overwhelm the dynastic rulers of the Middle East in the late 1960s had, by the mid-1970s, been checked, if not repulsed. While Fred Halliday's class-based analysis of revolutionary forces across Arabia anticipated a political order "with-out sultans," direct British support for and direct involvement with monarchical regimes remained crucial to the creation of the United Arab Emirates (UAE) as it emerged out of the paternalistic embrace of the Trucial States.[2] Nowhere, however, was such British involvement more critical than in the Sultanate of Oman. Faced with an ongoing rebellion in its Dhofar region aided and abet-ted by the newly independent People's Democratic Republic of Yemen (PDRY) and with Omani dissidents, supported by Ba'athist Iraq, threatening to desta-bilize the Trucial States, British involvement was crucial in securing a dynastic order whose ultimate security came to rest upon that social contract peculiar to the Middle East—the rentier state—to ensure its broad-based acceptance, if not legitimacy, among Omanis.

While Whitehall officials remained keen to ensure that British military foot-prints remained faint, several memoirs and indeed one excellent study of the insurgency in Dhofar detail the extent of British military involvement in the sultanate. During the period 1970–73 such involvement in the form of special forces and seconded or contract officers and soldiers in particular, proved crucial in containing the main insurgent group, the Marxist-inspired Popular Front for the Liberation of Oman and the Arabian Gulf (PFLOAG).[3] They may not have had the grandeur or romance of the "Great Game" of the nineteenth century but events in Oman certainly echoed its tribal complexities whose fidelities, so often a transient commodity, were deemed crucial to securing the longevity of the sul-tanate and with it, continued access to the oil of the Arabian Peninsula.

Equally however, these studies present little of note regarding the use of intelligence throughout the Oman campaign, a surprising omission perhaps given the link between an effective counterinsurgency (COIN) campaign and the absolute requirement of timely, effective intelligence. Where intelligence is mentioned, its utility in the literature remains limited to a circumspect discussion of operational deployments by the Sultan's Armed Forces (SAF) across the Dhofar region, with little reference to its wider role in securing the sultan's dispensation across the rest of Oman.[4] Only one systematic study has ever been published that analyzes the evolution of intelligence structures in Oman throughout this period, a study that, while informed by a historical narrative, remains focused on the ethnographic evolution of Oman's intelligence services from its dependence on British tutelage to its control by indigenous expertise by the 1990s.[5]

It is therefore the transformation of the intelligence structures in Oman between 1970 and 1976, and the way that they came to inform the political consolidation of the sultanate, that concerns this chapter. As such, this chapter highlights the complexities of constructing an intelligence relationship between "patron and client" in the course of a conflict but where such linear association—as the term suggests—had never previously been defined by the legacy of direct colonial rule.[6] As this chapter argues, in its attempt to defeat the PFLOAG insurgency, happenstance as much as the patient accumulation of material—both political and operational—defined the role of intelligence in ensuring the ultimate triumph of the Sultanate of Oman.

Fiddling while Rome Burns

The origins of the insurgency in Oman and the province of Dhofar in particular lay in the increased resentment among expatriate Dhofari workers over the archaic and isolationist rule of Sultan Said bin Taimur. This found expression in the formation of the mainly nationalist Dhofar Liberation Front (DLF) in 1964. At a time when Oman lacked even the basic infrastructure of a modern state despite the discovery and production of oil in commercial quantities by 1967— radios were banned, there existed few improved roads, while education was limited to those deemed necessary to run the country—such opposition remained understandable. Indeed, lying some six hundred miles from the capital Muscat, Dhofaris considered themselves distinct from the Arabs of Oman in language, history, and culture.[7]

The actual agenda of the DLF remained vague but it did eschew formal integration into the sultanate in preference of Dhofar's independence. From 1967 onward however, the program of the DLF became subservient to, and eventually subsumed by, the more radical policies pursued by the PFLOAG. The emergence of PFLOAG was a direct result of the establishment in 1967 of the PDRY, following the final withdrawal of British troops from Aden in 1967. The new republic, dominated by a Marxist-inspired government, began to exercise increasing influence over the political and military direction of the insurgency in neighboring Dhofar. This influence manifested itself not only in the desire to impose a Marxist order throughout the Dhofar region, but also extended to the overthrow of the Sultanate of Oman itself.[8]

While British ties to Oman dated back to the late eighteenth century, a 1958 treaty codified the military relationship between Muscat and London. In return for control of air facilities on the island of Masirah and Salalah in Dhofar, Britain agreed to help with the development of the Sultan's Armed Forces (SAF). This included the provision of some officers on secondment from the British armed forces. Contract officers—a preferred nomenclature for mercenaries—made up the rest of the numbers, though according to Colonel David Smiley, who commanded the SAF between 1958 and 1961, their quality was decidedly mixed.[9] By the late 1960s, the growing magnitude of the insurgency presented the United Kingdom with the prospect of two main overlapping strategic threats. London's attempts to cohere the Trucial states of Abu Dhabi, Dubai, Sharjah, Ajman, Umm al-Qawain, Ras al-Khaimah, and Fujairah into a single state structure—eventually to become the UAE—would be threatened by the success of an insurgency in neighboring Oman inspired by an ideology antithetical to the concept of a state grouped around tribal hierarchies. Moreover, given the material support proffered to the PDRY by the Soviet Union, the overthrow of the sultanate would have appeared to give Moscow hegemony over the strategic Musandam Peninsula guarding the Strait of Hormuz and thus the capability to interdict Western supplies of oil in times of crisis.[10] While very much a "worst case" scenario, taken within the ongoing context of the Cold War such thinking played an important part in deliberations by the Joint Intelligence Committee (JIC) throughout 1968 as it tried to plan for the protection of British oil interests in the Gulf amid a continued commitment to withdraw militarily from the region by 1971.[11]

Time was decidedly of the essence: PFLOAG guerrillas had, by August 1969, captured the administrative center of western Dhofar, Rakhyut, and by February 1970 were bombarding the Royal Air Force base at Salalah at regular intervals. Sultan Said bin Taimur's reliance upon the SAF to combat the insurgency was seldom matched by a similar commitment from him to its logistic support, nor, as proved crucial, in using increased revenues from the production of oil to modernize the archaic infrastructure of the state, a prerequisite in the overall struggle for the "hearts and minds" of the Dhofari people. Worryingly, he had also become increasingly estranged from the tribes and their leaders, whose traditional conservatism had acted as a bulwark against "progressive ideologies."

The febrile nature of the sultanate extended to the realm of intelligence. Omani intelligence structures were inadequate to the task, poorly resourced, and viewed with distrust by the sultan. Oman simply did not possess an effective "in house" structure capable of producing reliable intelligence through the systematic collection, collation, and assessment of material. A skeletal intelligence service did exist within the order of battle of the SAF under a British contract officer, Major (later Brigadier) Malcolm Dennison, but until 1970 it remained staffed predominantly by seconded British officers—known as Sultan's Intelligence Officers (SIOs)—on two-year fixed tours of duty, who never numbered more than twelve officers.[12] Aside from the obvious concerns over developing an "institutional memory," there existed little in the way of indigenous capability upon which colonial intelligence structures traditionally depended. His hostility toward Dhofaris, for example, had seen the sultan remain resolute in his opposition to their presence in the ranks of the SAF, let alone recruitment into Oman's nascent intelligence structures.[13] Despite his best efforts, Dennison had never been allowed by the sultan to develop a coherent intelligence service, even with a strong recommendation by Smiley that this capability remained crucial to the longevity of the sultanate. Fear of the subversive potential of an intelligence organization, as well as a personal dislike of Dennison for an alleged snub, best explains the sultan's styptic attitude.[14] Such suspicion extended to the SAF, with bin Taimur refusing to allow any Arab—Omani or otherwise—to hold the rank of major in the SAF, his view being that political coups in the Arab world were led invariably by high-ranking officers who had been allowed to establish a power base within the armed forces from which to launch a putsch.[15] As Major-General John Graham, the SAF commander, noted of his time in the sultanate in the late 1960s : "Although we had [Sultan's] Intelligence officers living, with their stalwart Omani assistants, near the main centres of population, their ability to obtain from a largely unhelpful citizenry accurate information about clandestine activities was in truth less than we at the time believed."[16]

Intelligence and Northern Oman

On 23 July 1970, Sultan Said bin Taimur was overthrown and replaced immediately by his son, Qaboos bin Said.[17] Sultan Qaboos was, and remains, a staunch Anglophile. Educated at Sandhurst, he had spent time as an infantry officer with the British army in Germany before returning to Oman in 1964. His perceived liberalism earned him the wrath of his father, who, fearful of his son's progressive values, had him placed under virtual house arrest. Circumstantial evidence of various provenances has attributed his accession in part to Britain's Secret Intelligence Service (SIS). Certainly, Qaboos was close to one SIO, Timothy Landon, a contemporary at Sandhurst who allegedly had been trained by SIS and maintained close ties with several of its personnel.[18] Rumors of an impending coup had in fact been commonplace among Muscat's merchant class by the late spring of 1970. In a cable to the British Political Resident, Persian Gulf (PRPG) Sir Stewart Crawford, the consul general in Muscat wrote:

> If there is a general feeling in the country [Oman] now it is that the Sultan's rule cannot go on, since it will lead to a takeover after what might prove to be a bitter period of fighting by the young Omanis encouraged by their Communist supporters. The only alternative it is generally considered is for Sayid Tariq and Talib bin Ali with or without Qabus [sic] to take over the government. Hopefully, this would be done with British acquiescence, thus avoiding bloodshed but, if necessary, we would have to be shown the error of our ways (previous support for bin Taimur) since it is assumed we are against the communists as well. This is an interpretation of the current mood in this country I have received from several sources, notably from G2Int SAF.[19]

But if any doubt existed regarding the urgency for supporting "regime change," this was cast aside amid growing reports of insurgent unrest in the north of Oman in and around Nizwa and the Musandam Peninsula. Given the paucity of human intelligence (humint), Dennison and his colleagues were now faced with a potential rebellion about which they knew little, a situation compounded by "the growing tendency of Omanis to withhold information."[20] At a time when the insurgents in Dhofar appeared to be in the ascendant, the prospect of the sultanate collapsing under the weight of a two-pronged guerrilla offensive appeared very real.

Officials in London were, however, aware of the severity of the challenges now facing the sultanate prior to July 1970. Three months *before* the coup, a senior officer from 22 Special Air Service Regiment (22 SAS) had visited Dhofar in order to make a detailed appreciation of the insurgency. This visit in March 1970 would not have been sanctioned without the express wish of a Labour government, soon to be ousted from office by a narrow Conservative victory. It suggests that, domestic political differences aside, both Labour and Conservative parties recognized the strategic importance of Oman, both in terms of maintaining Britain's energy needs as well as in the wider context of countering perceived Soviet subversion. Thus, the view that growing British involvement in Oman represented a clear policy shift between the Labour and Conservative governments needs to be tempered, suggesting as it does that the anticolonial zeitgeist within the Labour party, which had supported wholesale withdrawal from the Gulf, had now come to be exorcised by a more profound strategic reality.

The recommendations produced by the SAS centered on the development of five key areas—overt military action, civic aid, veterinary aid, psychological operations, and intelligence and covert operations—over three discreet phases, with each one building upon the expected success of its predecessor. Of note, however, is the complete paucity of both political and operational intelligence, admitted to by default in the document regarding the scale and scope of the challenge posed by PFLOAG. The document highlights the urgent requirement to "establish a viable unit responsible to the SAS commander to gather intelligence on the rebel groups, prepare orbats [orders of battle], establish identities, rebel contacts, cells, define hideouts, caves, routes and feeding areas; identify leaders and sympathizers and confirm tactics, habits, and intentions." Phase two looked to entice the surrender of enemy personnel, while phase three looked to actually eliminate (i.e., kill) the identified leadership of PFLOAG as well as any Chinese advisers.[21]

However, it was to be events in the north of Oman and the Musandam Peninsula, rather than Dhofar, which dominated the immediate concerns in London. Britain was still clear in its intent to leave the Gulf by 1971, having overseen the creation of the UAE, that amalgam of dynasties that would still owe political fidelity to Britain. But by the autumn of 1970, reports of dissident activity centered on the peninsula threatened to undermine this exercise in state creation. In particular, the Emirate of Sharjah, as well as Oman, was seen to be under threat from dissident Omanis, sponsored by Ba'athist Iraq. If one emirate were to fall under a radical republican regime, the perception across the Middle East would have been of a declining imperial father having sired a dynastic child incapable of resisting a new Arab order in the Gulf. Such sentiments were certainly shared by the Commander, British Forces in the Gulf, who noted in one report to London: "Clearly, we cannot allow the Musandam Peninsula to become as the Yemen was to the South Arabian Federation."[22]

While such parallels undoubtedly exercised the minds of decision makers in London there was one crucial difference: the death of Gamal Abdel Nasser in 1970 marked the end of Cairo's attempt to usurp all British influence in the Gulf. In his effort to court the West and in particular the United States, the new Egyptian president, Anwar Sadat, soon came to support the idea of dynastic regimes, and in 1971 fully encouraged Oman's attempts to join the Arab League. Even so, reports from June 1970 onward reaching the JIC suggested that Omani exiles had launched a series of attacks against both government and commercial interests in Izki, Nizwa, Sumail, and Muscat. It was also suggested that these attacks, while ineffectual, nonetheless gave the impression of the emergence of an insurgent group—the "National Democratic Front for the Liberation of Oman"—with a real potential to make common cause with PFLOAG.[23]

The capacity of the SAF, including G2Int (the Sultan of Oman's Intelligence Service), to counter the emergent rebel threat in and around the Musandam Peninsula and the north remained limited, even with the presence of experienced British officers, either on loan or on contract to the SAF. As such, the willingness of London to sanction Operation Intradon, which involved the direct use of the SAS in a counter-guerrilla role, reflected a recognition that reliance on the subcontracted nature of Oman's military structures had reached its limits. With the backing of the JIC, Intradon was designed to eliminate a group of seventy "dissidents" who, it was thought, were attempting to sow dissent among the Shihu, a tribe whose apparent hostility to any centralized control matched the extreme environment in which they survived. In the event, Intradon proved something of an anticlimax. With the overland exit and entry points to the Musandam Peninsula secured by the SAF and the neighboring Trucial Oman Scouts, and the sea lanes guarded by a small flotilla of the Royal Navy, the SAS entered the villages of Bukha and Ghumda on 18 December meeting no resistance. Indeed, aside from the arrest of three suspects and the discovery of three thousand rounds of small-arms ammunition, the threat from the dissidents had been exaggerated and "the local [Shihu] tribesmen seemed friendly."[24] Other than underlining the pressing need for good intelligence, the only real value of Intradon was as a statement of intent by the new regime in Muscat: the far reaches of the sultanate would no longer remain deprived backwaters, ripe for exploitation by dissident activity. Even so, it would take time for the use of "rent" derived from the sale of oil to have a real impact on wider Omani society, and as such, accurate and timely intelligence remained at a premium in allowing the sultanate to distribute its finite military resources to best effect.

By 1971, G2Int was renamed the Omani Intelligence Service (OIS), and two years later had become an autonomous, though not a wholly independent, service in its own right, with a premium placed upon timely political as opposed to operational intelligence.[25] The need was pressing. In October 1972, a Dhofari rebel who had changed sides identified a suspected PFLOAG member, Mohammed Talib, in Muscat. Talib, identified as a former political commissar with "the Lenin Unit," was placed under surveillance. It was only after another former member of the *adoo* (enemy) corroborated his identity that Talib was eventually arrested and interrogated on 18 December. While he at first claimed to have been a student in Beirut, he finally revealed that he had in fact been operating in the north of Oman for over a year, preparing a "second front." He went on to disclose that PFLOAG had established an active organization in northern Oman, whose various cell members, both inside Oman and across the border in the UAE, numbered over sixty and included Omani officers serving in the SAF. Of great concern to the British embassy were the large quantities of arms and ammunition smuggled into Oman that, if distributed to cell members, would have led to a campaign of terror being launched across the north of Oman over the New Year period 1972–73.[26] This campaign would have entailed not only attacks on commercial and military targets but the assassination of identified G2Int officials—including seconded Jordanian officers serving in intelligence as well as the SAF—and their contacts. This, in effect, would have blinded the intelligence effort in northern Oman and made it easier for PFLOAG to ease pressure upon its faltering guerrilla campaign in Dhofar by expanding its struggle across the sultanate.[27] Similar tactics had been adopted by the National Liberation Front (NLF) in Aden, which had destroyed, by 1967, any effective humint capability the federal authorities may have once possessed.[28]

On 23 December 1972, Operation Jason was launched to apprehend over forty suspects identified by Talib. Three concerns—one political, the other two operational—dominated the immediate intelligence horizons of the OIS throughout the operation. Politically, the service was taken aback by the social profile of those involved in the PFLOAG cells. They included serving Omani officers in the SAF, one of whom—Hamid bin Majid—confessed under interrogation to joining PFLOAG after being the alleged victim of "offhand treatment by British officers in SAF."[29] Others included teachers seconded to the SAF, officials of the Oman Gendarmerie, as well as women whose very gender was deemed the perfect cover for delivering messages between various members. Of note was that, while they were divided into typical cell structures, organized into five main districts across northern Oman and controlled externally by a central committee based in Aden, none of those arrested displayed any avowed ideological conviction. Indeed, opposition to a dynastic order dependent upon British tutelage, rather than any avowed support for a new socialist order, provided the dominant rationale for many to align themselves with PFLOAG. Familial links, however, did play some part in the recruitment process. Members of the al-Kiyumi and al-Ghassani families, for example were active in three of the five districts, while it was of note that many of those individuals identified as instructors had traveled to Aden and Iraq, as well as China, for training.[30]

In a dispatch to London, the British ambassador to Muscat, Donald Hawley, impressed upon the foreign secretary, Alec Douglas-Home, how "close run" the discovery of the PFLOAG organization had been. Indeed, rather than patient counterintelligence work uncovering the network, it had been the happenstance of a disillusioned rebel that had alerted authorities in Muscat to the attempt by PFLOAG to expand the war beyond the Dhofar. As Hawley noted, "Oman's own intelligence organisation urgently requires strengthening on the civil side."[31] Such a sentiment certainly echoed the views of Commander, Sultan's Armed Forces (CSAF) Major General Timothy Creasy who, in a written report to Sultan Qaboos, highlighted both the need for a more integrated body charged with making collective decisions over national security and an examination of "our present deployment of military forces and allocation of intelligence effort. . . . I do not consider the present deployment of forces in the North to be the most effective militarily to prevent recurrences of subversive activity."[32]

Operationally, Creasy was only too well aware that the sheer numbers rounded up under Operation Jason were beyond the limited ability of either the OIS or indeed the SAF to interrogate effectively or indeed efficiently. He was also concerned that the boat that had landed the arms just outside the port of Sur, having traveled from Yemen, had not been detected, despite the close proximity of the headquarters of the Oman Gendarmerie. This suggested either incompetence on the part of the Gendarmes or worse, collusion with the plotters. Creasy therefore turned to London for help in supplying the requisite expertise and equipment needed to undertake interrogations, and the subsequent collection and collation of intelligence that could hopefully be derived. This request caused much interdepartmental soul-searching in Whitehall. While eventually condoning the sale of recording devices to the OIS, the Foreign and Commonwealth Office (FCO) initially proved reluctant to allow British service personnel on secondment to the SAF to become involved in actual interrogations. In part, the sensitivity was informed by the recent furor regarding the disclosure of British interrogation techniques in Northern Ireland, but equally, it was also out of a desire by the Heath government to ensure that London's support for the sultan remained as discreet as was possible. But the FCO was only too aware that such a request could only have been made with the blessing of the sultan, and to withdraw or withhold British expertise would be damaging to Anglo-Omani relations.[33] As one official noted, if meeting requests for such aid by the sultan fell short of participation in "interrogation procedures which we ourselves are using in Northern Ireland," it would by default question the moral efficacy of those selfsame methods being used by the British in Ulster.[34]

To assuage such concerns Hawley, in a telegram sent on 4 January 1973, went some way to qualify the nature of the support sought by the CSAF. This looked for the loan of two senior intelligence officers to collate and administer information gleaned from the interrogations, assistance that would help expedite a more integrated appreciation of the PFLOAG structure without having to rely on the sparse number of SIOs upon whom already heavy demands were being made in Dhofar.[35] The British foreign secretary, Alec Douglas-Home, initially balked at the request, suggesting instead that the Saudis or Iranians be called upon to conduct the interrogations. This in turn provoked Hawley to remind Douglas-Home that the methods of the Saudis were "notorious," in sharp contrast to those employed by British seconded and contract officers, which were described by the British military attaché to Muscat, Colonel C. E. Welch, as being "conducted in a most gentlemanly manner." In a dispatch to London on 6 January, Welch noted that while much information had been gleaned from those arrested, details of PFLOAG contacts in other countries and future intention had "not been forthcoming." In a forthright manner he wrote:

> If the Omani security authorities, and this means SAF, are to capitalise on this important breakthrough against subversion/armed revolt, then the missing information that an interrogation centre with its proper system of questioning, recording, collating can produce could be critical. For instance, we know pistols were brought in with the arms. None of these have been recovered. We believe they have been distributed. Imagine the furore if one or two are used by PFLOAG hotheads to assassinate Europeans in the Muttrah suq. . . . If the war in Dhofar is to be prosecuted successfully, the North Oman must be kept quiet at this moment. A second front here could bring SAF to its literal knees with unfortunate repercussions, the least of which would be a request for more British aid.[36]

In the event, the defense secretary, Lord Carrington, approved the request for loan personnel to help with the administration of the interrogation center and to initiate Omani officers in British interrogation techniques, but made clear that such aid was finite, it being restricted to a period of just one month.[37] Even so, the arrest of further conspirators soon after in the UAE suggests that the loan of these British intelligence officers was crucial to forestalling any recrudescence of PFLOAG cells in north Oman and beyond.[38] All forty of those arrested in the initial stages of Operation Jason were sentenced to death after a brief trial. Of that number, twenty-two had their sentences commuted to various terms of imprisonment. The rest, including six army officers, were all executed by firing squad on three consecutive days in late June 1973.

In the immediate aftermath of Operation Jason, Creasy recommended that an integrated body be established tasked with security, intelligence coordination, and oversight at a national level. Hitherto, Qaboos had been reliant for matters pertaining to national security on his defense secretary, Colonel Hugh Oldman. However, as Hawley reminded the sultan, "It had become an anachronism that a British subject should hold what amounted to a ministerial post." This view was held by rulers of neighboring states, not least by the Saudi potentate King Faisal on whose political goodwill Oman greatly depended.[39] In March 1973, the National Defense Council (NDC) was formed. In effect a cabinet decision-making body, the NDC was chaired by the sultan, and included the minister of state for foreign affairs, the CSAF, the economic adviser to the sultan, the commissioner of police, the sultan's adviser on national security, and the director of intelligence.

Dennison was now appointed as the adviser to the sultan on national security in February 1972, with responsibility for overseeing the functioning of the OIS (soon to become in 1974 the Oman Research Department—ORD) and, in the light of Operation Jason, monitoring the tribes of the interior and their political proclivities. In his place was appointed Lieutenant Colonel Ray Nightingale, a Rhodesian by birth whose experience of dealing with the Mau-Mau insurgency in Kenya, as well as operating in Dhofar, instilled in him the importance of obtaining first-class intelligence. While noted for his rather direct style, Nightingale was credited with making the OIS "more professional," a task helped by large funds made available to the service by other Gulf states as well as the training assistance that was being provided by both the United Kingdom and Iran.

Still, the British military attaché observed that the OIS was a "strange creature," adding that it was "not quite SAF, not quite a service of its own, still trying to define what purpose it meant to serve, still not certain who its master is."[40] But if tension did exist between "master and commander," this was understandable. Living in what was tantamount to house arrest prior to July 1970 had prevented Qaboos from establishing the networks from which suitable candidates could be drawn into the OIS. Yet it is clear from the defense attaché's report that he would welcome the day "when sufficient corporate skill and experience" existed among Omanis to enable London at last to relinquish its role as master. Moves toward this end, while tentative, were certainly visible by 1974. A division of labor and territory came to define the newly named ORD between 1974 and 1976, with a clear emphasis on wider national security—including political intelligence—defining its remit, a remit very much defined by its evolution into a civilian bureaucratic endeavor. In the aftermath of Operation Jason, the

ORD concentrated most of its efforts in the tribal hinterland in the north of the sultanate, placing emphasis on establishing credible networks of informants designed to forewarn the authorities of any future dissident activities, real or potential, among the tribes.

Intelligence and Dhofar

In contrast to the increasing emphasis on political intelligence that now defined the ORD, the main intelligence effort based in Salalah was dictated by the exigencies of the insurgency and, in particular, the need to deny the PFLOAG the hitherto unfettered access it had enjoyed to Dhofar from the PDRY. It had always been recognized in London that a real intelligence vacuum existed in Dhofar. This vacuum hindered the SAF undertaking offensive military operations that had any real hope of denying the guerrillas sanctuary in the *jebal* (mountains) and wadis, from where they were free to interdict the tenuous lines of communication held by government forces along the coastal plain. Early on, it was suggested that a team consisting of one troop (drawn from the 22 SAS) of approximately thirty men, two interrogators, a psychological warfare officer, and two attached personnel from the intelligence corps would form the nucleus of a new intelligence structure.[41] Under the generic code name Operation Storm, elements of the 22 SAS were sent to the Dhofar under the cover of British army training teams from the end of 1970 onward. It was a designation that allowed London to disguise their deployment. But Whitehall was to remain sensitive to any long-term commitment of the SAS to the Dhofar campaign, lest discovery of their activities give rise once more to accusations of neo-imperialism at a time of declared British military retrenchment from the Gulf.

The extent to which the SAS actually engaged in covert action *across* the border into the PDRY remains a matter of some conjecture. The main supply base in Hauf, just over the border from Dhofar, was attacked by the Sultan of Oman's Air Force on 27 May 1972, an action that, in private, drew the opprobrium of the Foreign and Commonwealth Office. While no documents have ever been released that suggest official sanction was ever given to cross-border operations into Yemen, there is secondary-source evidence of some repute to suggest that British contract officers did indeed conduct covert missions into the territory of South Yemen. One, it is alleged, drove with his *firqa* (unit) to a fort deep inside the Yemen used to supply PFLOAG guerrillas. Having surprised the garrison, he then proceeded to destroy the fort with a series of explosive charges packed into old Bedford trucks. This account also claims that an SAS team did indeed penetrate into Yemen, its role being to disrupt operations of the PDRY army in support of the *adoo*.[42] Such operations may have occurred in the context off "hot pursuit operations." If so, they were of sufficient concern for the JIC to authorize a series of reconnaissance flights over the Oman-PDRY border, in an attempt to "define the alignment" of a large section of that boundary between the sultanate and its Marxist neighbor.[43]

From 1971 onward, SAS soldiers were involved in several fierce engagements but their primary task remained the covert training of the *firqas*, groups of former guerrillas or surrendered enemy personnel who had deserted their erstwhile comrades in the PFLOAG and had, in turn, been formed into irregular units used to counter the *adoo*. While never fully reliable in terms of intelligence gathering—tribal and factional infighting often degraded their effectiveness— they were nonetheless crucial to the sultanate as symbols of tribal fidelity to a new monarchical order.[44] Moreover, because their loyalties often denied efficacy to state boundaries, tribes were used by the CSAF to foment dissent in Yemen. For example, under Operation Dhib SAS soldiers instructed tribesmen from the Mahra in the arts of guerrilla warfare, with a view to conducting ambush operations against the *adoo* and military targets inside the PDRY.[45] In the aftermath of Operation Jason, Major General Creasy made clear his intention to recycle the arms, mines, and explosives recovered from the various caches to "the Firqat al-Bedayit for use in the 6th Governate of the PDRY."[46]

That so many of the *adoo* came over to the government side was in large part due to the alienation many felt toward a largely atheist liberation movement, a weakness again played upon by the SAS. While some analysts have maintained that PFLOAG never circumscribed Islam per se—only certain social aspects such as polygamy were condemned as regressive—invocation of Islam by government forces proved extremely effective, particularly among those whose involvement with the PFLOAG had occurred largely as the result of the digestion of the DLF.[47] When coupled with the incremental improvement in the well-being of the people throughout the Dhofar as the socioeconomic reforms introduced by Qaboos began to tell—roads were built, new wells sunk, clinics and schools established, and great strides made in land cultivation and treatment of cattle—the counterinsurgency campaign in Dhofar began to reap significant dividends. In this process, the involvement of the SAS between 1970 and 1976 was of crucial importance. The ability to train and organize the *firqas* allowed the government access to regions of Dhofar that reliance upon the ethnically diverse SAF would previously have denied. SAS-led *firqas* were the first to challenge the hegemony exercised by the PFLOAG over the Dhofari interior away from the coastal plain. This in turn allowed for the eventual construction of secure bases from which the SAF was able to re-impose the sovereignty of the sultanate over the entire Dhofar region by the end of 1976.

Conclusion

Given the narratives that have informed our understanding of the insurgency in Oman, it would be easy to conclude that the production and use of intelligence remained a purely British affair. From the assessments of the JIC through to the role of SIOs and the SAS, British personnel and personalities undoubtedly dominated a realm in which Omani involvement was certainly subservient. Yet this occurred by default rather than by design, which would normally define a "patron–client" relationship in which the former derives the main benefit. A legacy of distrust, personified in the figure of Sultan Said bin Taimur, had denied efficacy to intelligence and the indigenous means by which this could be realized by Omanis themselves. When coupled with the particular dynamic that defined relations between London and Muscat—Oman was never a crown colony— dependence upon Britain to provide the necessary expertise to staff Oman's intelligence structures, in whatever guise, became for London the only option. As such, and while mindful of too visible a footprint in the Omani sands, Britain was prepared to sanction both intelligence support for the sultan, as well as the proportionate deployment of special forces to secure the sultanate between 1970 and 1976. Such use of British forces in general, and the SAS in particular, was kept on a tight leash and balanced against the real concern of fulfilling treaty obligations to the sultan while avoiding becoming enmeshed in a conflict seemingly without end.

The assessments of the JIC certainly informed the broader strategic context in which the insurgency was played out, but equally, officials in London always placed clear caveats on how and when special operations could be sanctioned. As for the OIS, it should not be forgotten that its greatest triumph, Operation Jason, came about through chance rather than good intelligence work. Without the legacy of a bureaucratic tradition upon which to graft appropriate structures, Omani intelligence was always trying to balance internal security with external surveillance on a fulcrum of inadequate numbers of trained personnel. While 1974 marked a watershed in the development of the OIS, it should not be overlooked that the inexperience of those associated with the PFLOAG network in northern Oman certainly worked in the OIS' favor at a crucial time when the OIS lacked sufficient networks in the tribal hinterlands. This, however, should not disguise the central point: the use of intelligence and, indeed, special operations in Oman between 1970 and 1976 always remained subservient to strict political-military objectives that recognized the sovereign authority of Sultan Qaboos, but with it the perpetuation of British influence amid the process of physical withdrawal from the Gulf. Even so, to echo the words of the Duke of Wellington, it remained a close run thing.

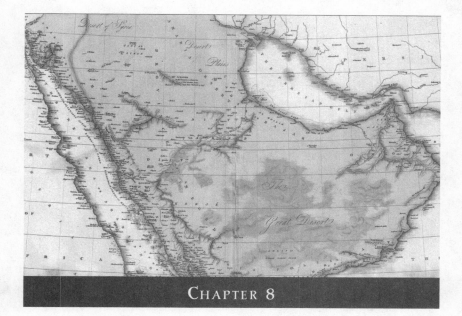

CHAPTER 8

In Brzezinski's Forge

Fashioning the Carter Doctrine's Military Instrument

Frank L. Jones

S
unlight angled in through the windows and warmed the Oval Office, the weather surprisingly mild for mid-January 1981. Jimmy Carter, thirty-ninth president of the United States, sat behind his carved oak desk and, with a neat draftsman-like signature, signed the document before him: Presidential Directive/NSC-63, Persian Gulf Security Framework. Carter was pleased with the progress his administration had made to improve the U.S. security posture in the Persian Gulf as well as fashioning the beginnings of an effective security framework.[1]

This directive would continue the trend to protect U.S. vital interests in the region, as he declared in his State of the Union address nearly a year earlier. The December 1979 Soviet invasion of Afghanistan had been foremost in his mind that evening when he spoke to the joint session of Congress. Never mind that the military force necessary to back the warning he articulated in his address was largely nonexistent. It was the perception of resolve that mattered. Since the pronouncement, his administration had worked diligently to develop a set of feasible and suitable plans and programs to meet the commitment he made. The directive was the culmination of that effort to deter Soviet control of Middle East oil. It was also anticlimactic. He would be out of office and on his way home to Georgia in fewer than five days.

Today, the former president's declaration, known as the Carter Doctrine, still influences U.S. policy in the region as each of his successors built upon the framework articulated in his final national security directive. This chapter examines the fashioning of the military instrument that gave credence to Carter's pronouncement. It explores the strategic context, the refinement of U.S. defense policy and strategy after his address, and military activities undertaken to realize his declaration. In examining this subject, it also considers how bureaucratic politics, interservice rivalry, North Atlantic Treaty Organization (NATO) planning concerns, and budget constraints nearly scuttled the president's policy enterprise.

From Review to Decision

The Carter administration did not differ from its predecessors in its attempt to examine existing U.S. foreign policy and promote its own worldview and policy initiatives shortly after inauguration. These initiatives were largely a reaction to and a criticism of Richard Nixon and Gerald Ford's approach to the Soviet Union, the lessons of the Vietnam War, and the administration's determination to place its own mark on foreign policy issues it considered a priority.[2] The day after Carter's swearing-in, the White House instigated several interagency policy reviews as well as a major assessment of the U.S.-Soviet global rivalry. Initially, the National Security Council staff was to conduct this task, but the State and Defense Departments opposed the assignment. State argued that it had the lead for formulating foreign policy, while Defense contended that the nation's security was its responsibility. The parties compromised and on 18 February 1977 Carter directed, in Presidential Review Memorandum (PRM)/NSC-10, a comprehensive net assessment and military force posture review, consisting of two parts undertaken simultaneously.[3]

The first part examined a wide range of alternative military strategies, with commensurate force posture and programs in support of the various options. Secretary of Defense Harold Brown would head this effort. Brown was an accomplished scientist with impressive academic credentials and extensive national security experience, having served in a high-level position in the Office of the Secretary of Defense during Secretary Robert McNamara's tenure, and ultimately as secretary of the Air Force during Lyndon Johnson's presidency. Brown believed that the most critical military threat for the new administration was a NATO–Warsaw Pact conflict in Europe; therefore, the primary national security objective should be the strengthening of NATO. The 150-page study he approved in June clearly underscored this belief by making it the preeminent theater of operations.[4] Nonetheless, the Defense Department study included several recommendations on how conventional forces might be used in non-NATO contingencies. The underlying concept of operations was to build existing forces flexible enough to be capable of acting independently of allied operating bases. The Persian Gulf was one of the areas where this concept could be applied.[5]

The second part was a net assessment under the leadership of Zbigniew Brzezinski, assistant to the president for national security affairs. It reviewed and compared the overall trends in the political, diplomatic, economic, technological, and military capabilities of the United States, its allies, and potential adversaries, with particular attention to the adversaries' objectives and strategies and the appropriate U.S. response.[6] Brzezinski, a former Columbia University political scientist known as "Vitamin Z" by students because of his intensity, and who served in the Department of State during the Johnson administration, was regarded as a hardliner toward the Soviet Union. He wanted what he called "bite" in U.S. policy toward the Russians.[7] He assigned Samuel P. Huntington, a political scientist on leave from Harvard University and serving as the head of strategic planning for the National Security Council staff, to lead the assessment, directing him to "tell us how we're doing in the world vis-à-vis the Soviet Union."[8]

Huntington was determined to make the assessment a "lineal descendant" of NSC-68,[9] President Harry Truman's directive initiating U.S. Cold War containment policy. Ultimately, Huntington and his team produced about a dozen interagency study-group products, a number of "special studies," and an executive summary of approximately three hundred pages. When Huntington and his group concluded their preliminary assessment of the military balance, the State Department and several members of the NSC staff disputed its findings as "too pessimistic." Huntington's team contended that Warsaw Pact conventional forces had attained supremacy over NATO forces in central Europe (the area along the West German border) and would quickly overcome NATO resistance. A revised study was issued to correspond with the State Department's view that there was an approximate balance of military capability in the region, but the trends were adverse because of decline in U.S. defense expenditures and the steady growth in Soviet military capacity. Within the Department of Defense, Secretary Brown, under pressure from the Joint Chiefs of Staff, rejected as flawed the force structure recommendations proposed by a senior member of his staff. Huntington's vision that the comprehensive review would be the equivalent of NSC-68 became, in the words of one contemporary, "an exercise in confusion."[10]

After further wrangling among his senior advisers, Carter articulated the administration's strategic guidance in Presidential Directive (PD)/NSC-18, U.S. National Strategy, signed on 24 August 1977, which focused on U.S.–Soviet Union relations, describing them as a combination of competition and cooperation. The U.S. national strategy would seek to counterbalance, with its allies and partners, Soviet military power in three key areas: Europe, East Asia, and the Middle East. The emphasis was decidedly on Europe and South Korea. Nonetheless, the directive declared that in a crisis, the projection of U.S. forces into the Middle East region must be considered as high a priority as that of reinforcing South Korea. The president further charged that the United States maintain a deployment force of light divisions, supported by naval, air, and land forces from the United States, designed for use against Soviet force projection in the Middle East or Persian Gulf. The force was Huntington's idea based on his assessment in addition to discussions with NSC staff members responsible for U.S. policy in the Middle East. These experts held that with potential internal challenges to the shah of Iran's rule and other discord in the region, the Persian Gulf was the area of the world most susceptible to Soviet pressure and the likely place for a conflict requiring the deployment of U.S. forces.[11]

The Year of Indifference

The Defense Department paid scant attention to the president's direction for the formation of a deployment force. It was not immediately affordable, and the White House was determined to achieve sizeable defense savings as part of a campaign pledge Carter had made. Further, Carter, Brzezinski, and Secretary of State Cyrus Vance agreed with Brown that NATO needed reinvigorating after its neglect during the Vietnam War.[12] A focus on the Persian Gulf would divert scarce resources. Given these political aims, the secretary of defense launched, with the assistance of Robert Komer, his special adviser for NATO affairs, a series of NATO projects. These ventures, consistent with the president's direction, were designed to prepare conventional forces to conduct a short, intensive war in central Europe, a NATO-first strategy. To signal further its vow to strengthen NATO, the administration increased the U.S. defense budget modestly to meet the funding levels that the alliance members agreed to in the 1977 Long-Term Defense Program: 3 percent real growth per annum for the next five years.[13]

The State Department made no effort to advance the concept with friendly nations in the region either.[14] Vance, a steady, self-effacing Wall Street attorney and former senior official in the Kennedy and Johnson administrations who practiced a plodding form of "turtle diplomacy," believed that the most urgent priority in U.S. foreign policy was to conclude a new strategic arms limitation treaty with the Soviets.[15] Career diplomats in the State Department supported his agenda, but for a different reason. One senior State Department official with substantial experience in the Arab world acknowledged that the decision not to engage diplomatically concerning a potential U.S. military presence in that region was the result of years of conditioning in the belief that it was unnecessarily inflammatory.[16] Continuing the current policy wherein the U.S. presence was not highly visible was optimal because of U.S. support of Israel. Arab radicals could use a more overtly pro-U.S. policy on the part of their leaders to disrupt and possibly destabilize moderate Arab regimes.[17]

Thus, throughout 1978, no effort commenced to bring the force into being, although Brown issued guidance to the Joint Chiefs that directed that U.S. forces prepare to counter a Soviet "blitzkrieg" in central Europe while concurrently handling a Soviet "brushfire" in the Persian Gulf. The language of the order was hardly forceful: "But we are unsure of the utility of U.S. military power in the Persian Gulf contingencies." Thus, the Carter administration's force planning continued to be based on a "1½" war concept, NATO and a lesser contingency, with the Korean Peninsula to be the most likely location for this lesser conflict to occur. The Joint Chiefs also dutifully conducted a strategy review that summer in response to PD-18 that implicitly acknowledged the need for a rapid deployment force (RDF) to handle a lesser contingency, but nothing more.[18]

The administration, meanwhile, concentrated on the Arab–Israeli peace process and attended to pressing domestic issues such as runaway inflation. In doing so, it gradually adopted the Persian Gulf strategy favored by the Nixon and Ford administrations. Called the "twin-pillar" policy, it relied on the shah of Iran (and to a lesser degree, Saudi Arabia) to help protect Western interests in the region. It also fundamentally gave a blank check to the shah's regime to purchase modern arms and build its military strength to ensure internal stability and the capability to defend against Soviet-supported threats in the Gulf. Provided the Soviet Union did not try to extend its influence or threaten U.S. interests in the region, important interests but not clearly articulated as vital, the Carter administration could live with this approach.[19]

A Turn of Events

A few months after Carter signed PD-18, however, several events suggested potential Soviet threats in the Horn of Africa, the Middle East, and the Persian Gulf region. The first occurrence was the Soviet Union's decision in November 1977 to abandon its support for Somalia and back its rival, Ethiopia, in their war over the Ogaden region because it better suited Soviet interests and provided them a foothold in the Arabian Sea. The Soviets provided massive military aid and Cuba contributed 17,000 soldiers, while Brzezinski and Vance disagreed as to what the American response should be. Vance argued that the Soviets had no "genuine strategic concept of projecting power into that region," it was "opportunism" and had no major impact on U.S. interests. For Brzezinski, the Soviets' movement of forces and matériel into Ethiopia in an abbreviated period demonstrated the complete opposite; never before had the United States seen them exercise such an operation over substantial distances while disregarding the airspace of other countries to do so.[20]

Concerns heightened sharply in April 1978 with the local Communist coup in Afghanistan, creating a Soviet client state adjacent to pro-U.S. Iran. Further, throughout the summer and autumn of 1978, intelligence and diplomatic reports from U.S. officials in Tehran described the shah's gloomy disposition regarding radical opposition forces within his country. In mid-January 1979, he was forced to flee the country because of domestic turmoil. On 1 February, the exiled Ayatollah Khomeini, the shah's foremost political opponent, arrived in Iran, followed by the stunning collapse of the pro-Western government of Shahpur Bakhtiar on 11 February 1979.[21] Border incursions by pro-Soviet South Yemen into the territory of the Yemen Arab Republic, its neighbor, a month later, led to the shipment of $400 million of emergency U.S. military assistance, prompted by Saudi anxieties. The administration also dispatched the USS *Constellation* carrier battle group to the Arabian Sea, and deployed four airborne warning and control system (AWACS) aircraft to Saudi Arabia to augment Saudi air defenses and reassure the monarchy.[22] Additionally, U.S. intelligence made the administration progressively more aware of the Soviet Union's focus on increasing its force projection capabilities, which included emphasis on the Middle East with planning and exercises dedicated to a Soviet invasion to capture and control Middle East oil fields.[23]

These incidents only confirmed Brzezinski's perception of the strategic landscape, particularly his perspective on the area running from the Middle East to Pakistan, which he described in a much-quoted January 1979 interview as an "arc of crisis." He insisted that the fragile political and social structures located in this region were of vital importance to the United States and threatened by fragmentation. If that happened, powers antagonistic to U.S. values and agreeable to its enemies would fill the chaotic political vacuum. He added that the arc's center of gravity was Iran.[24] This stance, which he also put into a classified memorandum to the president, ignited substantial debate among the administration's top officials as to whether Western Europe should continue to be the region of principal concern. However, the administration took no action as the NATO allies remained fearful of the growing Soviet military buildup and were not amenable to the Carter administration abandoning the long-term plan to improve the alliance's defenses.[25]

Nonetheless, public statements made by other prominent administration officials intimated that a revised perception of U.S. interests in the region was gaining consensus. After traveling to the Middle East in February 1979 to assure partners in the region of U.S. security commitments, Secretary Brown stated that the United States had vital interests in the region and would use military force, if necessary, to ensure the flow of oil. However, he hedged by stating that the use of force was not always necessary. Secretary of Energy James Schlesinger also avowed that U.S. interests in the region were vital and that to protect them, military force or presence might be necessary, but he too quibbled, commenting that actual deployment was not necessarily the preferred option.[26]

Sensing that two cabinet officers now shared his strategic vision for the Persian Gulf region, Brzezinski, on 28 February 1979, sent a detailed memorandum to the president in which he offered his thoughts about major policy changes that were required to protect Western interests, particularly the NATO allies and Japan, which were highly dependent on Middle East oil. He also expressed his beliefs about the necessity of thwarting Soviet influence as well as blunting the budding power of radical Arab groups in the Middle East and Gulf region. The prescription, he claimed, was the formulation of the "consultative security framework for the Middle East," which he had surfaced a year previously as the mechanism for reasserting U.S. influence and power.[27]

Brzezinski also included an action plan with the memorandum that required the United States to develop a real force projection capability for rapid deployment in the region. In his view, making this capability manifest required four steps: improved military basing on the British island of Diego Garcia in the Indian Ocean (a portion of which the United States leased), the conduct of military exercises in the region, increased naval presence in the Arabian Sea, and formation of a military command with its headquarters in the United States but capable of deploying quickly to the region. He conceived of the security framework in broad strategic terms, consistent with other major Cold War initiatives such as the Truman Doctrine, the Marshall Plan, and the establishment of NATO. While he preferred the European allies to support such a massive undertaking, he believed they would not act until the United States made a substantial investment.[28]

Carter did not respond to Brzezinski's memorandum. A few weeks later, the national security adviser tried again, this time sending the president a copy of Comprehensive Net Assessment 1978 (CNA-78), an update of PRM-10, which concluded that the Persian Gulf and Southwest Asia remained flash points and that the Department of Defense had made no progress in creating the RDF needed to meet U.S. objectives. The president read his adviser's analysis and annotated the copy with his agreement concerning the importance of the RDF. Brzezinski then forwarded a copy of his memorandum and CNA-78 to Vance and Brown, along with the president's notation. Vance replied with a bristling rejoinder that the United States did not need a standing military force capable of deploying to the region, but Brown embraced the idea, finding Brzezinski's views consistent with his own growing concerns.[29] By May, all three agreed on one point at least: the United States had vital interests in the region. A month later, Carter expressed this consensus position to Soviet premier Leonid Brezhnev at the Venice summit. Still, when Brzezinski asked the Defense Department shortly thereafter what progress had been made on an RDF, the response was a guarded "not much."[30]

Soothing Zbig

While officials in the Office of the Secretary of Defense expressed unease about the lack of movement toward setting up the RDF, the military services did not share this trepidation, continuing to argue that budget constraints precluded creation of the force. The size of the defense budget had been a source of discord between the Joint Chiefs of Staff and the White House since the beginning of the administration.[31] From the Joint Chiefs' viewpoint, the RDF would not be constituted without a comprehensive discussion of a concomitant increase in force structure, budget levels, and readiness.

Brzezinski did not relent and sent a second memorandum to Brown. His pique prompted two results. First, Gen. David C. Jones, chairman of the Joint Chiefs of Staff, directed in April 1979 the initiation of planning for the RDF at the "joint level" among the Office of the Joint Chiefs of Staff and the armed forces. For the remainder of the year, desultory planning efforts were undertaken to placate Brzezinski. His memoranda, however, encouraged a dialogue between the NSC staff and the Department of Defense, first with the Office of the Assistant Secretary of Defense for International Security Affairs, and later drawing in the Joint Staff and other Pentagon offices. These discussions and the Pentagon's planning exposed the political and military difficulties associated with the region together with the underlying friction between the Departments of Defense and State. When Brzezinski, Brown, and Vance met in June, there were still limited military options available, but it remained clear that the State Department stood firm against the United States being involved militarily in the region.[32] In June, Brown directed the Joint Chiefs to study force options that could be used in the event of a conflict in Southwest Asia. They responded in August, but could not agree to an approach. Brown, sensitive to the depredations of inter-service rivalry, found a compromise by taking features from the two options presented, but that ended the effort.[33]

In September, based on intelligence reports, some members of the NSC staff grew increasingly alarmed about the Soviets committing combat troops to Afghanistan to prop up the pro-Soviet regime. However, the Defense Department believed that the evidence did not "warrant undue alarm" and that Soviet troop movements along the border were more likely for training purposes, while CIA analysts concluded that despite the worsening conditions for the leftist regime, it did not augur the direct participation of Soviet combat forces. Nonetheless, the deputy national security adviser, David Aaron, tasked the Central Intelligence Agency and the Department of State to develop papers exploring what actions the U.S. government should take if the Soviets intervened in Afghanistan. Brzezinski continued to fret about the probability of a Soviet invasion and urged the president repeatedly to authorize public statements from administration officials remonstrating against potential Soviet meddling in Afghanistan. The State Department thwarted his efforts, refusing to participate or to clear background papers.[34]

Enter "Blowtorch Bob"

On 19 October 1979, the U.S. Senate confirmed Robert Komer as Brown's new undersecretary of defense for policy. In Komer, Brown found a person ideally suited for the functions the defense secretary had envisaged when he established the position. Komer had sterling policy and strategy credentials accumulated over nearly three decades of public service in the Central Intelligence Agency and as a member of the National Security Council staff under Presidents John F. Kennedy and Lyndon Johnson, responsible for the Middle East and South Asia portfolio. Johnson made him his special assistant for Vietnam pacification in 1966, where he acquired the nickname "Blowtorch," because one diplomat likened his abrasive and aggressive personality to having a blowtorch aimed at the seat of one's pants. This assignment was followed by nearly two years in South Vietnam as Gen. William Westmoreland's deputy for pacification on the Military Assistance Command staff; he was then appointed U.S. ambassador to Turkey until April 1969. Before becoming Brown's adviser on NATO, he had been employed by the RAND Corporation as a senior analyst, studying counterinsurgency and, when money for that topic vanished, NATO issues.

For the first two weeks after commencing his new duties, Komer devoted a substantial portion of his time to pushing the NATO programs Brown and he had devised. However, two events turned his and the administration's immediate attention elsewhere. The first occurred in Iran on 4 November 1979 when radical anti-American demonstrators took over the U.S. embassy compound in Tehran in support of the Islamic revolution and held fifty-two occupants hostage. The incident provoked a heated debate in Washington as to why the United States failed to anticipate this outcome, and led to a tangle of accusations and alibis. Some blamed the State Department and the U.S. ambassador to Iran for suppressing the pessimistic and farsighted cables of his subordinates. Other critics censured Brzezinski's theory of bolstering "regional influentials." They argued that its basic assumption was discredited and flawed by an overly naïve equation that military power plus oil wealth equaled political stability. He had failed to consider how corruption, mismanagement, and religious opposition could undermine the shah's legitimacy among his own people.[35] On 4 December at an NSC meeting, Carter directed Brown to make an RDF operational immediately and for the Departments of State and Defense to develop plans for attaining access to air and naval bases in the region. Brzezinski recommended Somalia, Oman, and Kenya.[36]

The second critical event followed on 25 December when the Soviet Union invaded Afghanistan. The operation, according to Brzezinski, represented "not a local but a strategic challenge."[37] Soviet premier Brezhnev told Carter that events internal to Afghanistan required the USSR to save an unstable pro-Soviet government there. Carter and his principal advisers perceived the Soviet Union's use of force to increase its domination beyond its borders for the first time since the late 1940s as portending ominous designs in the Persian Gulf, potentially invading a militarily weakened Iran.[38]

Carter was initially stunned and felt personally betrayed and disappointed by the Soviet invasion because of his efforts to win ratification of the second Strategic Arms Limitation Treaty (SALT II). He recovered and seemed to one of his close aides to toughen, become more forceful and ready to act.[39] The first sign of his determination came on 30 December when he told journalists that the United States now confronted in the Persian Gulf a wider strategic challenge that would necessitate a broad response.[40]

Brzezinski followed Carter's lead a few weeks later, by remarking in an interview that "three central strategic zones" now existed where the United States had vital interests: Western Europe, the Far East, and the newly emerged area, the Middle East. Further, he saw these zones as interdependent: a threat to the security of one was a threat to the other two. Almost simultaneously, he sent a memorandum to the president laying out the long-term objectives needed to cope with the consequences of the Soviet action in Afghanistan, reiterating the regional strategic framework he had advanced before and underscoring that an increased defense budget would be required for a sustained effort.[41] A year earlier, when he had first suggested the new security framework, he had also recommended the president declare his plans publicly in a major speech. Carter had demurred then.[42] Now the time was ripe and the president's upcoming State of the Union address would be the venue.

Declaring a New Doctrine

In his State of the Union message on 23 January 1980, President Carter articulated the new United States policy on the Persian Gulf region, using language Brzezinski furnished the White House speechwriters. "Let our position be absolutely clear. Any attempt by any outside force to gain control of the Persian Gulf region will be regarded as an assault on the vital interests of the United States of America, and such an assault will be repelled by any means necessary, including military force."[43]

Détente was dead. Brzezinski now enjoyed Carter's complete support and approval. No longer was the president fluctuating between the national security adviser and his secretary of state to maintain harmony, the result of which had been incoherent U.S. foreign policy. Brzezinski was the bureaucratic victor: the Soviet invasion justified his long-held views that challenging the Soviets was the best stance. However, the new "Carter Doctrine," as the press soon named it, required more than rhetorical flourishes.[44]

To provide a basis for an embryonic Persian Gulf security framework, Brig. Gen. William Odom, Brzezinski's military assistant, delineated a number of activities, categorized as military, diplomatic, economic, and intelligence issues, which required immediate implementation.[45] The first visible indication of the new military approach was the president's fiscal year 1981 budget request, which included a substantial increase in defense spending for that year, approximately $35 billion more than the previous year's request to Congress.[46] As Secretary Brown informed Congress, "The President and I believe the prospect for renewed turbulence in the Middle East, the Caribbean, and elsewhere, and the possibility of new demands on our non-nuclear posture, require additional precautionary actions. As a consequence, we will accelerate our efforts to improve the capability of our Rapid Deployment Forces."[47] Such a tangible budget increase, in addition to the declaratory policy, dictated that the halfhearted planning for an RDF that had been ongoing for months must now be an immediate priority for the Defense Department.[48]

Komer was even more specific about the RDF at a Senate hearing on the subject where he articulated the strategic vision he had in mind, based on improving U.S. capabilities to respond quickly to deter conflict or defend vital interests. The RDF, in his view, would have to rely on speedy movement of personnel and equipment to the region using a concept he had promoted for rapid NATO reinforcement, prepositioning of matériel. To this end, the Defense Department budget request, he informed the members, was approximately $300 million, $220 million for the floating bases (maritime prepositioning ships) and $81 million for developing suitably large transport planes, the Air Force's C-X program.[49]

With the 1980 presidential election only months away, the decision to proceed with the RDF was also good politics as Carter was badly sagging in the polls. The defense budget increase and his forceful declaration could possibly bolster his support among some constituencies, silence his critics, and give him an advantage over his potential Republican adversary. However, the commitment was not complete; there were still reservations at the Defense Department, where some officials complained about declining readiness of the forces and the lack of funding to replace older, increasingly less reliable weapons.[50]

Assembling a Force, Shaping a Strategy

A distraction quickly materialized after Carter's declaration: the Army and the Marine Corps started vying for command of the new force as soon as Carter decreed its immediate creation in December. Both services nominated strong candidates, but Brown designated Maj. Gen. P. X. Kelley (USMC), promoted to lieutenant general, the new force's first commander in December 1979, with the headquarters to be established formally at MacDill Air Force Base in Tampa, Florida, on 1 March 1980. The RDF, renamed the Rapid Deployment Joint Task Force (RDJTF), would be a headquarters of a few hundred personnel only. Under this concept, there would be no new combat units but a "reservoir of forces" drawn from the four services, which was largely based in the United States and configured in a variety of force packages tailored to meet various crises. Although originally not dedicated to a specific region, the Persian Gulf area was recognized as the most likely use for the new task force, but Brown did not make this definite until August 1980 after the Joint Chiefs approved a revised charter for the RDJTF. As to command and control, it was under the operational control of the commander of U.S. Readiness Command, led by a four-star Army general.[51]

With that issue settled, Komer, in February 1980, asked Gen. David C. Jones, chairman of the Joint Chiefs of Staff (JCS), for a paper on Middle East military strategy, since it was the Joint Chiefs' responsibility to formulate such a strategy. Brzezinski was already pestering the Pentagon for the document. Jones told Komer that there was no chance of obtaining such a document because of a lack of agreement among the service chiefs on how the subject should be approached.[52] Instead, Jones suggested that Komer and his staff develop the strategy. If he found it acceptable, he would tell Brown that he did, and if Brown approved it, then the document could be forwarded to the White House. Komer agreed and soon had a thirteen-page paper that laid out military options in the Persian Gulf, primarily in response to a Soviet incursion, but other contingencies were envisioned. His paper proposed the rapid deployment of forces and an active defense in the Zagros Mountain passes of Iran. It was a high-risk concept but if successful, it would either deter the Soviets or hold them off long enough to deploy a more robust force and defend well forward of the vital oil fields in the

Persian Gulf. Jones liked the paper, suggested a few changes, and so did Brown before sending it to the White House. Brzezinski and his staff were pleased with it as well and it was distributed to the other relevant agencies. At a subsequent NSC meeting, the document was approved as the basic outline of a new Middle East strategy.[53]

In essence, the Carter Doctrine, as Komer envisioned it, changed the very foundation of the U.S. defense strategy when it came to the security of Europe, that is, NATO, and the reinforcement of South Korea. The new strategy he offered consisted of fighting a major theater war in Europe, with forces for two simultaneous smaller contingencies or "half wars," Korea and the Persian Gulf.[54]

In March, Secretary Brown publicly revealed the major tenets of the new strategy, and while he stressed that it consisted of "non-military components," it was clear that the emphasis was on conventional deterrence of Soviet aggression. The military components consisted of increased peacetime presence in the Persian Gulf, prepositioning of equipment, enhanced mobility using air and sealift capabilities, access and transit rights, and frequent deployment and exercises in the area.[55] With the fall of the shah, the United States sought out locations where U.S. forces could have access, but as Odom underscored the administration did not want to make itself "dependent upon the survival of a single regime in order to protect [our] access."[56] By August, the Departments of State and Defense concluded such arrangements with Oman, Somalia, and Kenya, which Brzezinski had originally recommended.

Turning Metal into Gold

Komer now spent his time developing specific program initiatives to give substance to the strategy. The Army and Air Force were unenthusiastic about shifting funds in their budgets from NATO to the Persian Gulf. The Marine Corps was not eager either, but they now had the mission of leading the RDJTF. In addition to building up Diego Garcia's air and naval facilities, at an estimated cost of nearly $1 billion, the RDJTF would have equipment on board twelve maritime prepositioning ships (MPS). The Marines were concerned that if the funding were applied to these vessels, then the Marine Corps would lose funding for amphibious ships, which it needed to perform its core mission. Thus, the attitude among the services was that if the president and the secretary of defense wanted such a force, then the funding should be in addition to current levels. It would have to be directed, which is exactly what Komer did.[57] He created a document called the Defense Planning Guidance, signed by the secretary, to get compliance. It provided specific direction regarding RDJTF priorities and ensured that strategic planning was not disconnected from the programs needed to execute the strategy.[58] Komer also allayed the Marines' fears by assuring them that funding for the MPS would be additive, as would be the supplies on board the ships needed to support Marine brigades.[59]

Working with Russell Murray, the assistant secretary of defense for program analysis and evaluation, Komer had the secretary approve the Consolidated Guidance (CG). This document set both the direction and goals for RDJTF-related programs in the department's Five-Year Defense Plan (FYDP) beginning with the fiscal year 1982 budget request. Murray's staff was also able to identify most of these programs as discreet items in the FYDP. The result was a paper that permitted useful high-level debates about options.[60]

Komer then directed his staff to examine the services' Program Objective Memoranda (five-year financial plans) using this information and determine if they were complying with the CG language that directed placing emphasis on the Persian Gulf. If they found that the services were not funding these requirements, then they were to inform Komer. In turn, Komer and Brown would find the offsets needed to fund the requirements. The means now existed to ensure that a strategy-funding mismatch did not exist for the task force and that RDJTF initiatives were protected in the budgeting process.[61]

Komer recognized that basing in the Indian Ocean and projecting forces into the Middle East meant a crucial problem in time compression. Ideally, the United States wanted to project its forces overseas before a conflict began so that it could deter it. Rapid deployment was essential, but Komer questioned the meaning of the word "rapid." To deploy three divisions to the Persian Gulf would be an enormous undertaking, especially in terms of logistical support. The distance between the United States and the region was 12,500 nautical miles by sea and eight thousand nautical miles by air. The emphasis had to be on projecting combat capability. Supporting these forces for an extended period could not be done simultaneously. Komer had an answer for that and it again came from his NATO experience. The supply and support would have to come from the local governments. This assumed that the task force would be operating in a "permissive environment," relying to some degree on local ports and airfields.[62]

In mid-1980, Brown, at Komer's recommendation, enunciated a policy that the Defense Department would rely on its allies and friends worldwide to meet American initial fuel and lubricant requirements from their stockpiles. Komer's view was that the Defense Department would approach governments in the Persian Gulf region and make it known that if they wanted U.S. security, then they would have to construct hardened storage and distribution facilities and to stock them with the needed products.[63]

Komer reasoned that the logic of this approach could be extended to other supplies. He knew that the second most important commodity that U.S. forces would need in the Persian Gulf was water. Consequently, the Gulf States built large desalination plants. Additionally, the governments in the region would provide the infrastructure necessary to sustain U.S. forces logistically, such as ports and repair installations. For example, the Saudis were acquiring Hawk missiles, in addition to which the manufacturer, Raytheon Corporation, sold them a maintenance facility operated by contract employees hired by Raytheon. If U.S. Army troops deployed to the region, their Hawk missiles could be repaired at that facility. Komer urged the Saudis to overbuild the facility so that it was capable of processing and reworking more missiles. His view was that the Saudis would be willing to finance that upgrade provided the facility remained a Saudi Arabian installation.[64]

By the fall of 1980, disbelievers complained that the RDJTF, while largely a "tripwire" force, still politically destabilized the region. Others ridiculed it, remarking that after several months it was essentially a toothless fraud. The units designated for the task force were currently lined up for the defense of Western Europe and Korea in various war plans. This was tantamount to a shell game. Additionally, while rapid deployment necessitated substantial airlift and sealift capabilities to deploy forces to the region in time to blunt a Soviet invasion, this problem was exacerbated by the Army's penchant for procuring tanks that were too heavy to transport on cargo airplanes, while the Navy and Air Force did not place emphasis on lift capability.[65]

Komer acknowledged these deficiencies would require additional funding, and dealt with them in the fiscal year 1982 Defense Department budget request along with the planned future budgets, recognizing that it might be years before these operational shortcomings were rectified. Nonetheless, as an indicator of the administration's commitment, over the five-year defense program the funding request would be nearly $10 billion, more than $6 billion for airlift capabilities and $3 billion for the additional prepositioning ships.[66]

Another flaw from Komer's perspective was that the administration had not adequately addressed its military assistance requirements in the Persian Gulf, yet regional cooperation and capabilities were critical. He complained to the White House, with Brown and the Joint Chiefs' support, but the Office of Management and Budget opposed any additive funding for security assistance, as did the State Department. Komer then pressed for a presidential decision on the subject given its criticality to the Persian Gulf initiatives. David Aaron, the deputy national security adviser, set 7 November, Election Day, as the date for a joint

State-Defense paper outlining various options.[67] Komer realized that he was racing against time and he had his doubts that Carter would be reelected.

On 7 November, time ran out: Carter lost his reelection bid. Less than a month later, at a National Security Council meeting, the president insisted on a directive codifying the Persian Gulf Security Framework.[68] This final national security issue, acted on in the waning days of Carter's presidency, ultimately enshrined the administration's policy while also serving as one of its legacies.

Concluding Thoughts

The historical record supports Brzezinski's assertion that the rapid deployment force, as a concept, was an NSC staff initiative, and it also demonstrates that Brzezinski was its most fervent advocate. However, in the three years between President Carter's approval of PD-18 and the establishment of the RDJTF, it remained largely an objective. Brzezinski and his staff could do little to advance it beyond the conceptual stage because the president had no interest in it and did not view it as a priority. Brzezinski learned what his predecessors discovered: "Counselors advise but presidents decide."[69]

Nevertheless, while Odom recounts his and Brzezinski's frustration with the lack of Defense Department planning in support of the RDF concept, he attributes this principally to bureaucratic resistance. He discounts several points critical to effective policy implementation and to its corollary, presidents decide but bureaucrats complete. First, there is no evidence that the NSC staff pushed or offered incentives, financial or otherwise, to the Defense Department to pursue such a course of action. Second, the NSC staff did not seek an interim change in the administration's national strategy to emphasize the concept or refine its elements to compel concrete planning. As Robert Komer pointed out, the direction in PRM-10 "was far too general and had failed to set in motion specific planning guidance."[70] Third, the RDF concept was not one of Carter's foreign or defense policy priorities until the situation demanded it, and it was not one of Brzezinski's ten priorities, which he delineated for Carter in early 1977. It was not even an issue for consideration until it surfaced in the PRM-10 studies and language was wedged into the ensuing presidential directive. The only coherent element of the Carter foreign policy with respect to conventional forces was NATO. Strengthening the alliance's capabilities was a priority—politically and financially. Fourth, Brzezinski and Vance's deeply divided approach to U.S.-Soviet relations marred the Carter administration's foreign policy direction in its first two years, compounded by Carter's ambivalent style of governance. This tension created inconsistent foreign policy, which in turn produced a disjointed defense strategy. Brown essentially decided to make do with gradually increasing defense budgets for NATO, and lived with indecisive political direction on all other matters.[71] In short, the NSC staff won a bureaucratic victory when the RDF concept was included in the PD-18 language, but in typical NSC staff fashion, they expended little effort to ensure its execution.

Whereas the creation of the RDJTF demonstrated a clear change in administration policy and instigated a dramatic increase in defense funding, it did not lead to the diminishment of a "NATO first" approach, or a change in strategic priorities "at the expense of America's capabilities to defend its Northwest Asian or European allies."[72] PD-62, *Modifications in U.S. National Security*, which Carter approved in January 1981, clearly states, "NATO will retain first call on force deployments in peacetime for wartime operations."[73] Additionally, the administration did not abandon the 1½-war strategy. Instead, it added another half war. This change was essentially a modification of strategic intent, because there was no increase in the U.S. conventional force structure to build a capable Persian Gulf force. As contemporary detractors stressed, the United States in all likelihood did not have sufficient forces flexible enough to protect interests outside of NATO.[74] Jeffrey Record, one of the skeptics, observed, "The Carter Doctrine for the first time formally committed U.S. military power to the defense of Southwest Asia. . . . In doing so, the Carter Doctrine imposed new and exceedingly difficult obligations on U.S. conventional forces already severely overtaxed by traditional commitments in Europe and the Far East."[75] More realistically then, the RDF was a repudiation of the Nixon Doctrine. The United States was now underlining its willingness to intervene in other parts of the world outside of Western Europe, the Korean Peninsula, and when required, the Western Hemisphere.

Lastly, the Persian Gulf Security Framework was more an outline than a coherent strategic vision or an overarching strategic concept, despite Odom christening it a strategy. He honestly characterizes it in an article on the subject as "a list of things to be done."[76] An inventory of activities is not a strategy and this lack of a comprehensive strategy was one of the weaknesses of the administration, especially since the skeletal PD-18 remained unrevised until the end of the administration. As Brzezinski opined, he and Carter did not share a grand strategy and the president did not think in broad conceptual terms. Carter acted issue by issue.[77] It was not until January 1981, five days before Ronald Reagan's inauguration, that Carter promulgated the framework as a coherent presidential directive, the purpose of which was to capture the guidance as a legacy document and to goad the incoming administration into continuing its thrusts.

The lack of a revised and comprehensive strategy meant that the Defense Department had the ultimate chore of fashioning one to implement the Carter Doctrine. This is not surprising as military power was the principal instrument, with diplomacy, intelligence, and economic instruments in supporting roles. The controversy ultimately, as James Noyes argues, centered on "the means rather than the ends,"[78] and the means before the fiscal year 1981 president's budget request were scarce. The force, jury-rigged and underfunded, was a long shot, even as a deterrent, given its force composition, the distances it had to deploy, and the logistical challenges it confronted. Thus, if U.S. interests in the region were truly vital, as Carter, Brzezinski, Brown, and Schlesinger depicted them, these policy makers were remiss in not acting before 1980. The Carter administration had willingly allowed a "gap between U.S. military aspirations and resources"[79] to grow until the worsening international situation demanded the United States enhance its military power.

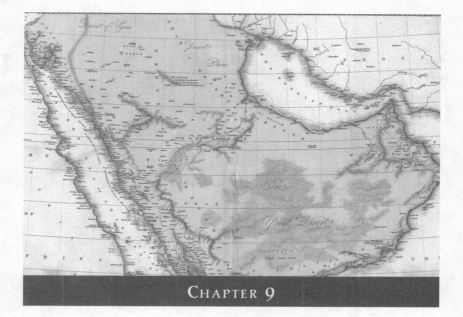

CHAPTER 9

The Ties That Bind

The Events of 1979 and the Escalation of U.S.-Saudi Security Relations during the Carter and Reagan Administrations

Jason H. Campbell

The defense of Saudi Arabia is vital to the defense of the United States of America.

—PRESIDENT FRANKLIN D. ROOSEVELT, 1943

T he year 1979 was pivotal with regard to American policy in the Middle East. It began with the fall of Iran's shah and longtime U.S. ally, Reza Pahlevi, in January and ended with the Soviet invasion of Afghanistan in December. In the span of one calendar year one of the "twin pillars" in the Middle East had fallen and the long-dreaded Soviet expansionism was seemingly taking place. The Carter and, subsequently, Reagan administrations concluded that guaranteeing stability in the region would require both an escalation of assistance to remaining allies as well as more active American participation in security matters. As a result, in American national security circles Saudi Arabia quickly became elevated from valued ally to vital partner.

The abrupt departure of the shah of Iran created a gaping strategic void in the Middle East. Almost overnight, a staunch regional ally of the United States was replaced by an Islamic fundamentalist government that detested the West and blamed the United States in particular for supporting an autocratic regime that for years ignored the plight of the Iranian people. Thus, Saudi Arabia, long the lesser of the two primary U.S. regional allies, was thrust to the fore as the somewhat unlikely epicenter of geostrategic consideration. Joe Stork and Martha Wegner argue, "Sparsely populated Saudi Arabia was never a serious candidate to play a role comparable to Iran. The real 'second pillar' of U.S. strategy in the Middle East was Israel, but Israel's political liabilities severely limited its usefulness in the Gulf."[1] This was especially true when it came to safeguarding the free flow of the region's vast supply of oil. Over the following decade relations between the United States and Saudi Arabia would progress substantially and have a profound effect on the future of American security commitments to the region.

In responding to a direct threat, the Carter administration first focused its energy on making it known that America would not sit idly by if aggression were to proliferate. In early 1979 Secretary of State Cyrus Vance asserted that America considered "the territorial integrity and security of Saudi Arabia a matter of fundamental interest."[2] This statement would prove to be a harbinger of forthcoming policy goals that would endure through a change of administration and define U.S.-Saudi relations for a generation. This process would be characterized by two broad guidelines: availing the Saudis of some of the most advanced weapons technology available and devising ways to increase U.S. presence in the Gulf or, at the very least, position American forces and matériel in closer proximity should they be needed to aid in the Gulf's defense. First, however, it is constructive to understand how U.S. domestic politics helped to set the stage for greater ties shortly before the shah's overthrow.

Prelude to an Escalation: The Carter Administration Changes Tack

Though the dramatic international developments of 1979 provided the impetus for the escalation of U.S.-Saudi security relations, it was domestic political concerns prior to these events that helped precipitate closer ties. In the 1976 general election, Jimmy Carter secured the presidency thanks in no small part to a proposed foreign policy based not on aggressive deterrence of the perceived Soviet threat, but on the defense of human rights and the de-escalation of nuclear proliferation and arms sales. In practice, however, this proved quixotic, and public opinion began to wane, as evidenced by the approval rating of President Carter's handling of foreign policy issues rapidly dwindling from 48 percent in July 1977 to 22 percent in July 1978, according to polling done by Harris surveys.[3] Facing what was sure to be a difficult reelection campaign, Carter began by 1978 to grow more hawkish in confronting the Soviets. Thus, he became less concerned about the United States acting as arms merchant and more focused on supporting friendly nations.[4] Saudi Arabia would soon become a beneficiary of this policy shift.

In early 1978, referring to recommendations made in a 1974 survey identifying the need for the Saudis to replace their aging fleet of British Lightning fighter jets, the Carter administration proposed a $2.5 billion sale of sixty U.S. F-15 aircraft to the Kingdom.[5] The deal was originally part of a larger proposal that included similar hardware being sold to Israel and Egypt but, due to congressional concerns, was detached and assessed separately. After much debate on Capitol Hill and loud protests from Israel, an accommodation was reached whereby the Saudis would receive the F-15s, though with certain conditions attached. The configuration of the Saudi F-15s would not include "fast pack" conformal fuel tanks that extended the range of the fighter, wing racks capable of holding air-to-ground missiles, or the most advanced radar and payload capacities. Additionally, the Saudis would not be permitted to base the F-15s at Taif, the Kingdom's closest installation to Israel.[6] Regardless of the apparent slight, the deal was significant in that it marked the first time the Saudis had received American consent to purchase such advanced weaponry. Once the fate of the shah became more apparent by the end of 1978, however, the Carter administration realized that arms sales would not suffice in addressing the new concerns brought about by the abrupt toppling of America's main "pillar" in the Middle East. More immediate action would be necessary to keep the instability in Iran from permeating to its strategically critical neighbors. Though enhanced arms sales would be reconsidered at a later date, the attention of the administration first turned to utilizing U.S. forces as a barrier.

The Stakes Are Raised: The Rapid Deployment Force and New Arms Negotiations

In February 1979, immediately after the fall of the shah, the Carter administration moved quickly to capitalize on a perceived opportunity to deploy U.S. forces to Saudi Arabia, as a means of containing the unrest in Iran and guaranteeing the free flow of Persian Gulf oil. Defense Secretary Harold Brown traveled to Riyadh and promised "training and equipment better than any in the world" in hopes of obtaining permission for the United States to finance and construct a base on Saudi soil, but he was flatly denied.[7] Seeking to avoid the fate of the shah, the Saudis were adamant to avoid the perception that they had to rely on an outside (particularly Western) power to ensure their security. Because of this, a delicate balance had to be reached whereby the United States could provide necessary support without it seeming that Riyadh was subservient to Washington. As National Security Adviser Zbigniew Brzezinski penned in his memoirs, "Something much looser than a formal alliance was needed to convey our recognition of the political sensitivities of the countries and yet at the same time provide a sufficiently explicit assurance of American involvement."[8] This statement would encapsulate U.S.-Saudi discourse in the intervening years and provide the basis for future negotiations. For the time being, however, the administration remained undeterred by the Saudis' refusal and began contingency planning for increased Gulf security in lieu of basing rights.

As early as 1977, Brzezinski, seen by many as Carter's most hawkish adviser, reconstituted an idea that had been present since the Vietnam War: the formation of a U.S. military force capable of being rapidly dispatched to the Persian Gulf or elsewhere in the Third World.[9] The problem was that such an undertaking would have been perceived as counter to the ideals of de-escalation and détente championed by the bulk of the administration, and the plan was once again shelved. However, once the shah was toppled, the justification for the rapid deployment force (RDF) became more pronounced. In October, Carter announced its formation, although whom it would comprise and what its mission would be was left undetermined. A significant challenge in the early going was motivating the military services to make the RDF a high priority and devote scarce resources to the effort. This changed with the Soviet invasion of Afghanistan in December 1979, as the administration could now repackage the threat in a more familiar light. The RDF was now needed not only to provide stability in localized Third World conflicts, but also to halt the spread of Communism. In a short time President Carter would seize on this anti-Soviet fervor and, before an international audience, all but renounce the foreign policy principles that had heretofore defined his tenure in office.

During the annual State of the Union address on 23 January 1980, Carter issued a stern warning to the Soviets and any other foreign party wishing to destabilize the Middle East, thus jeopardizing American access to oil. "The Soviet Union is attempting to consolidate a strategic position that poses a grave threat to the free movement of Middle East oil," he stated. He went on to proclaim, "Any attempt by an outside force to gain control of the Persian Gulf region will be regarded as an assault on the vital interests of the United States and will be repelled by any means necessary, including military force."[10] This subsequently became known as the Carter Doctrine. With a reelection campaign looming, it was no secret that Carter's political advisers wanted him to appear tough on East-West issues.[11] With the Soviet invasion of Afghanistan occurring only three weeks earlier, this provided the ideal setting for Carter to emphasize the Soviet threat and justify such a dramatic departure from the administration's previous platform of increased negotiation and détente. Once again, domestic political concerns would contribute to a shift in President Carter's policies vis-à-vis U.S. strategy in the Middle East.

The Carter Doctrine once more placed the Soviet Union in the crosshairs of U.S. defense policy. Such renewed focus on the known enemy helped to motivate Pentagon planners and gave the RDF the shot in the arm it needed. As Stork and Wenger point out, "When Carter spoke these words, the Rapid Deployment Force was more a state of mind than reality. It had no equipment, and its troops would have to be requisitioned from U.S. forces assigned to other commands."[12] Only days after the speech, Secretary Brown released the Department of Defense's *Annual Report* for fiscal year 1981. The $159 billion request called for "special attention and resources on the improvement of capabilities to get personnel and equipment quickly to potential trouble areas like the Middle East, Persian Gulf, and Arabian Sea areas."[13] With increased budgetary support, Lt. Gen. P. X. Kelley (USMC) was named commander of the RDF, and MacDill Air Base outside of Tampa, Florida, was selected as the headquarters. In the very initial planning stages, the RDF was seen as a force numbering approximately 100,000 troops. However, by late 1980, with the fall of the shah and the Soviet invasion of Afghanistan still very much on the minds of military planners, the proposed composition ballooned to a 200,000-man force backed by 100,000 reservists, and it continued to expand.[14] As Lieutenant General Kelley stated during a June press conference, "There's not an upward number, upper limit" on the RDF. "We're talking several hundred thousand."[15]

Though on paper the RDF seemed to be coalescing into a formidable fighting force, for a few reasons it was in reality far from it. First, nearly all the forces earmarked for the RDF were already assigned to more pressing missions with NATO in Europe or the Far East. Second, the military's strategic lift capabilities were nowhere near sufficient enough to transport the bulk of the RDF forces into the trouble spots they were tasked with defending. Finally, with such lift capacity a distant hope, the United States required access to bases with greater proximity to the region in order to obtain legitimacy. In congressional testimony on the RDF in April 1980, Undersecretary of Defense Robert Komer stated, "The viability of this military policy depends critically on our access to facilities in the area."[16] Over the coming years U.S. policy makers would continue to find ways to achieve such regional access for the burgeoning rapid deployment forces. While some inroads had been made with Kenya, Somalia, and Oman, these alone would not suffice, as they granted access to facilities that were either of limited capability or geographically distant from the strategic epicenter of the Persian Gulf. It was clear that Saudi Arabia provided U.S. forces the best combination of proximity and infrastructure necessary to address regional security threats. Obtaining access to the Kingdom would entail years of continued negotiations and tradeoffs. Yet another dramatic turn of events in the latter part of 1980 would further hasten closer ties.

On 22 September 1980, Iraq invaded Iran, beginning what would become a bloody eight-year war of attrition. With open conflict commencing on their borders, the Saudis quickly turned to the United States. Merely four days after Iraq's initial invasion the CIA station chief in Riyadh dispatched an urgent message to Washington stating that the Kingdom wanted U.S. military assistance.[17] High-level Carter administration officials met to discuss options on how they would respond, no doubt with the notion that this was their chance to press for a greater presence of the rapid deployment forces on the Arabian Peninsula. Having earlier been rebuffed by the Saudis in securing basing rights within the Kingdom, Brown and Brzezinski were more measured in their expectations. Nevertheless, both believed that the situation offered the United States the opportunity to transport forty F-14 fighter jets from the aircraft carrier USS *Eisenhower*, already in the Arabian Sea, to Saudi airbases as a first step in escalating American military presence in the region.[18] Secretary of State Edmund Muskie, however, was more cautious. In his view such a move would call into question on an international scale the stated neutrality of the United States in the war and, perhaps more importantly, jeopardize a pledge of mutual nonintervention Muskie had agreed to only the day before with his Soviet counterpart, Andrei Gromyko.[19]

By the end of the opening month of hostilities Brown, Brzezinski, and Muskie came to the conclusion that the United States would send four Air Force airborne warning and control system (AWACS) aircraft to Saudi Arabia, pending a formal request from the Kingdom, and keep the F-14s on board the *Eisenhower*. By early October, the AWACS were providing constant surveillance on Iraqi and Iranian aerial movements with their state-of-the-art radar capabilities. Most importantly from the American perspective, official U.S. military personnel on the ground in Saudi Arabia doubled from four hundred to eight hundred in only a few weeks. In addition, U.S. authorities retained full discretion in analyzing any intelligence gathered, and passed on to the Saudis only that which was deemed necessary for their defense.[20] M. S. El Azhary argues that this ultimately provided "an ideal means by which the United States could demonstrate its concern for the security of Saudi Arabia without provoking the Soviet Union by introducing new 'offensive' military systems."[21] Ideal as it may have been, such an arrangement would come at a price. While Riyadh was appreciative of Washington's robust commitment, it was eager to boost its own military capabilities. Like the Carter administration in early 1979, the Saudis now saw a chance to press their ally for greater concessions.

Saudi officials were quick to try to leverage the increased regional instability into a new arms package that included the F-15 enhancements they had been denied in 1978 as well as AWACS planes of their own. Their desire for such a package was first voiced to Brzezinski during his visit to Riyadh in February 1980 and reiterated to Brown during meetings in Geneva the following June.[22] On each occasion it was communicated to the Saudis that such a deal, particularly with the inclusion of the AWACS planes, was politically sensitive and would require congressional deliberation. The only consolation the Saudis took away was a U.S. pledge to conduct an air feasibility study to better assess the requirements of the Kingdom. However, the events of late September and the subsequent U.S. presence in Saudi Arabia changed matters for both sides. From the American perspective, the Iran-Iraq War constituted the most pressing menace to the flow of Persian Gulf oil yet. Revisiting a potential arms deal with the Saudis could both strengthen a vital ally and warm them to a more robust, lasting American presence. For the Saudis, observing the capabilities of the AWACS firsthand reinforced their desire to obtain them. From their perspective, the imminent threat of attack raised the stakes to the point that such a deal constituted a test of the U.S.-Saudi relationship. It was in this context that the Carter administration began in earnest to consider such a substantial arms sale that was sure to be controversial both at home and with other regional allies, particularly Israel.

Evidence shows that by the fall of 1980, closed-door discussions had commenced between senior U.S. and Saudi officials on how best to address heightened security concerns. A settlement was soon reached between Brown and Prince Sultan bin Abdul Aziz, the Saudi defense minister, by which Saudi Arabia would provide oversized "warehousing and infrastructure facilities" for "prepositioning" U.S. equipment for the RDF. In return, the United States would assist Saudi Arabia in acquiring the most modern command, control, and communications (C3) systems as well as the previously proposed AWACS and F-15 enhancements, should the findings of the pending air feasibility study support it.[23] Such an arrangement would give the United States the adequately positioned bases deemed vital to the RDF, as well as allow U.S. forces to compensate for a lack of strategic lift capability by prepositioning supplies in the Kingdom in case American intervention became necessary. The one caveat was that all of this had to be done clandestinely so as to avoid political sensitivities to the presence of foreign forces on Saudi soil. As Undersecretary of Defense Komer would later state, "No country in the region is prepared to accept U.S. bases in peacetime. They are willing to let us . . . design the systems . . . even operate them, but not under the American flag. We have got to fly their flag."[24] This was an acceptable accommodation since it would guarantee the presence of thousands of specially trained American military and civilian personnel to be stationed throughout the Kingdom in order to provide operational and maintenance assistance. Gen. F. Michael Rogers (USAF), then head of Air Force Logistics Command, wrote that ties developed by military sales "provide a subtle leverage when one considers the long-term logistical support required for modern weapons."[25]

Despite all of the backroom dealing and a sense that Congress might be supportive considering recent regional events, Carter would never have the opportunity to officially announce the new arms deal. Particularly fearing renewed protests from pro-Israeli groups similar to those that accompanied the 1978 F-15 sale, the administration agreed with the Saudis that they would wait until after the 1980 election to formally proceed.[26] Unfortunately for Carter, the domestic repercussions of an economy in shambles and an ineffectual foreign policy, typified by an unsuccessful attempt to free U.S. hostages in Iran, were too much to overcome, and Ronald Reagan won the presidency handily. Nevertheless, recognizing the strategic importance of the Saudi agreement, the administration kept its word and pressed on with the deal. This was affirmed in a joint letter from Muskie and Brown to Senator Carl Levin dated 1 April 1981. In it they state that their assessments following the election led them to become "favorably disposed" to a sale of both the F-15 enhancements and AWACS to the Saudis.[27] In addition, this judgment was conveyed to Reagan aides in the transition period. During a 20 November meeting at the White House, Carter took the opportunity to inform President-elect Reagan that this was an issue he would have to deal with early in his administration.[28] As will be seen, the Reagan years would usher in a new era of U.S.-Saudi relations, both building on what Carter had started and developing new commitments that would draw the countries closer than ever.

The Reagan Administration Takes Over

The new Reagan administration was virulently anti-Communist and ranked Soviet expansionism as the primary threat to the Persian Gulf region. In his first eighteen months in office Reagan stressed the need for "strategic consensus" among Middle Eastern nations opposed to the increase of Soviet influence, beginning with the regimes of the Persian Gulf. The Saudis shared these ideological convictions, as evidenced by the key financial role they played in stemming Communist influence in Egypt, Zaire, the Yemen Arab Republic, and Somalia during the 1970s.[29] In remarks to newspaper editors in fall 1981, Reagan acknowledged the mutual sentiment, asserting that the Saudi royal family was "as concerned about the threat to the Middle East by the Soviet Union as, I think, we are. They have seen those puppet governments installed around them with the proxy troops and so forth. . . . I think they want to be a part of the West. They associate more with our views and philosophy."[30]

This mutual perception of the Soviet threat to the region provided Riyadh and Washington with an ideological base from which to grow their relationship. As Terry Deibel argues, "[T]he Carter administration reacted to events, moving more out of necessity than conviction. But for the Reagan administration, strengthening and expanding American alliances has been a primary element in restoring American power."[31] Key members of Reagan's cabinet wasted little time echoing the president, pronouncing their staunch support of increased security ties to the region in general and Saudi Arabia in particular. Newly confirmed Secretary of Defense Caspar Weinberger was previously a senior executive with Bechtel, a construction conglomerate with major interests in Saudi Arabia. Only weeks after Reagan took office he stated, "[W]e want to do everything we can to assist [the Saudis] in providing the additional security that they need."[32] In a March interview with *Time* magazine, Secretary of State Alexander Haig, when questioned about the Carter Doctrine, stated, "Western industrialized societies are largely dependent on the oil resources of the Middle East region and a threat to the access of that oil would constitute a great threat to the vital national interest. That must be dealt with; and that does not exclude the use of force."[33] Only a few short months into his presidency, Reagan would not only reaffirm his predecessor's commitment to Gulf security but also add a new caveat designed to further solidify the Saudis' trust in America.

On 1 October 1981, Reagan made a major pronouncement when he declared, "We will not permit Saudi Arabia to be an Iran."[34] Later that same month, when the president was to elaborate on that statement, he made it unambiguously clear that the United States had a vested interest in both the external and internal stability of the Gulf states by criticizing his predecessor: "I don't believe that the Shah's Government would have fallen if the United States had made it plain that we would stand by the Government and support them in whatever had to be done to curb the revolution and let it be seen that we still felt we were allied with them."[35] Such sentiment reflected a new commitment by the Reagan administration to forge closer ties with countries dedicated to the "rollback" of Communism. This expanded the scope of the Carter Doctrine by placing both the internal and external security of such states within the purview of vital U.S. interests and would become known as the Reagan Doctrine. Not satisfied with providing the Saudis only verbal backing, however, Reagan made the addition of more tangible support one of his initial foreign policy priorities.

The AWACS Debate

The new administration was quick to back up its strong rhetoric regarding security assistance to Saudi Arabia with substantive action. Equipped with a ready-made, albeit tacit, agreement with the Saudis and the due diligence of his predecessor, Reagan made what would become known as the AWACS/F-15 enhancement package one of the first priorities in his foreign policy agenda. As early as 3 February 1981, Defense Secretary Weinberger was proclaiming publicly that an arms deal was in the works, though there was no mention of AWACS. Citing a "serious deterioration" in Western security interests, on 6 March the administration announced its plans to sell the Saudis a new arms package, including additional equipment that would enhance the capabilities of their F-15 fleet as well as an undisclosed aerial reconnaissance component.[36] On 21 April the White House revealed that five AWACS aircraft would be included as part of an $8.5 billion package that would also comprise conformal fuel tanks for F-15s, AIM-9L Sidewinder missiles, KC-3 aerial tankers, and an upgrading of the Saudi ground radar network.[37] The Reagan administration was convinced that such a significant commitment would both ensure the trust of a critical ally and provide the United States with a stronger foothold in a strategically crucial region. There was also a considerable economic aspect to the inclusion of AWACS that proved influential in the final decision, brought to light by Gen. David C. Jones (USAF), chairman of the Joint Chiefs of Staff. Of the $128 million the Saudis agreed to pay for each plane, an estimated $60 million would go to the U.S. Treasury as a partial repayment for previous government research and development expenditures.[38] However, the optimistic sentiment previously felt by President Carter regarding the prospects of such a deal would prove misguided, as initial reaction from Congress and Israel was intensely critical. Sensing a potential defeat, the administration agreed to delay an official vote to allow for extensive congressional consultations with the State and Defense Departments as well as a more focused lobbying effort.

Congress had serious doubts about the proposed deal for two central reasons. First, the unexpected fall of the shah was still fresh in the minds of many and the stability of the Kingdom was in some doubt. This was particularly the case in the aftermath of the 1979 terrorist seizure of the Grand Mosque in Mecca and minority Shia unrest in the oil-rich Eastern Province during this same period. The second, more pressing, major concern for Congress was the likelihood that some of America's most advanced military technologies could fall into the hands of the Soviets. The administration attempted to forestall such fears by offering the Saudis only a watered-down version of the AWACS that would be stripped of some of the most sensitive enciphering and jamming capabilities. Nevertheless, congressional opponents of the sale worked to grow a coalition to block the sale. On 24 June 1981, fifty-four senators, led by Robert Packwood (R-OR), sent a letter to the president expressing their "strong belief" that the proposed arms package was "not in the best interest of the United States" and requested that it not be submitted to Congress.[39] Their efforts were buoyed by strong opposition from the Israelis that incorporated not only their influential lobby in the United States but also the efforts of the Israeli prime minister, Menachem Begin. It became apparent that the AWACS/F-15 enhancement package would be a true test of the nascent Reagan administration, and a significant amount of political capital would need to be expended to gain approval.

The administration moved quickly to address mounting concerns. To assuage Congress, the State Department addressed questions of the stability of the Saudi state in its talking points, classifying Saudi Arabia as "one of the most stable Arab states."[40] A staff report prepared for the Senate Committee on Foreign

Relations in September 1981 helped to back this up. While it mentioned some broader concerns with regard to future trends within the Kingdom, the report also conveyed that Saudi Arabia was at the present time stable and that Saudi leadership lacked significant political opposition.[41] In responding to fears of Soviet transgressions, proponents of the sale pointed to two key facts. The first was that Saudi Arabia had no diplomatic relations with any Soviet bloc countries. With AWACS and AIM-9L missiles already either based abroad or in the hands of a number of U.S. allies it was more likely that any technological compromise would stem from countries where the Soviet intelligence apparatus was more entrenched. Furthermore, considering that the delivery date of the main elements of the package would not occur until at least the latter part of 1985, even if a "worst-case scenario" were to come to fruition the blowback would be limited. Overall, the administration argued, the potential strategic gains of the sale made such risks acceptable.

Appeasing Israel proved yet another difficult proposition. Both the Defense and State Departments rallied to assure Israeli authorities that the most sensitive aspect of the proposed sale, the AWACS, would not pose a serious threat to their security. Undersecretary of State James Buckley argued that the relatively slow, modified Boeing 707 aircraft could be easily shot down by Israeli defenses should they stray into its airspace. The Air Force attempted to demonstrate this by giving a team of Israeli military and technical experts a nine-hour flight across the United States to show the limitations of the AWACS.[42] All of this, however, was unconvincing. By September, Begin became personally involved in building support against the sale. During a trip to Washington he met with a number of pro-Israel lobbyists as well as several U.S. legislators to discuss strategy in blocking the package. The situation became so contentious that Reagan reportedly warned Begin implicitly not to interfere in U.S. domestic policy, a charge Begin denied.[43] Evidence suggests that such a direct challenge from a foreign entity reinvigorated Reagan and prompted his tireless personal lobbying effort in the weeks before the vote.

With the congressional vote imminent and resistance to the proposed sale persisting, the Reagan administration soon adopted an all-hands-on-deck effort to stanch the negative momentum. The administration pressed Congress to consider in greater detail the strategic importance of the deal. A background paper released by the State Department on 24 August illuminated the ways in which U.S. military capacity in the region would be bolstered. The AWACS deal, the report stated, "will provide the basis for a comprehensive military command, control, communications, and logistics infrastructure, which could be compatible with U.S. tactical forces' capabilities and requirements and could become the nucleus of support for U.S. forces if we are asked by regional states to respond to a crisis."[44] National Security Adviser Richard Allen argued that the AWACS sale "assures the presence of the United States in Saudi Arabia's security future."[45] In a letter to the Senate shortly before the vote, Reagan took the opportunity to echo each of these points. The "practical consequence" of the sale, he argued, was to "extend U.S. involvement in Saudi AWACS operations and activities well into the 1990s."[46] He went on to point out that the Saudis had agreed to share all information acquired through the AWACS with their American counterparts, giving U.S. forces in the region an additional outlet of potentially critical intelligence should tensions escalate.

By September, it was widely recognized that the stakes of the sale had become extremely high. The repercussions of a negative outcome would be potentially severe, as it would serve as a poor reflection on the new administration and create doubt with a critical (and anxious) regional ally. Leaving nothing to chance, Reagan became more personally involved with garnering congressional support in the weeks leading up to the crucial vote. To lobby Congress to his side, Reagan enlisted the help of an array of former presidents, secretaries of defense and state, national security advisers, and chairmen of the Joint Chiefs of Staff. This impressive list included Richard Nixon, Gerald Ford, Henry Kissinger, Donald Rumsfeld, McGeorge Bundy, and Zbigniew Brzezinski.[47] In addition, he worked tirelessly behind the scenes. Between 11 September and the 28 October vote, seventy-five out of one hundred senators had been called to the White House to hear the pitch in person, with forty-four receiving one-on-one sessions with the president.[48] When the final tally was announced the AWACS/F-15 enhancement package passed in the Senate by the slimmest of margins, 52–48.

The approval of the AWACS/F-15 enhancement package was a pivotal development in U.S.-Saudi security relations. As will be seen, the sale paved the way for greater bilateral cooperation on a host of issues of mutual concern and increased American military access in the strategically vital Persian Gulf region. Though his lobbying efforts cost Reagan a good deal of political capital, his willingness to face adversity to get the deal through instilled in the Saudis more confidence than ever that the United States could be a trusted ally. With such a crucial hurdle cleared, American contingency planning for the security of the Gulf would intensify, and the Saudis would continue to revamp their military installations to accommodate U.S. forces should they be needed to defend the Kingdom.

After AWACS

Buoyed by an increased confidence that the Saudis would be more accommodating in granting access to the Kingdom's strategically located facilities, Reagan soon escalated America's military commitment to the region. On 1 January 1983, President Reagan announced that the RDF would be converted to U.S. Central Command (CENTCOM), a unified command reporting directly to the secretary of defense.[49] This was seen as the next step by the United States to increase its rapid-response capability to stymie Soviet transgressions in the region. The CENTCOM mission, as outlined in a "secret" 1982 Defense Department guidance, stated: "Our principle objectives are to assure continued access to Persian Gulf oil, and to prevent the Soviets from acquiring political-military control of the oil directly or through proxies."[50] Initially, CENTCOM faced many of the same criticisms that had been leveled at the RDF, particularly with regard to the lack of dedicated forces and the inadequacies of strategic lift capabilities. However, the Reagan administration did make immediate efforts to address such concerns. For instance, the number of ships stationed off Diego Garcia containing supplies for an intervention force was increased from seven to seventeen.[51] Central Command was also given authority to requisition an increased number of troops, between 300,000 and 350,000, although most were still based in other theaters. Finally, budget allocations for "power projection" increased significantly throughout the 1980s.[52] Had the United States not been able to count on the Saudis to revamp and modernize their military facilities and offer at least tacit prepositioning rights, it is unlikely that CENTCOM would have materialized. Access to land basing was vital to any increased commitment. Former undersecretary of defense Robert Komer, in emphasizing the importance of such Saudi cooperation, stated shortly after the passage of the AWACS package: "I see absolutely no other viable way to deter against aggression or defend Persian Gulf oil. And there is no other competent military judgment that I know of that there is another way."[53] Some obvious flaws notwithstanding, the formation of CENTCOM was important in reaffirming America's commitment to Gulf security, and would play a significant role in coalescing other pro-American Arab states to deal with mutual security threats in a more coordinated manner.

In May 1981, the nations of Saudi Arabia, Bahrain, Kuwait, Oman, Qatar, and the United Arab Emirates formed the Gulf Cooperation Council (GCC) in response to the regional instability created by the Iranian Revolution and the subsequent Iran-Iraq War. Though the GCC was notoriously stricken by infighting and political posturing, it provided an important vehicle for the United States to improve its standing in the region, particularly with the Iran-Iraq War becoming a prolonged affair and the added credibility engendered by the formation of CENTCOM. Most appealing from the U.S. standpoint, Saudi Arabia was the most influential member of the GCC and provided added legitimacy to U.S. interests among some of the more cynical elements. It also allowed for the United States to work more constructively with the Saudis in a multilateral manner that otherwise would have been difficult given political sensitivities. Through the GCC the United States was able to stage formal military exercises that provided an opportunity to train with member states. This also served as a barometer of how the Gulf states, and particularly the Saudis, progressed, which was of particular interest given the substantial amount of state-of-the-art technology obtained by the Saudis and other GCC nations during the decade. Such an influx of military hardware made the GCC's force strength, at least on paper, formidable enough to counter regional aggression brought on by any country other than Israel. For instance, by 1984 Saudi Arabia was in possession of 185 modern fighter jets (with an additional 115 such jets owned collectively by the other GCC states) that were far more superior in number and capabilities to the sixty to seventy aged F-4 Phantoms and handful of F-14s Iran boasted. Taking this into consideration one U.S. official, in explaining the general American view of what role the GCC states should play in reacting to Iranian aggression, stated: "The feeling here is that they should get bloodied first."[54] Despite the apparent force advantage, though, military exercises conducted with the GCC exposed some serious questions. This was particularly apparent following the Peninsula Shield exercises held in late 1983. The mixed reviews were perhaps best summarized by one U.S. official who stated: "The maneuvers showed us how far the Gulf states have come, but also how badly they need us."[55] Without the formation of the GCC, the United States would most likely have been deprived of such a thorough examination of the Gulf states' capabilities. This would prove valuable as, by the mid-1980s, the specter of a Soviet invasion of the Gulf gave way to a much closer threat.

Departing from its earlier philosophy regarding threats to the Middle East, by 1984 the United States began to refocus on forming the political and military framework for creating "strategic consensus," this time directed not at the Soviet Union but Iran.[56] With Tehran gaining the upper hand in its war of attrition with Baghdad, both the Saudis and Americans feared that reprisals on the Kingdom were imminent. The infrastructure that was the lifeblood of the Saudi oil industry was fragile and vulnerable to damaging attacks. Even more menacing, Iran was clearly aware of this. In a radio interview in May 1984, Iranian president Hashemi Rafsanjani warned, "The lifestyle of the littoral states of the Persian Gulf . . . depends on ports, installations, and their oil pipelines. All of them could be destroyed by shelling, let alone air attacks."[57] In April 1984, Deputy Secretary of State Richard Murphy and Rear Adm. John Poindexter, head of the Crisis Pre-Planning Group on the National Security Council, traveled to Riyadh to reaffirm Washington's commitment to Saudi security and gently push for permission to store added ammunition, food, and weapons to be used by U.S. intervention forces should they be formally invited by the Saudis.[58] In May, Reagan used emergency appropriations to skirt congressional stipulations for a direct sale of four hundred advanced anti-aircraft Stinger missiles to the Saudis, boldly stating, "We don't put conditions on friends."[59] Perhaps the clearest sign that America was willing to accept significant risk to support the Saudis occurred in June when U.S. AWACS and KC-10 refueling tankers assisted the Royal Saudi Air Force in shooting down two Iranian F-4 Phantom jets over the Gulf.[60] Though the threat from Iran persisted through the decade, such a show of American cooperation undoubtedly affected Tehran's decision calculus. With many of their security fears at least somewhat pacified, the Saudis continued throughout the 1980s to finance and build new military facilities that were far in excess of their modest capabilities, making it clear that they were realistic about their need for a drastic increase in American military presence should the instability in the Gulf escalate and spread.[61] Ironically, the country that would eventually force the Kingdom's hand in formally requesting the presence of U.S. forces on Saudi soil was neither the Soviet Union nor Iran, but a nation for which little contingency planning had been undertaken.

Epilogue: U.S. Forces Get the Call and the Legacy of 1979

In August 1990, Saddam Hussein ordered the Iraqi army to invade Kuwait. Shortly thereafter, following entreaties from Saudi authorities, President George H. W. Bush began deploying U.S. forces to the Kingdom. After nearly a decade of substantial transformation, the Saudi military infrastructure was able to not only provide state-of-the-art facilities for the torrent of troops but also afford a ready-made interoperable network that allowed U.S. and coalition troops optimal command, control, communications, and logistics capabilities. Beginning shortly after Iraq's invasion of Iran in September 1980, Saudi Arabia spent nearly $50 billion on building a Gulf-wide air defense system to U.S. and NATO specifications. By 1988, the U.S. Army Corps of Engineers had designed and constructed a $14 billion network of military facilities across the Kingdom. Equally unfortunate for Iraq was that the end of the Cold War meant that redeploying hundreds of thousands of U.S. troops to the region was now strategically feasible. Once Operation Desert Storm commenced in January 1991, the Iraqi army was routed in a matter of days. While an eventual triumph for the U.S. and coalition forces was virtually guaranteed in most any scenario, victory was achieved much sooner than even the most optimistic of planners could have predicted. This was due in no small part to Saudi military investment throughout the 1980s, made possible by technology provided by the United States.

The tremendous success of Operation Desert Storm can be traced back to the incidents of 1979 and the subsequent events that contributed to Saudi Arabia becoming the preeminent U.S. ally in a strategically critical region. The fall of the shah thrust Saudi Arabia to the fore as the last remaining pro-Western bulwark in the Gulf and created the base from which U.S.-Saudi discourse would escalate over the next decade. While this was the central event in drawing the two sides closer, it alone was insufficient to motivate the American bureaucracy to fully carry out ambitious presidential objectives. The concurrent reinvigoration of the Soviet threat served as the catalyst in cultivating a sense of urgency. It was not until the Soviets invaded Afghanistan that Carter rallied the necessary support to make the RDF a priority within the Pentagon. Subsequently, the Reagan administration continuously alluded to the Soviet threat to the Gulf in defending the formation and expansion of CENTCOM throughout the 1980s, even after it became apparent that the Soviets had become bogged down in Afghanistan and the most imminent threat was spillover from the Iran-Iraq War. It can be argued that had the Soviets not invaded Afghanistan in 1979, subsequent U.S. military commitments to the Gulf could not have been as robust, thus making the need for Saudi basing rights less pronounced and impeding the willingness of Presidents Carter and Reagan to push for advanced weapons deals in the face of public opprobrium.

Such a vast escalation of military commitments to the Gulf did not go unchallenged, however. During this time many argued that American policy in the Middle East, particularly in the Persian Gulf, was overly fixated on resolving perceived threats militarily, eschewing diplomatic avenues and counterintuitively perpetuating the threat by inserting more troops and enabling regional states. The fall of the Soviet Union helped to substantiate such fears as hundreds of thousands of U.S. troops became available for permanent assignment within CENTCOM almost overnight. Despite this, sustainable stability in this strategically vital region has remained elusive. What is evident is that the legacy of the events of 1979 continues to pose difficult questions for American policy makers.

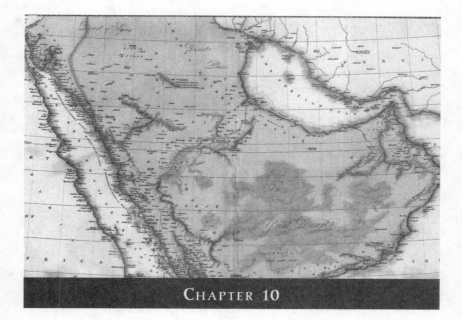

CHAPTER 10

India's "Monroe Doctrine" and the Gulf

James R. Holmes and
Toshi Yoshihara

An Article of Faith

Scholar C. Raja Mohan, arguably India's foremost foreign-policy pundit, proclaims that a kind of "Monroe Doctrine" constitutes the prime mover for his nation's pursuit of power and influence in the Indian Ocean basin. Writing in the journal *The American Interest*, Mohan observes that India has long asserted "an exclusive sphere of influence in South Asia," an "Indian version of the Monroe Doctrine for the Subcontinent, aimed at preventing other major powers from intervening in the region, became an integral element of India's policy."[1] Nor is this mere whimsy; declares Mohan, the Monroe Doctrine as interpreted by New Delhi "has not been entirely successful in the past, but it has been *an article of faith* [our emphasis] for many in the Indian strategic community."[2]

In their nation's novel bid for great sea power, then, Indians look to the nineteenth-century U.S. policy declaration that barred European imperial powers from territorial conquest or from rule by proxy in the New World. President James Monroe and Secretary of State John Quincy Adams, the framers of the doctrine, President Grover Cleveland, who saw Monroe's precepts as a writ for U.S. hegemony throughout the Western Hemisphere, and President Theodore Roosevelt, who gave the doctrine a forceful twist, may have indirectly molded the character of Indian sea power.

No less a figure than Jawaharlal Nehru connected America then with modern-day India. Post-independence India's founding prime minister Nehru delivered a speech before the Indian parliament in 1961 in which he justified the resort to arms to expel the Portuguese from their coastal enclave of Goa. The Portuguese had been ensconced along the southwestern coast of the subcontinent since 1510, the age of Alfonso de Albuquerque and Vasco da Gama. The prime minister's remarks are extraordinarily rich and thus worth quoting at length:

> [E]ven some time after the United States had established itself as a strong power, there was the fear of interference by European powers in the American continents, and this led to the famous declaration by President Monroe of the United States [that] any interference by a European country would be an interference with the American political system. I submit that . . . the Portuguese retention of Goa is a continuing interference with the political system established in India today. I shall go a step further and

say that any interference by any other power would also be an interference with the political system of India today. . . . It may be that we are weak and we cannot prevent that interference. But the fact is that *any attempt by a foreign power to interfere in any way with India is a thing which India cannot tolerate, and which, subject to her strength, she will oppose. That is the broad doctrine I lay down.*[3] [Our emphasis]

While a European presence on the Indian landmass—and thus adjoining Indian territory—precipitated his doctrine, Nehru took the opportunity to warn *all* external powers against *any* actions, anywhere in the region, that New Delhi might see as a danger. In effect, he argued that Indian security was indivisible from affairs anywhere in the region, and thus that any interference by any external power was something India must resist to its utmost power. Indeed, the prime minister carried his vision of an Indian Monroe Doctrine well beyond anything Monroe or Adams had contemplated when they warned the European powers against seeking new dominions in the Americas. Nehru's starkly worded injunction against outside meddling laid the groundwork for a policy of primacy in the Indian Ocean.

Despite the expansive terms in which he framed his "broad doctrine," Nehru nonetheless acknowledged realities of power and geography. India remained weak by most measures in 1961, a scant fourteen years after independence. But the prime minister contemplated enforcing his security doctrine with new vigor as Indian national power grew, supplying new means and new political options. He vouchsafed that New Delhi could put his precepts into effect beyond the subcontinent. Indeed, the Monroe precedent suggested those precepts might apply throughout the Indian Ocean basin. It was up to future prime ministers to decide how far beyond Indian frontiers a policy of noninterference could and should be applied, taking into account constraints of interest, power, and distance.

Like Monroe and Adams, Nehru asked no one's permission to articulate a hands-off doctrine, and he made no attempt to codify his views in a treaty or other international compact. His doctrine, then, had no legal standing. It was a unilateral policy statement to which New Delhi would give effect as national interests demanded and national means permitted. India did expel the Portuguese from Goa, as Nehru urged—affixing an exclamation point to his words. Whether Nehru's doctrine will gain the same grudging acceptance from fellow governments that the Monroe Doctrine accumulated by the late nineteenth century remains to be seen—especially as the interests of powerful outsiders grow in the Indian Ocean.

Each generation applies the principles bequeathed by its founders differently. In the post-Nehru years, accordingly, Indian statesmen interpreted and applied his security doctrine not by rote but according to their own appraisals of India's surroundings, its interests, and its power. Indira Gandhi and Rajiv Gandhi were especially inventive about adapting India's security doctrine to contemporary needs and interests.[4] Nehru's original pronouncement was ambitious in principle if modest in execution. His successors cast off the restraints imposed by limited political, economic, and military power, with varying degrees of success. Three shifts in Indian foreign policy were noteworthy:

- *From the Subcontinent Outward.* New Delhi projected Nehru's "broad doctrine" beyond the Indian landmass, intervening around the maritime and terrestrial periphery where Indian interests dictated and Indian power allowed. Not only direct challenges on the subcontinent but crises elsewhere in the Indian Ocean region merited action on New Delhi's part. While more dramatic than evicting the Portuguese from Goa, widening the scope for Indian diplomatic and military action was consistent with Nehru's concept that Indian security was inseparable from that of the Indian Ocean region.

- *From Defensive to Offensive.* The defensive action at Goa corrected a historical aberration, namely foreign occupation and the fracture of Indian territorial unity. Prime ministers Indira and Rajiv Gandhi implemented Nehru's hands-off policy not only forcefully but offensively, construing threats to "the political system established in India" more and more expansively as national power grew. As a more assertive diplomacy became viable, threats to Indian interests beyond the subcontinent's immediate neighborhood seemed to warrant offensive action.

- *From Reactive to Proactive.* Indian diplomacy took on increasingly preventive overtones. The idea of keeping threats from fully forming made its way into the Indian strategic calculus. Nehru was one of the architects of the global nonaligned movement of the Cold War years, while New Delhi saw itself as the guardian of a nonaligned bloc of South Asian states. In keeping with his outlook, succeeding prime ministers considered India the rightful protector of regional security from rival blocs—particularly the U.S.-led West. By policing insurgencies, natural disasters, and other crises, New Delhi could deny meddlesome external powers any excuse to aggrandize themselves in the Indian Ocean, posing an eventual threat to India and its neighbors.

Not only vigorous diplomacy but also limited military operations flowed from India's security doctrine. From 1983 to 1990, most notably, New Delhi exerted political and military pressure in an effort to put an end to the Sri Lankan civil war. It waged a bitter, inconclusive counterinsurgent campaign on the island, in large part because Indian leaders feared the United States would gain a new geostrategic foothold at Trincomalee, along India's oceanic flank. One commentator depicted New Delhi's politico-military efforts as "a repetition of the Monroe Doctrine, a forcible statement that any external forces prejudicial to India's interests cannot be allowed to swim in regional waters."[5] India's Monroe Doctrine reflex combined with nonalignment impelled the leadership to erect a barrier to a nearby U.S. naval presence.

India's security doctrine resurfaced in 1988, when Indian forces intervened in a coup in the Maldives, and again in a 1989–90 trade dispute with Nepal. Devin Hagerty sums up Indian doctrine thus: "India strongly opposes outside intervention in the domestic affairs of other South Asian nations, especially by outside powers whose goals are perceived to be inimical to Indian interests. Therefore, no South Asian government should ask for outside assistance from any country; rather, if a South Asian nation genuinely needs external assistance, it should seek it from India. A failure to do so will be considered anti-Indian."[6]

This flurry of activity subsided after the Cold War, as New Delhi embarked on economic liberalization and reform while enhancing its armed forces. Influential pundits—even those who doubt the existence of an Indian security doctrine—nonetheless continue to speak in terms of an Indian Monroe Doctrine.[7] In a similar vein, we postulate that the Monroe Doctrine has entered into the Indian foreign-policy lexicon. Because the doctrine was and remains an intensely maritime concept—the influential sea-power theorist Alfred Thayer Mahan was an outspoken "disciple of Monroeism"—we use it to discern possible futures for Indian maritime strategy.[8]

Two assumptions guide our inquiry. First, the Monroe Doctrine is not simply a slogan Indian political leaders use to justify regional hegemony. These leaders take the lessons of U.S. history seriously and are attempting to fit these lessons to India's distinctive geographic, political, and military circumstances. Second, a rough consensus on the meaning of Monroe's principles informs Indian foreign and military policy, notwithstanding the vagaries of domestic politics.[9] Indian opinion makers uniformly favor regional primacy for their nation, frowning on outside meddling in what they deem an Indian preserve.[10] Although they agree on the principles, however, putting principles into action is another question. Lively debates rage on with regard to the doctrine's geographic sweep, with some voices advocating confining it to waters immediately adjoining the subcontinent and others clamoring for extending it beyond the Indian Ocean proper. The South China Sea, the Mediterranean, and even the Atlantic occasionally put in appearances as arenas for Indian influence. Indians have clearly widened their strategic aperture to encompass the sea, says scholar Rahul Roy-Chaudhury, but their grand strategy "still falls far short of an 'Indian Ocean policy'" that would let New Delhi maximize "its growing interests in the Indian Ocean region."[11]

What would an Indian Navy inspired by James Monroe look like, and how would it conduct business? Each generation of Americans interpreted Monroe's "general principles" of American diplomacy depending on its own needs, aspirations, and capabilities. Similarly, Indians will filter the axioms enunciated by Nehru and Monroe through their own traditions, geopolitical circumstances, and national power.[12] Tracing the impact of ideas on statecraft—especially ideas imported from abroad—is no simple endeavor. But it is a worthwhile one.

Manifest Destiny Goes to Sea

It is safe to say that an Indian Monroe Doctrine will display a strong saltwater component, just as the United States' hands-off doctrine once did. And indeed, strategists in New Delhi phrase their analyses of India's maritime surroundings—and the proper responses to those surroundings—in bracingly geopolitical terms. Vessels enter and exit the Indian Ocean through narrow seas like the Strait of Malacca and the Bab el-Mandeb Strait. The 2004 *Indian Maritime Doctrine*, the original "apex" document for Indian sea power, declares that control of such maritime chokepoints "could be useful as a bargaining chip in the international power game, where the currency of military power remains a stark reality."[13] The 2009 *Indian Maritime Doctrine* statement conjures up the subcontinent's painful past, noting ruefully that India never lost its national independence except to a seaborne conqueror, the British Empire. Neglect of the sea exacts a high price: "The lessons of ignoring the ability to control the seas around India are thus embedded in the colonisation of India and three centuries of European, mostly British, rule. Post independence, India has attempted to regain her maritime moorings. With its rapidly increasing dependence on the seas for her economic and social well-being, it is also laying adequate emphasis on developing commensurate maritime-military power. The process may well be regarded as [a] 'Work in Progress.'"[14]

Such language pervades official statements issuing from the naval establishment. India's 2007 *Maritime Military Strategy*, New Delhi's most authoritative appraisal of the strategic surroundings and how the Indian Navy should cope with them, contends that India's geopolitical rise and quest for prosperity necessitate "a concomitant accretion of national power, of which the military power will be a critical dimension." Proclaimed Admiral Sureesh Mehta, then serving as chief of naval staff:

India's primary national interest . . . is to ensure a secure and stable environ-ment, which will enable continued economic development and social uplift-ment [sic] of our masses. This in turn will allow India to take its rightful place in the comity of nations and *attain its manifest destiny*. . . . [W]e do not harbour any extra-territorial ambitions, but aim to safeguard our vital national inter-ests. Therefore . . . our *primary maritime military interest* is to ensure national security [and] provide *insulation from external interference*, so that the vital tasks of fostering economic growth and undertaking developmental activities can take place in a secure environment. Geographic, historic, and economic imperatives, then, are driving India to the sea.[15] [Our emphasis.]

Admiral Mehta packs considerable substance into this passage. First, eco-nomic development requires secure surroundings. Second, India can only real-ize its "manifest destiny"—the choice of term cannot have been accidental—by erecting a military buffer against outside interference. And third, assuring India's freedom to use the seas "under all circumstances" requires maritime forces able to discharge missions ranging from traditional combat to humanitarian assis-tance and disaster relief to constabulary missions such as sea-lane security.[16]

The absolute terms in which official statements from New Delhi are framed, and certain ambiguities in these documents, cry out for analysis. What consti-tutes "outside interference" for Indian officials and scholars, and what kind of "insulation" against it do they mean to provide? To what extent does the analysis found in the *Indian Maritime Doctrine* and *Maritime Military Strategy* encompass the Persian Gulf region—a region that appears in Indian commentary mainly as an afterthought? To get some purchase on these questions, we survey past devel-opments in Indian foreign policy and strategy, which, as it turns out, shed con-siderable light on how contemporary India sees the Gulf region.

A "Free-Rider" Navy

First of all, consider the original understanding of the Monroe Doctrine. In 1823, spurred by a dispute over Russian territorial claims in the Pacific Northwest, President Monroe informed Congress that "the American continents, by the free and independent condition which they have assumed and maintain, are hence-forth not to be considered as subject for future colonization by any European power."[17] To deter European aggrandizement, Monroe further declared that the United States would consider:

any attempt on [European governments'] part to extend their political sys-tem to any portion of this hemisphere as dangerous to our peace and safety.

With the existing colonies and dependencies of any European power we have not interfered and shall not interfere. But with the governments who have declared their independence and maintained it . . . we could not view any interposition for the purpose of oppressing them, or controlling in any other manner their destiny, by any European power in any other light than as the manifestation of an unfriendly disposition towards the United States.[18]

Roughly speaking, then, the 1823 message to Congress forbade any expansion of European control over American territory beyond that which the European powers already exercised. Monroe and Adams did not assert U.S. control of the hemisphere. They considered their policy a common defense of the American states. The geographic reach of the doctrine, moreover, was a matter of debate. Taken to its logical extreme, Monroe's language implied that it applied throughout the hemisphere, but it remained unclear whether the United States should or could enforce it that widely.

Nor did Monroe's precepts qualify as international law, which derives its force from the consent of states. They were unilateral policy. If U.S. leaders wanted to enforce the doctrine, therefore, they needed a navy able to unilaterally defend against European encroachment. The United States possessed no such fleet, but it did have a silent partner: the Royal Navy. Great Britain had an interest of its own in keeping rival imperial powers out of the Americas. British naval mastery granted America a strategic holiday that lasted for much of the nineteenth century. In effect the United States free-rode on maritime security supplied by the Royal Navy until the 1890s, when the first modern U.S. battle fleet took to the seas. Sheltering behind Britain's wooden walls allowed Americans to concentrate resources on westward expansion and economic development. Resources not needed for defense went into territorial expansion, internal improvements, and industrialization—fueling the economic growth that ultimately made world power possible.

Finally, it bears mentioning that Monroe and Adams were agreeable to cooperation with external powers—even an erstwhile foe like Britain—provided it did not imperil U.S. interests. Indeed, Monroe's 1823 message reported that British and U.S. squadrons were jointly policing the Caribbean for slavers. Formal alliance entanglements were unthinkable, but informal cooperation could serve mutual interests. This "Free-rider" paradigm from early U.S. naval history has much to commend it. Applying this to India's position depends on permissive strategic conditions in the Indian Ocean, including the presence of a dominant U.S. Navy to assure maritime security. Accepting the U.S. security guarantee allows India to pursue its uppermost priority—economic development—just as accepting British protection indirectly supported U.S. economic development.

What kind of Indian Navy would a Free-rider policy demand? Military power would rank lowest among the implements of national power under this policy, while New Delhi would restrict its maritime efforts primarily to the sea lines of communication crisscrossing crucial expanses—namely the northern Indian Ocean. Indian officials would welcome cooperation with the U.S. Navy and other external navies to reduce the burden of maritime defense. Indian officials, moreover, would remain fairly comfortable depending on outside suppliers for military hardware, since such reliance would entail little risk.

One immediately deployable aircraft-carrier task force would likely satisfy a Free-rider policy's requirements for naval diplomacy, humanitarian and disaster relief, maritime security, and lower-end combat missions, so long as the United States remained a reliable custodian of Indian Ocean security. The U.S. Navy's thumb rule—that two to three aircraft-carrier strike groups are necessary for one to be fully trained, in excellent repair, and ready for immediate overseas deployment—implies a Free-rider Indian Navy composed of two to three carrier groups organized into one fleet.[19] Since local and regional commitments would not impose the same wear-and-tear that worldwide operations exact from U.S. equipment and personnel, the lower figure would probably suffice. Exact numbers depend on New Delhi's tolerance for risk and the navy's ability to maintain its fleet in peak condition.

The navy would continue developing an undersea nuclear deterrent manifest in fleet ballistic-missile submarines (SSBNs). Conventional attack submarines would suffice for operations in nearby expanses such as the Arabian Sea and the Bay of Bengal—the foci of a Free-rider doctrine. Nuclear attack submarines (SSNs)—boats able to range throughout the Indian Ocean basin and beyond—would take lesser priority for a Free-rider navy. As long as the nautical milieu remained fairly tranquil, New Delhi could exploit this strategic interlude to upgrade its maritime forces, work with fellow navies to improve tactics and procedures, and pursue fleet experimentation.

"Strongman" of the Indian Ocean

As U.S. economic and military power surged in the nineteenth century, U.S. leaders were less and less willing to entrust maritime security to outside sea powers whose goodwill might prove fleeting. Emboldened, many Americans inferred new prerogatives from the Monroe Doctrine. Diplomats took to insisting that any canal dug across the Central American Isthmus must be in U.S. hands, not those of France or Great Britain. They considered European empires untrustworthy stewards of the sea lines of communication that would come into being with an isthmian canal.[20]

The 1890s, in short, marked the "Strongman" phase of the Monroe Doctrine. In 1895, Richard Olney, President Grover Cleveland's secretary of state, interposed himself—uninvited—in a territorial dispute between Venezuela and British Guiana. The United States' "fiat is law" on matters of vital interest, proclaimed Olney. The United States now possessed the moral standing and the maritime might to enforce its will throughout the hemisphere.[21] Washington wanted to mediate a settlement, underscoring its claim to regional hegemony.[22] Three points are worth noting about Cleveland's Strongman doctrine:

- Material power encouraged U.S. leaders to assume a more energetic stance in times of crisis—vindicating the witticism that problems look like nails to statesmen who brandish hammers. Naval power was the hammer for U.S. hemispheric policy in the 1890s.

- The Cleveland administration projected the Monroe Doctrine outward. A Strongman policy required a U.S. Navy preponderant not just in U.S. coastal waters but throughout the Americas. It was the embodiment of Olney's "fiat is law" maxim.

- The administration confronted Great Britain, long the guardian of maritime security in the New World. No longer, it seems, were U.S. leaders content to free-ride on the Royal Navy, accepting the political risks such dependence involved.

Similarly, an Indian Strongman doctrine would demand the military capacity to dominate the Indian Ocean basin. Naval power would be the tool of first resort in difficult times. Indian officials would further widen their strategic gaze to encompass all of the Indian Ocean and the Red Sea, perhaps mounting a forward defense of Indian interests in the South China Sea, the western Pacific, or even the Mediterranean and the Atlantic.

Indian naval planners would vest little trust in foreign military suppliers under the Strongman paradigm. Completing a self-sufficient, indigenous defense-industrial base, therefore, would assume high priority for the Indian military. In force-structure terms, a hegemonic Indian Navy would likely feature six to nine carrier task forces, four to six SSBNs, and a fleet of SSNs. At least three carrier groups thus would be available for speedy deployment. Indian forces would be organized into east- and west-coast fleets, providing immediate military options in both the Arabian Sea and the Bay of Bengal, while the remaining assets would constitute a third, expeditionary fleet for power-projection missions farther from Indian coasts—in all likelihood beyond the confines of the Indian Ocean.

The logic for an expeditionary fleet would be the same as for the forward-deployed U.S. fleets that now anchor the overseas U.S. naval presence. A Strongman navy would offer maximum flexibility in stressful times—albeit at considerable expense and effort.

A Naval "Constable"

Cleveland's Strongman approach met with skepticism. Mahan, a prominent critic, saw the strategic geography of the Americas not as a realm of U.S. hegemony but in narrow defensive terms. He espoused enforcing the Monroe Doctrine only in the Caribbean basin, a zone of vital U.S. economic and military interest.

In particular, the geostrategic value of secure sea communications with the Isthmus, the "gateway to the Pacific for the United States," could hardly be overstated.[23] The canal then under construction would spare East Coast–based shipping the arduous voyage around South America, shorten communications with the modest Pacific empire won from Spain in 1898, and let the U.S. Navy concentrate its Atlantic and Pacific fleets for battle with relative ease. Mahan's chief concern was to keep the great powers—primarily Imperial Germany, which craved "a place in the sun" of maritime empire—from establishing naval bases from which their warships could menace shipping bound to or from the canal.[24]

To do so, maintained Mahan, the U.S. Navy needed a battle fleet "great enough . . . to fight, with reasonable chances of success, the largest force likely to be brought against it." This meant local superiority of naval force to "beat off an enemy's fleet on its approach" to the Caribbean.[25] Since the entire Royal Navy or German High Seas Fleet was unlikely to venture across the Atlantic for a decisive fleet action, the U.S. Navy could afford to prepare against smaller naval contingents. In short, a battle fleet symmetrical with European fleets was unnecessary.

President Theodore Roosevelt agreed with Mahan's logic. In his day, imperial powers typically dispatched warships when weak American governments defaulted on their foreign debts. They seized customhouses, using tariff revenues to repay their aggrieved creditors. This left Europeans in possession of American territory. Roosevelt fretted that they might use debt collection as an excuse to wrest away naval footholds in the Caribbean.

In 1904, accordingly, he fashioned a "Corollary" to the Monroe Doctrine. When the Dominican Republic went into default, threatening to trigger European intervention, "TR" informed Congress that "chronic wrongdoing" or governmental "impotence" keeping Caribbean states from meeting their foreign obligations justified preventive U.S. intervention.[26] Washington would forestall violations of the Monroe Doctrine by stepping in itself. Proclaimed Roosevelt, "If we intend to say 'Hands Off' to the powers of Europe, then sooner or later we must keep order ourselves."[27]

He thus asserted the right to deploy "an international police power" when governmental incompetence or malfeasance in the Caribbean basin threatened to leave American territory in the hands of European navies. Three aspects of TR's "Constable" paradigm bear on Indian politics today:

- As noted above, geopolitics was central to his Corollary, but Roosevelt jettisoned Olney's overweening interpretation of the Monroe Doctrine, which needlessly affronted Latin American sensibilities. He believed the United States had neither the need, nor the naval power, nor the forward bases to police the vastness of a hemisphere. Local preponderance in the Caribbean was enough.

- TR exercised the police power with forbearance. The Dominican enterprise meant little more than stationing a warship in Dominican waters for deterrent purposes, and negotiating a treaty empowering U.S. customs agents to administer repayment of the Dominican Republic's foreign loans. Roosevelt in effect saw the United States mediating tactfully between weak Caribbean governments and rapacious great powers.

- The United States no longer needed British help to fend off European threats to the Americas. London and Washington struck a tacit bargain under which the United States minded British interests in the Americas under the Roosevelt Corollary, while the Royal Navy withdrew from American waters to address more pressing concerns—namely the German High Seas Fleet then building in the North Sea.

Having become a sea power in its own right, then, the United States could usher foreign sea powers out of the Americas, assuming the mantle of maritime police duty. TR remained agreeable to temporary cooperation with extrahemispheric navies when there was little prospect of European aggrandizement— a confident, strong United States had less and less to fear—but his default stance was that the United States and "advanced" Latin American states could police the New World themselves.

An Indian Constable, then, would occupy a middle ground between a Freerider and a Strongman India. The military instrument would be an important tool for implementing a Constable policy, but not the most important one.

While New Delhi would remain amenable to collaborating with outside powers on a case-by-case basis, it would take a warier view because of the potential for emerging threats. With a greater sense of menace, increasing national confidence, and the "hammer" of potent naval capabilities would come a tendency to apply India's security doctrine more broadly from a geographic standpoint—probably from the Horn of Africa to the Strait of Malacca.

The boundary between a Constable and a Strongman navy would blur from a force-structure standpoint, making net assessment a less reliable indicator of Indian policy and strategy. An Indian Constable would step up its efforts to improve its defense-industrial base, relying less on foreign suppliers. The Indian Navy would probably construct four to six carrier task forces, two to three SSBNs, and a mix of nuclear and conventional attack submarines. It would array these assets into two fleets, one stationed on each coast. At any time, then, at least one carrier group would be available for immediate service in the Arabian Sea and another in the Bay of Bengal.

So equipped, New Delhi would stand a good chance of attaining TR's twin aims of deterring or beating back outside aggressors and discreetly policing its extended neighborhood. Indian leaders would enjoy greater political leeway than under a Free-rider policy—but less than they would have if a third, Strongman expeditionary fleet were in existence. This modest posture would befit an Indian Constable.

Whither Indian Naval Strategy?

Toward which archetype of the Monroe Doctrine will Indian naval strategy tend? At present, the Indian security doctrine most closely approximates the Free-rider model. Despite the bleak outlook conveyed in the *Indian Maritime Doctrine* and the *Maritime Military Strategy*, New Delhi evidently views the strategic milieu with equanimity. In the strategic interlude they perceive, Indian officials have courted close ties with the U.S. Navy and Coast Guard to refine tactics and procedures, break down bureaucratic barriers between the sea services, and police the region for scourges such as weapons proliferation, piracy, and human trafficking. They appear undisturbed by the leisurely pace at which the three-carrier, blue-water Indian Navy they envision is taking shape.

Over the longer term, the Constable paradigm represents the most likely outcome for Indian sea power. Theodore Roosevelt's vision of benign supremacy over vital seas will prove attractive for India, a nation with a tradition of nonalignment and its own aspirations to regional primacy. Assuming the nation's drive for economic development continues to provide new resources for naval development, New Delhi will ultimately pursue something resembling the two-fleet, bicoastal navy foreseen in our Constable analysis. In the words of the *Maritime Military Strategy*, this seagoing force would provide sufficient "insulation from external interference" as long as security conditions in the Indian Ocean remained fairly benign.

What would drive New Delhi to abandon its nonaligned posture, pronouncing itself an aquatic Strongman? If China forward-deployed nuclear submarines in India's backyard, or if the United States used regional waters lavishly for strikes on Iranian nuclear sites, such wild cards could precipitate a doctrine that shut all external great powers out of the Indian Ocean. Alternatively, mixed circumstances—say, Chinese naval encroachment coupled with continued good relations with the United States at sea—could give rise to a variable-geometry Indian Monroe Doctrine. Under such a doctrine, the Indian Navy would focus its strategic and force-structure efforts on countering the Chinese naval threat while contenting itself to follow the U.S. lead on constabulary matters such as combating proliferation and piracy.

The Strongman and the Free-rider could coexist, then, letting India concentrate its energies where needed most. There are signs that a hybrid doctrine is taking shape in the minds of Indian naval strategists, who resist function cooperation with China for fear of granting a Chinese forward presence legitimacy, and who welcome tactical and operational ties with the American sea services but have sought to overrule higher-level relations with even a friendly United States. Such attitudes will influence Indian policy—especially once embedded in bureaucratic politics.[28] In parting, then, a cautionary note is in order. Analysts of Indian sea power should not assume India will apply its Monroe Doctrine in mechanical fashion:

- Certain geographic differences between the Indian Ocean and the Western Hemisphere hold policy implications. Whereas keeping Europeans out of Latin America was Monroe's chief concern, the southern Indian Ocean holds less to beckon Indian strategists' gaze southward. Barring an overbearing great-power threat, this will diminish the appeal of a Strongman navy for Indian strategists.

- As noted above, New Delhi could apply different models of the Monroe Doctrine to different external powers. Indeed, TR sorted the imperial powers into a strategic hierarchy, deeming Germany a serious threat, Britain a threat that could be deterred through asymmetric means—namely a counterstroke against Canada—and France and the lesser naval powers minor nuisances at most. New Delhi may assign strategic priorities of its own.

In short, Indians will take a variegated view of their strategic surroundings and of effective naval strategy. No security doctrine—even one bequeathed by the likes of statesmen such as James Monroe and Jawaharlal Nehru—is a foolproof predictor of real-world statecraft.

India's Monroe Doctrine and the Gulf

How will all of this apply to the Persian Gulf region? Any answers are provisional at best. In principle, India's Monroe Doctrine seemingly spans the entire Indian Ocean region, just as America's Monroe Doctrine spanned the entire Western Hemisphere. Manmohan Singh, India's prime minister, declares, "India's growing international stature gives it strategic relevance in the area ranging from the Persian Gulf to the Strait of Malacca," seemingly envisioning the Gulf region as a theater of Indian interest.[29] Yet Indian strategists pay little attention to the mechanics of asserting influence in the Gulf. This raises a host of questions. Can the region be safely entrusted to American stewardship at a time of U.S. naval decline? How can New Delhi reconcile its strategy with Iranian claims to regional primacy? Does it consider the Gulf a theater where regional powers must sort things out for themselves? What tripwires would prompt Delhi to take a more active hand in the Persian Gulf?

Nineteenth-century U.S. history echoes again. The original Monroe Doctrine ran up against limits on U.S. power, while U.S. interests never demanded suzerainty over the entire hemisphere. Washington seldom worried about, say, an Italian or French threat to the Caribbean, while fin de siècle Germany topped the Theodore Roosevelt administration's list of challenges. Enforcement efforts remained confined to the Caribbean Sea and the Gulf of Mexico. Like Washington, New Delhi will presumably apply its security doctrine selectively.

The 2009 edition of the *Indian Maritime Doctrine* certainly counts the Gulf as part of the Indian Ocean region, delimiting the northernmost bound of the region at latitude 30°N—that is, along the northern coast of the Gulf.[30] This harks back to K. M. Panikkar's analysis. Writing in 1955, Panikkar observed that the "bays and bights of the Indian Ocean," foremost among them the Persian Gulf, "require special consideration." He depicted the Gulf as a "protected landlocked sea with [Hormuz] commanding the entry."[31] Despite the attention lavished on the region by India's godfather of geopolitics, the *Indian Maritime Doctrine* mentions energy security only in passing while saying little beyond how important Gulf oil and gas are to Indian economic development. The document's only reference to Iran, furthermore, is a mention of the "tanker wars" of the 1980s, and even this example is proffered to illustrate the potential of commercial war at sea.[32]

Indian political leaders and maritime strategists, then, pay the Gulf little attention as of yet. Seldom does the Gulf region figure in commentary on the Indian sea services, although the *Maritime Military Strategy* observes that extra-regional navies take an interest in Middle East affairs.[33] New Delhi has reached various accords with Qatar and Oman but has assigned a single defense attaché to manage relations with four of the Gulf Cooperation Council countries.[34] This apparent indifference represents an interesting finding in itself, considering the scope and magnitude of Indian interests in secure energy shipments. One small example: a recent volume on maritime security in the Indian Ocean contains only one chapter with any real assessment of maritime challenges pertaining to the Gulf region. The author, Peter Lehr—a non-Indian—speculates on how the Islamic Republic of Iran would deploy naval forces in wartime. Even Lehr's work includes Iranian strategy as a minor part of a chapter on state, substate, and non-state actors with maritime war-fighting capacity.[35] The other Gulf states' sea services are conspicuously absent, as is any analysis of interactions among the many navies in the region. What explains this seeming lack of urgency on the Indians' part? A few hypotheses:

- *Other Fish to Fry.* No government can manage every security-related challenge in its geographic neighborhood. Indians have a long list of priorities. Recurrent acts of terrorism on Indian soil, notably the 2008 bloodletting in Mumbai—an attack launched overseas—have kept New Delhi's attention on Pakistan and Kashmir. A spike in piracy off the Horn of Africa induced Manmohan Singh's government to dispatch warships for patrol duty, acting under the aegis of a series of United Nations (UN) Security Council resolutions empowering UN member states to strike at pirates at sea and ashore.[36] Chinese efforts to acquire basing rights in the Indian Ocean region attract intense scrutiny. In particular, the Chinese-financed seaport facility at Gwadar, in western Pakistan, has occupied Indians' analytical energies. And so on. Unless some pressing security challenge issues forth from the Persian Gulf—an unlikely possibility so long as the U.S. force posture there remains robust—the Gulf region will stay low on the scale of Indian priorities. Policy drift constitutes acceptable policy for the time being.[37]

- *Geographic Separation.* The partition of India in the 1940s interposed a new state, Pakistan, between India and the broader Middle East, a region with which India shares close historical and cultural ties by virtue of centuries of interaction and the age of Mughal dynastic rule. No longer does India share a land frontier with one of the Persian Gulf states, while the Strait of Hormuz separates the Gulf from the Indian Ocean, despite the fact that it is a bay or inlet in the larger body of water. One result has been a sense of remoteness from Persian Gulf affairs. New Delhi does not see itself as the leading power in the Gulf region the same way it fancies itself the steward of maritime security in the Indian Ocean region writ large.

- *Amicable Ties with Iran.* New Delhi has assiduously courted good ties with the Islamic Republic, despite the long-simmering dispute over Iranian nuclear-weapons aspirations and qualms about the radicalism of President Mahmoud Ahmadinejad. This is good geopolitics and conforms to Indian strategic traditions. Kautilya's venerable *Arthashastra*, or manual of statecraft, portrays a kingdom's immediate neighbors as natural antagonists, and the kingdoms beyond those immediate neighbors as natural allies.[38] The impulse to stay on good terms with Tehran, then, finds solid footing in Indian traditions of realpolitik.

  The Indian leadership can assume, reasonably enough, that it has neutralized the Gulf as long as relations with the Gulf's preponderant state remain cordial. Interestingly, officials in New Delhi tend to think of Iran not in maritime terms but as a unit with Pakistan and Afghanistan. Indeed, the Indian Ministry of Foreign Affairs groups the three nations bureaucratically—hence New Delhi's pronounced landward orientation toward affairs to the subcontinent's west and northwest.[39] In short, there is no obvious threat to divert Indian strategists' attention from the Arabian Sea, Bay of Bengal, Gulf of Oman, and Gulf of Aden to the Persian Gulf.

- *Free-Rider Mentality Reigns.* Again, New Delhi has its own strategic hierarchy. None of the Gulf states has any evident motive to endanger Indian interests in the Gulf region, while Iran is the only state with any real capacity to cause trouble. The U.S. Navy remains dominant in Gulf waters, it remains an adequate check against any Iranian mischief that might transpire at sea, and its leadership has cultivated a partnership with the Indian Navy and Coast Guard. Accordingly, Indians assume they can safely entrust their interests in the Gulf to the United States, just as they remain content to free-ride on the U.S. security guarantee throughout the Indian Ocean. The Gulf, then, will take a back seat to planning for contingencies in the broader Indian Ocean unless (a) the United States proves itself an unreliable or untrustworthy custodian of maritime security in the Gulf, or (b) some threat comparable in magnitude to piracy off the Horn of Africa emerges, engaging New Delhi's interest in helping police regional seas. This would be especially true should China's People's Liberation Army Navy show an interest in taking up the slack for regional maritime security—triggering India's competitive reflex.

What might impel New Delhi to modify its complacency toward the Gulf? Trends or developments discrediting the assumptions and attitudes posited above might well prompt Indians to rank the region higher on their list of strategic priorities. Should the United States use the Gulf or the Arabian Sea to stage strikes against the Iranian nuclear sector, for instance, Indians might well start taking a dimmer view of the strategic partnership with Washington. Should China press its string-of-pearls strategy aggressively, obtaining a pearl in the Gulf, India would doubtless respond in some fashion.

It is possible, furthermore, that some "Black Swan" event will take place, drawing India's strategic gaze to the Gulf region.[40] Suppose the relative era of good feelings across the Taiwan Strait ends, bringing a return to military confrontation between Beijing and Taipei. Should war ensue, triggering U.S. intervention in the Strait, Washington would perforce commit the Pacific Fleet to battle. Should the United States risk its fleet and lose, it could suffer serious if not irreparable damage to its world standing in an afternoon. In all likelihood, its position in central theaters like the Persian Gulf would decline. If so, India could find itself entangled in the politics of the region owing to U.S. misfortune elsewhere in the world. New Delhi would discard its Free-rider assumptions, dedicating itself to becoming an Indian Constable. The Gulf would presumably fall within the Sino-Indian "rivalry arc" some Indian commentators now discern enclosing the entire Asian coastline.[41] If so, New Delhi can be expected to expand its own maritime interests and strategy to enfold the Gulf—much as it sees naval activities in the South China Sea as "a direct response to the growing Chinese presence in the Indian Ocean," in the words of Rahul Roy-Chaudhury.[42]

How to test these hypotheses? There is no substitute for keeping tabs on Indian commentary on Gulf affairs, as evidenced in statements of policy like the *Maritime Military Strategy*, the writings of current and retired naval and military officers, and editorializing in influential press outlets like the *Times of India* or *The Hindu*. While the Chinese counter-piracy mission off Somalia has aroused anxious commentary, for instance, Indians appeared to view the March 2010 Chinese naval visit to the United Arab Emirates with equanimity. The *Times of India*, arguably the subcontinent's leading news outlet, contented itself with reprinting a *New York Times* story about the Chinese navy operating in American preserves like the Gulf.[43] This small example suggests that, for now, Indians feel comfortable with U.S. Navy preeminence in the region and prefer to concentrate their efforts in the Indian Ocean proper. The Free-rider paradigm prevails in Indian strategy toward the Gulf.

This low-key response offers a baseline from which to chart future changes in attitude. Threat perceptions on display in such outlets would provide a leading indicator of a new naval strategy toward the Persian Gulf—alerting outsiders to begin considering how to adapt to a new, more forceful Indian policy in the Middle East.

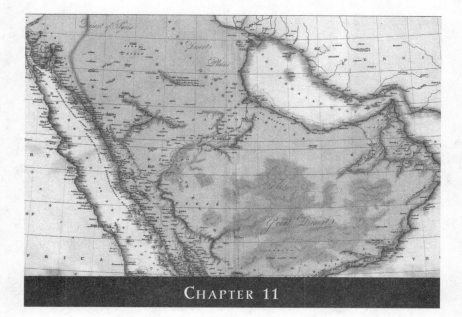

CHAPTER 11

China's Historic Return to the Gulf

Ben Simpfendorfer

T he strengthening of China's relations with the Gulf is one of the more important, yet less observed, events reshaping the global balance of power. The event is often overlooked, as China's relations with the Gulf have been almost non-existent for nearly four centuries, or since Admiral Zheng He's treasure ships visited the Gulf in 1421. Moreover, many of the changes have taken place in only the last five years, allowing limited time for observation. The changes are also largely limited to economics. This owes to China's preference to focus on economics, rather than politics. Yet the traditional focus for the region's observers is politics. Indeed, there are only a few books written on the region's economic problems, compared to hundreds on its political. This chapter relies on both a combination of empirical analysis and anecdotal observation to provide an explanation of China's growing role in the region.

◆ ◆ ◆

Admiral Zheng He, a Chinese Muslim, is believed to have made the last historic visit to the Gulf by a Chinese official. Between 1405 and 1433, the Ming government sponsored a series of seven naval expeditions; the intention was to demonstrate China's overwhelming power and establish tributary trade relations with the country's neighbors. Admiral He was put in command of the fleet, and over 317 ships and 28,000 crewmen participated in the first voyage, and He is argued to have visited the Gulf during the sixth expedition. However, records of the visit were later destroyed by the Ming emperor after the expeditions were abandoned, so it is not possible to convincingly prove the admiral did indeed visit the region. Nonetheless, it was from this point that China turned inward, abandoning its outward-looking stance, and there was limited official contact with the Gulf until the twentieth century.

The creation of the People's Republic of China in 1948 saw greater interaction between China and the Gulf in the 1950s and 1960s. However, China's support of revolutionary movements, especially in Oman and Yemen, and its treatment of its own Muslim population was an obstacle to stronger relations.[1] The Cultural Revolution, lasting from 1966 to 1976, further disrupted China's foreign policy, and relations with the Gulf states were generally not re-established until the late 1980s and early 1990s, with President Jiang Zemin making the first trip by a Chinese president to Saudi Arabia in 1999. Yet while the trip resulted in trade and investment agreements, China was only just emerging as a major economic power, and the agreements had limited practical effect. It was the two trips made by President Hu Jintao, Jiang's successor, in 2006 and 2009 that marked a genuine turning point in the relationship.

China's limited engagement with the Gulf over the past five hundred years has had a major bearing on its modern relationship, as its reputation in the region contrasts markedly with that of the major Western countries.

First, and more negatively, unlike Europe and the United States, China does not enjoy an established modern relationship with the Gulf. For instance, while China hopes to invest in the region's oil sector it must compete with long-entrenched American competitors. It was American oil companies that initially discovered oil in Saudi Arabia and helped the country to develop its domestic oil industry. European companies enjoy similar relationships in the oil and non-oil sectors. These relationships are reinforced by the number of Gulf nationals who have studied in Europe or the United States. For instance, in the 2008–9 academic year, there were 12,661 Saudi students studying in the United States, including members of the royal family.[2] Neither is Saudi Arabia the only example. The son of Dubai's ruler, Mohammed bin Rashid Al Maktoum, studied at Britain's Sandhurst Academy, an institution that produces some of the UK's leading military personnel and has educated a number of foreign rulers.

Second, and more positively, China was never a major colonial power in the region, unlike Europe and, some may argue, the United States. It is charges of imperialism that periodically spoil the West's reputation in the region. For example, the Arabic-language media have often cited America's occupation of Iraq as intended not to liberate the Iraqi population from a dictator but instead to forcibly acquire the country's oil wealth. China, by contrast, is more often seen as a victim of the same imperialism. The country was indeed attacked, and regions occupied, by colonial powers from the 1800s. The fact that Syria's *Al Thawra*, a state mouthpiece, argued that the unrest in Xinjiang province in July 2009, pitting minority Uyghur Chinese against majority Han Chinese, was an attempt by the United States to break up China demonstrates how the narrative of colonial victim persists today.[3] (*Al Thawra* made the link on the basis that Uyghur agitators were based in the United States.)

◆ ◆ ◆

China's commercial relations with the Gulf have expanded rapidly since the early 2000s. But it is trade in goods that has led the way. The Gulf's shopping malls are increasingly full of "made-in-China" furniture and electronic goods.

In turn, China is increasingly reliant on the Gulf's oil to run the factories that make the same consumer goods and to fuel the container ships that travel in growing numbers between the ports in Guangzhou and Dubai. A few figures underscore the significance of the change. China's exports to the Gulf rose from $6 billion to $42 billion between 2001 and 2009.[4] In the process, China overtook the United States in 2007 as the world's largest supplier to the Gulf, having overtaken the United Kingdom in 2002 and Germany in 2006. It was the first time the United States had lost its number-one position since the 1960s, or as far back as data are available.[5]

Most of the increase was accounted for by consumer goods, such as clothing, furniture, and household electronics. A detailed breakdown is not available for the entire region, but clothing and household electronics accounted for 21 percent and 30 percent, respectively, of China's exports to Saudi Arabia in 2009. The remainder is mainly made up of miscellaneous goods, such as toys and hardware. (By way of comparison, clothing and household electronics account for 13 percent and 25 percent, respectively, of China's total exports to the world, suggesting that low value-added exports of clothing account for a higher share of exports to the Middle East than to the rest of the world, in particular to Europe and the United States.)[6]

There are three important explanations for why China's exports to the Middle East surged after 2002. First, China's entry into the World Trade Organization in December 2001 resulted in a sharp reduction in trade barriers to its exports. For instance, all quotas on China's textile exports were eliminated by 2004, albeit temporary safeguard mechanisms remained in place until the end of 2008. China's exporters were suddenly more competitive and their exports to most countries surged, in particular their textile exports. Between 2001 and 2009, total exports rose from $266 billion to $1,202 billion, doubling in value every three years until the global crisis, after which shipments dipped modestly to their 2009 level.[7]

Second, China's government unofficially relaxed its visa policies around the same time. Most Arab traders simultaneously found it harder to visit Europe and the United States as a result of the events of September 2001. In 2008, the average Egyptian trader took eighteen days to receive a visa to visit the United States, based on U.S. State Department data,[8] whereas the same trader took just one day to receive a visa to visit China.[9] The number of Arab traders visiting China surged. An estimated 200,000 Arab traders, from a few thousand a decade earlier, annually visit the coastal city of Yiwu, a four-hour drive south of Shanghai, attracted by the city's status as China's largest wholesaler of small-consumer goods selling to both domestic and foreign markets.[10]

Third, oil prices started rising after 2004, buoying Gulf economies and pro-ducing stronger household consumption growth. Indeed, the Gulf grew at an average of 8.2 percent between 2003 and 2008, the fastest sustained rate of growth since the 1970s.[11]

It was not only China's exports to the Gulf that surged, but also its imports from the Gulf. These rose from $9 billion to $54 billion between 2001 and 2009.[12] Oil and oil-related imports accounted for almost the entire increase owing to the combination of China's rising oil consumption and rising interna-tional oil prices. (Indeed, China's oil demand increased by 2.5 million barrels, even as global oil consumption increased by just 2.9 million barrels during the same period, and so contributing greatly to the rise in international oil prices.) The question of oil imports is discussed in more detail later in the chapter. But, in brief, Saudi Arabia accounted for the largest share of the increase, as China turned away from more traditional, and smaller, suppliers in Oman and Yemen.

It is popularly assumed that China imports from the Gulf more than it exports and so runs a large trade deficit. Yet China's exports to the Gulf almost match its imports from it, and the trade balance was only modestly in deficit at $12 billion in 2009.[13] The deficit is difficult to measure by country owing to the tendency for a large share of China's exports to the Gulf to be transshipped through Dubai's Jebel Ali Port, but China is assumed to run a trade deficit against all of the oil-producing Gulf countries. (Dubai does not release detailed data on which countries transshipments are destined for.) The deficit will likely widen in time as China consumes more oil than it can sell consumer goods to the small Gulf markets.

The economic benefits of trade have a greater impact on the Gulf's economy than on China's. In 2009, China accounted for 6.5 percent of the Gulf's total exports.[14] Yet China's contribution to rising international oil prices means that its demand has positive effects on all the Gulf's oil exports. So Kuwait and the UAE, for instance, benefit from China's oil demand even though they export only small volumes of oil to China. The Gulf, by contrast, accounted for 5.1 percent of China's total exports, only marginally higher than the share of its exports to Africa (2.8 percent) and Latin America (4.7 percent).[15] Nonetheless, Chinese traders still speak of the Middle East, and the Gulf specifically, as a hot spot, or *jiao dian*, especially since demand in more established markets weakened. Moreover, profit margins are anecdotally higher in the Gulf than they are in most developed countries, a point often made in the Chinese-language media.

It was individual traders that led the charge to the Middle East. However, Chinese construction companies have more recently also made their presence felt. Many of these companies are engaged in low-cost construction of roads, roundabouts, and apartments. They provide both cheap labor and raw materials, much of them imported from China. They also anecdotally provide financing, with Chinese banks prepared to lend to Chinese-related projects. Still, the arrival of Chinese construction firms is unsurprising. In part, they are simply following in the footsteps of the Japanese in the 1980s and the Koreans in the 1990s. However, they have also built experience and scale as a result of China's two-decades-long investment boom. And Chinese construction companies, such as China State Engineering Construction Company, now rank among the world's largest, and are winning contracts globally.

The rapid growth of trade in goods and construction services testifies to the strengthening commercial relationship between China and the Gulf. But the economic data also disguise an important feature of the relationship that is markedly different from the relationship of the Western powers and the Gulf.

The trade is exceptionally labor-intensive, a term that implies large numbers of traders dealing in small volumes of goods. It is these entrepreneurs, buying for their own shops or street stalls, who are responsible for China's exports to the Gulf. The 200,000 Arab nationals who visit Yiwu annually were noted earlier. However, many thousands more visit Guangzhou and other Chinese cities. There are meanwhile an estimated 50,000 Chinese traders based permanently in the Gulf. This contrasts with trade between China and Europe or the United States, which is more likely to be conducted by large multinationals making multi-million dollar orders and with a limited number of purchasing managers flying between the two countries regularly.

The labor-intensive character of trade is evident on the ground. For example, the bi-annual Canton Trade Fair, in China's southern Guangdong province, has a halal canteen and provides Arabic-language directions to the nearest mosque. Saudi taxi drivers often speak a few words of Chinese, testifying to the growing numbers of Chinese traveling from the airport to their hotels. Trade in construction services is equally labor demanding. Chinese construction firms often bring their own labor to the Gulf, and the number of Chinese nationals working in the Gulf has grown significantly. An estimated 120,000 of the 200,000 Chinese working in the UAE are construction workers.

The increase in Chinese nationals in the Gulf is also reflected by the growing number of flights between China and the Middle East. Dubai's national airline, Emirates, had forty-nine direct flights to China and Hong Kong each week in December 2011, a steady increase from previous years. In the same period, Emirates was flying the same number of direct flights to the United States, its traditionally larger market. Neither is Emirates the only airline flying between the Middle East and China. China Air, Cathay Pacific, and Qatar Airways, among others, also fly.

◆ ◆ ◆

The labor-intensive character of China's commercial relations with the Gulf is a major risk for China's strategic interests in the Gulf. Labor conditions in the Gulf do not always meet international standards, and labor protests are increasingly common. The failure of a Gulf construction company to pay wages to its Chinese construction workers, for instance, could result in strikes. (Chinese workers on the Mecca light-rail project did indeed strike in late 2010, partly protesting over having to work in such hot conditions. However, the workers were employed by China Railway Construction as opposed to a local company, thus limiting the fallout from the incident.)[16] The fallout for foreign relations between China and the Gulf countries would not be disastrous, but it might act as an obstacle to their further deepening, especially if the Chinese-language blogs and media were to report such an event.

However, the bigger risk is that Chinese nationals are turned into political targets. If China was to find itself in conflict with Islamist extremists, for instance, then its nationals living in the region might suffer reprisal attacks, as have American nationals. Yet American nationals are smaller in number, and largely living in guarded compounds, thereby limiting their exposure to attacks. By contrast, Chinese nationals are larger in number and, while some live in guarded compounds, they do not necessarily enjoy the same level of protection.

It is still early days. And the Chinese government has yet to face a substantive attack in the region. However, the threat of reprisals by Al Qaeda in North Africa against Chinese workers in Algeria, in July 2009, is illustrative of the challenges. The threat was made in response to the Chinese government's crackdown on Chinese Muslims in Xinjiang province the same year. The threat was taken seriously enough for the Chinese embassy in Algiers to post a warning on its Web site. In the event, the threat came to nothing. But there are an estimated 32,000 Chinese workers in Algeria,[17] mainly construction workers, and they remain a target in the event that Islamist extremists again target China for its policies toward its own Muslim population, or toward Islamic countries in the region. It is not impossible to imagine a similar threat in Saudi Arabia, where there are extremist groups and a growing number of Chinese workers.

Chinese academics have spoken of the need for the establishment of private Chinese security companies, much like those in the United States, such as Xe Services and DynCorp International. These security companies would likely be formed by ex–People's Liberation Army soldiers. The Chinese leadership is wary of private Chinese militias. Indeed, unlike the Western colonial powers in earlier centuries, the Chinese state banned merchant ships from carrying arms, worried that rich and armed merchants would eventually create a threat to the state.[18] (Some economic historians point to this as the reason why Western colonial traders pushed aside their Chinese competitors so easily during the period. Their advantage was not cost, but arms.)

Private militias might also be perceived by the host country as a sign of Chinese imperial ambition. This would clearly break with China's long-standing policy of non-intervention in another country's affairs, except where the issue touches on China's core interests, such as in Tibet and Taiwan. The policy was first described by Chairman Mao Zedong and later by Premier Zhou Enlai at the 1955 Asian-African Conference in Indonesia, and has remained a cornerstone of the country's foreign policy since. Indeed, there are already some who question China's non-interventionist stance, especially as related to commercial interests. For instance, Libya's foreign minister, Musa Kasa, rebuked China in November 2009 saying that "China's presence in Africa is neo-colonialism and aims to rule over the continent." He continued, "True cooperation must include all fields of politics and economics. It must not be reduced to constructing roads or building schools."[19]

The threat to China's overseas population may thus emerge as one of the country's greatest strategic threats in the coming years. The threat will be greatest in the Middle East, a region that suffers from periodic instability and has a history of targeting foreign nationals. And it would be odd if China did not fall foul of such risks, no different to the world's other major powers and in spite of its policy of non-intervention. As such, China's relations with the Gulf might force a major change in the country's traditional policy of non-intervention and wariness toward private militias, or security companies. If so, the implications for China's relations with the rest of the world, especially Africa and Latin America, would be significant. It certainly would not be the first time that the Gulf and, more broadly the Middle East, has forced a change in the way a major power behaves on the global stage.

Neither is the threat limited to reprisals. In early 2010, an Arabic-language e-mail was distributed, mainly to Saudi nationals, calling on readers to bring Chinese nationals, both Muslim and non-Muslim, to an Islamic center in Saudi Arabia for religious instruction,[20] and it may be that the centers are an attempt by the government to counter criticism of the large number of Chinese nationals working in the Kingdom, especially on the Mecca light-rail project. The e-mail underscores the small, but not insignificant, risk that Chinese Muslim nationals bring back a more strict, or extreme, version of Islam to China. Certainly the country's public security services will be aware of the threat. But it is another reminder that personal exchanges between China and the Gulf are not entirely in China's interests. Like the old Silk Road, the new Silk Road will carry not only goods between countries, but also ideas.

◆ ◆ ◆

China is one of the Gulf's largest oil buyers. However, the importance of oil is easily exaggerated. Oil is a fungible commodity. While there are different grades of oil, the commodity is largely interchangeable on the global market. This means that oil produced in Saudi Arabia, for instance, becomes part of the global supply of oil. So if China was to buy more oil from Saudi Arabia, it would buy less from other countries, leaving the global supply and price of oil largely unchanged. It is a situation best imagined as if the world had only a single oil well. Neither can Saudi Arabia guarantee China's oil supply. A conflict in the Strait of Hormuz between Iran and the United States, for instance, would disrupt China's oil supplies. A similar argument can be made with respect to China's acquisitions of oil assets in Africa. These may allow Chinese oil companies to produce oil at a lower marginal cost, but the companies cannot protect against an African government nationalizing its oil assets and expelling Chinese oil companies. This makes it difficult for countries to pursue a "nationalist" oil strategy. More accurate is the phrase "oil interdependence."

China's oil imports from the Gulf have certainly grown significantly, rising from 1.33 million barrels per day (bpd) to 1.95 million bpd between 2006 and 2009. (The data series has a short history.) Saudi Arabia and Iran account for the largest increase from 480,000 to 790,000 bpd and 340,000 to 500,000 bpd, respectively. Together, they account for 66 percent of China's imports from the Gulf. The remainder is accounted for mainly by Oman (250,000 bpd), Kuwait (150,000 bpd), and Iraq (140,000 bpd).[21] The increase is explained by China's surging oil demand. China became a net oil importer in 1994, and its oil imports had risen to 4 million bpd in 2009, equal to near 50 percent of the country's oil consumption. The International Energy Agency estimates that its consumption will reach 16.3 million bpd by 2030. Imports will account for the large share of this increase, as domestic production is expected to peak in 2015 at 3.8 million bpd.[22]

While oil is interchangeable, oil contracts are not, and there is a strong alignment of interests between China and the Middle East in the way oil is traded. The alignment of interests is especially strong between China and Saudi Arabia. Both prefer to transact on the basis of medium-term oil contracts. Such contracts are typically negotiated annually. The price of oil is set monthly according to a monthly benchmark. For Saudi Arabia, this is a benchmark determined by the average selling price of Dubai and Omani crude. The buyer also enjoys some "tolerance" during the course of the contract, and can purchase +/−5 percent of the originally contracted volume.

There are also other common interests between the two sides. In the case of China, oil security is an overwhelming concern. If Guangdong's factories or Beijing's automobiles no longer have sufficient oil, the implications are economic and, accordingly, social. Ensuring oil supplies through medium-term contracts is thus consistent with the country's strategic objectives. It is also consistent with the fact that there are only a limited number of companies allowed to buy crude oil, and all are majority state-owned. In the case of Saudi Arabia, the country must sell a vast 10.5 million barrels of oil a day, equivalent to 13 percent of the world's supply. This requires large capital spending to maintain and increase Saudi Arabia's production capacity; the country's oil-related capital expenditures were estimated to be worth $30 billion in 2010.[23] Medium-oil contracts assist the country to forecast future expenditures by creating a more stable operating environment. Saudi Arabia also only sells to end-users. This policy is consistent with Saudi Arabia's religious prohibition on speculation. It also allows the country to more accurately estimate final demand and regulate global oil prices. Were traders to build speculative stocks of oil, it would only increase volatility in the oil market. Saudi Aramco's company Web site explicitly includes this warning to potential buyers on its international sales and marketing page.

The upshot is that market forces mainly explain the sudden increase in Saudi Arabia's oil exports to China. Indeed, when China marginally overtook the United States, in late 2009, to become Saudi Arabia's largest oil buyer, it owed its success in part to the collapse in United States oil demand during the economic crisis. Again, while the event grabbed news headlines, market forces were the more logical explanation, rather than any secret agreement. Speculation of a secret agreement also comes unstuck when examining the difficulty Gulf oil companies have had building refineries in China. Saudi Aramco has jointly built a 240,000-bpd refinery in Quanzhou, in Fujian province, with Sinopec and Exxon Mobil. But this is the company's only investment to date, and anecdotally the company encountered delays in trying to negotiate this and other agreements. Similarly, Kuwait Petrochemical Company's joint-venture agreement with Sinopec to build a 300,000-bpd refinery in Zhanjiang, in Guangdong province, has met similar delays.

Chinese companies have had more recent success in Iraq. In November 2009, China National Petroleum Company (CNPC) and British Petroleum (BP) won a contract to jointly develop the Rumaila field. In January 2010, CNPC, Total, and Petronas also won a contract to jointly develop the Halfaya field. CNPC owed its success in part to its ability to draw on a large skilled work-force, more willing to operate in risk areas at relatively cheap wages, but also in part to its having access to low-cost financing from Chinese banks. By contrast, they have had less success in Saudi Arabia and other Gulf countries, where oper-ating conditions are more stable and governments are more eager for foreign oil companies to supply value-added technologies that raise oil recovery rates. And while Chinese oil companies are certainly moving rapidly up the value-added chain, they still struggle to compete with their Western competitors and even with some developing country competitors, such as Brazil's Petrobras.

◆ ◆ ◆

While there is a steady flow of consumer goods and oil between China and the Middle East, capital flows have lagged. There are still only limited examples of, for example, Gulf investors buying stakes in Chinese companies, or Chinese investors building factories in the Gulf. This is odd given that both sides have among the world's largest holdings of foreign currency reserves. The fact that China and the Gulf effectively peg their currencies to the dollar requires con-stant intervention in foreign exchange markets to maintain the pegs. And large current account surpluses, either as a result of oil or manufactured goods exports, mean their central banks must buy vast amounts of foreign currencies. These for-eign currencies are then invested abroad through public, and occasionally pri-vate, agencies. Yet while China and the Gulf have thus steadily acquired foreign currency assets—from U.S. Treasury debt to London residential apartments—they have invested only sparingly in each other.

There are two important explanations. First, China still imposes tight restrictions on the ability of foreign investors to buy majority stakes in estab-lished Chinese companies. Yet it is these types of transactions that are preferred by Gulf investors. Moreover, a limited number of transactions make the deals more expensive than those in, for instance, Africa, Europe, or the Middle East. Second, the Gulf's largest assets are typically state-owned energy assets and these are not usually for sale. Most private equity transactions relate to the consol-idation of small family-owned businesses, for which the deal-size is too small for China's foreign reserve managers. As a result, Chinese firms had made few acquisitions in the region by mid-2010. By contrast, European and United States investors, such as the American private-equity firm Carlyle Capital, were active in the Gulf in spite of the challenges.

◆ ◆ ◆

China's strengthening commercial relations with the Gulf have naturally led to assumptions that their military relations are also tightening. Yet there is limited evidence of such a change. The fact that military relations have not strengthened is surprising given that China's oil imports from the region have grown to account for such a large share of the country's total oil consumption. Conflict between Iran and the United States, for instance would have a material impact on China's domestic stability were it to temporarily stop oil shipments through the Strait of Hormuz. The country is building emergency oil reserves, and plans to have capacity to stockpile one hundred days' worth of oil consumption by 2020. Nonetheless, a temporary shortfall owing to a disruption of shipments, coupled with rising oil costs, would bankrupt factories and put thousands of workers on the street.[24]

China's military relations with the Gulf, however, face soft and hard constraints. The soft constraint is the country's long-standing policy of non-intervention in another country's affairs. Military intervention in the Gulf would break with this policy and potentially harm China's economic interests. For example, if Iran was to worry that China's military was prepared to take a more interventionist stance in protection of China's commercial interests, the Iranian leadership might be less willing to sign oil agreements with Chinese oil companies. The hard constraint is the country's limited blue-water navy. First, the navy was largely subordinate to the army before the 1990s and the collapse of the Soviet Union. Second, China had only limited economic interests beyond its own borders before the 1990s, as it was neither a major exporter of goods nor importer of oil. Third, a blue-water navy is both difficult to develop and expensive to maintain, and, until recently after the export sector flourished and foreign direct investment rose, the country was still relatively poor.

Nonetheless, policy is changing. China's growing international economic interests—such as in the commodity-rich Spratly Islands in the South China Sea or the Strait of Malacca through which 80 percent of the country's oil is shipped—imply a greater role for the navy. The navy has indeed modernized rapidly since the 1990s and there is public talk about the need for an aircraft carrier, with China, according to reports in early 2010, having purchased a scrap Soviet-era carrier from the Ukraine to assist its development program.[25] A more visible demonstration of China's changing policy was a port call by the Chinese navy outside the Strait of Hormuz in late March 2010. Two Chinese naval ships, a 135-meter frigate and a supply vessel, visited Abu Dhabi's Port Zayed. The visit was explained as a refueling stop, as the two ships had been part of the international naval force in the Gulf of Aden and, according to the state news agency

Xinhua, had escorted six hundred Chinese ships and foreign vessels during their six-month assignment.

Somali pirates and their disruption of shipping through the Suez Canal have provided China with good reason to participate in the international naval force. Europe is China's largest trading partner, with the combined value of exports and imports worth $423 billion in 2009. Europe was also China's largest export partner at $294 billion the same year.[26] So long as the trade sector remains a major driver of employment growth, China's trade with Europe is crucial to social stability. It is thus important that a large share of China's container trade with Europe travels through the Suez Canal. It is possible for container ships to travel around the southern end of Africa. However, this lengthens transit times from Shanghai to Rotterdam significantly. The delays are important, as they make it harder for China's export factories to meet rush orders, and would reduce the country's competitiveness against Eastern Europe.

Yi Zhuo, a senior researcher at the Naval Equipment Research Center, has raised the idea that China establish naval bases in the Arabian Sea and Indian Ocean in order to supply the country's recent naval activities in the region.[27] The suggestion attracted significant attention in the international media, including an article in *The National*, an English-language UAE newspaper, which was, in turn, later widely quoted by Chinese-language newspapers. China is still a long way from challenging the military dominance of the United States. However, a naval base in the region would be a small step toward establishing a more visible military presence in the Gulf, and the geopolitical implications would be significant.

There are a number of possible locations for a naval base. China's construction of a naval port facility in Sri Lanka, for instance, is popularly viewed as providing a naval foothold in the Indian Ocean region. The Hambantota Development Zone (HDZ) is a $2 billion joint-venture agreement between China and Sri Lanka that includes deep-water facilities for commercial and military vessels. Yet the facility's proximity to India risks damaging relations with one of China's strategic partners, and it is not clear whether the port is indeed being built for dual-use purposes.[28] More promising would be a naval port facility at Djibouti. The presence of other foreign naval forces would certainly provide China with an excuse to establish its own facility without significantly worsening tensions.

Moreover, growing instability in Yemen will have only hardened views on the need for a naval base. The risk for China is that, since Yemen and Somalia neighbor each other across the Gulf of Aden, if Yemen's government were to collapse, the risk of piracy would only grow. In 2009, the international community held a conference on Yemen in response to the worsening conflict between the government and Houthi rebels, and the attempted attack by an Al Qaeda sympathizer, Umar Farouk Abdul Mutallab, on a flight traveling between Amsterdam and Detroit on 25 December 2009, after having received technical assistance from Al Qaeda in Yemen. The Chinese government's "formal" response offered few clues to its concerns other than emphasizing the need to restore order to the country.

However, an article on China Energy Web voiced other "informal" concerns, arguing that unrest in Yemen may threaten China's oil imports from the region. The author said, "The United States recognizes Yemen's geographic ability to choke China's oil import life lines," and then hinted that the United States may bring the war on terror to Yemen, and "strangle China's oil imports and strangle China's economy."[29] The author was a reporter, not an official. But the fact that he was considering Yemen in this manner raises the possibility that officials are as well. China certainly has commercial interests in Yemen, primarily in the construction sector, and many of its top Arabic-speaking diplomats have also served in the country. So China is unlikely to remain passive should Yemen's collapse result in American intervention.

◆ ◆ ◆

The large number of Chinese nationals in the Gulf and the threat of piracy in the Gulf of Aden are a challenge to the sustainability of China's policy of non-intervention in affairs outside the country's core interests. But it is China's relations with Iran and Saudi Arabia that are arguably the most serious challenge.

It is tempting to assume, from reading the English-language press, that China's relations with Iran are stronger than its relations with other countries in the region. Certainly China has had a far longer relationship with Iran than it has had with most other Gulf countries. The two sides first established relations in 1971. China's exports to Iran have also grown from just $1 billion in 2001 to over $10 billion by 2009, while China's oil imports from Iran account for 13 percent of the country's total oil imports.[30] Yet China's exports to Saudi Arabia have grown at a similar rate during the same period, this in spite of the country's smaller domestic population of just 26 million, against Iran's 74 million. Moreover, its exports to Saudi Arabia remained strong during the economic crisis even as exports to Iran fell sharply. Equally, China's oil imports from Saudi Arabia account for a large 19 percent of its total imports. There is thus a case to make that Saudi Arabia is increasingly the more important economic partner.

Importantly, Iran and Saudi Arabia have often vied for influence in the region, and Iran's efforts to acquire nuclear capabilities, either for commercial or military use, have further exacerbated tensions between the two. The growing conflict between Sunni and Shia communities in the region has only further worsened these tensions, while Saudi Arabia has often been caught on the back foot by popular support for such Shiite groups as Hezbollah. The growing tensions between Riyadh and Tehran are a problem for Beijing. In the event of open conflict, China might be expected to take sides. On a 2010 visit to Saudi Arabia, the author found his audience most interested to hear about China's views on Iran, and while the majority of Saudis were not hostile toward China's non-interventionist stance, they certainly worry it is helping soften the impact of international sanctions.

China's position is thus increasingly complicated. China desires to maintain strong relations with Iran, given the country's importance as an oil exporter. Yet China's failure to support international sanctions may be perceived by the rest of the Gulf as assisting Iran in attempting to acquire nuclear weapons. If so, this would make it increasingly difficult for China to argue that it is indeed pursuing a policy of "non-intervention" in the region. China's position toward Iran was accordingly at an inflection point in 2010. There was no indication that Saudi Arabia was lobbying China to take a stronger stance toward Iran, but reports by the *Wall Street Journal* implied that the United States was certainly encouraging Saudi Arabia to take a stronger stance.[31] A visit by Israeli officials to China in February 2010, reportedly to talk about Iran, also underscored the challenges for China's policy of non-intervention.

It was thus interesting to read an article published by *Huanqiu*, a hardline Chinese-language foreign affairs magazine, in January 2010 that pointed to an increasingly nuanced position.[32] The author, Yin Gang, works at the Chinese Academy for Social Sciences. His views were not official policy, but they are indicative of official thinking. The type of language he used was also refreshingly frank, and a few points, in particular, are worth highlighting. Yin began by empathizing with Iran by saying, "China understands Iran's desire for nuclear deterrent capability. China's nuclear deterrent capability was difficult to achieve under Western pressure. But times have changed. China and Iran are both signatories to the non-proliferation agreement. We should respect these principles." However, he then more forcibly argued that "China cannot ignore global opinion. It very well understands that its Arab and Jewish friends don't want to see the Iranian nuclear problem end tragically." He later continues, "Under no conditions will China accede to Iran's demands, only to hurt the Arab and other countries' feelings." Yin wrote that China, as a member of the United Nations Security Council, has previously voted in favor of modest sanctions in order to make Iran "wake up." He voices his frustration, in particular, at Iran's decision to secretly build a second uranium enrichment plant. Iran's failure to restrain itself, according to Yin, could result in "another arms race" in the Middle East. In 2010, events were moving fast. However, it is this concern of another arms race, or growing tensions between China's major oil suppliers, which suggest the Middle East is more likely than other parts of the world to force China to take a more interventionist stance. The region has certainly in the past called on the major powers to take a side in conflicts.

◆ ◆ ◆

China's return to the Gulf is an event of great strategic significance. Symbolically, it echoes the historic visit of Admiral Zheng He and his treasure ships in the 1400s. In doing so, it draws parallels between China's successes today and those six centuries ago when the country was last both an economic power and still engaged with the global economy. It only hardens views that China's rise is not a blip, but rather part of a historic global rebalancing. This makes China a potential game-changer. It was not a colonial occupier in the Middle East. It does not have a large Jewish lobby. It is attempting, at least, to stay clear of the region's politics. It will eventually be a larger oil importer from the region than either Europe or the United States. It is already a growing military competitor to the United States, and its threat will grow further with the inevitable creation of a blue-water navy.

Yet China need not be a threat. First, it has similar objectives in the region to the United States. It desires a stable Middle East that exports oil without restriction to the rest of the world, and with governments capable of curbing the extremist elements that are a growing threat to foreign nationals. Second, China is potentially a positive economic influence, such as by constructing cheap infrastructure, or extracting oil from high-risk countries. For these reasons, the Western powers must be ready to welcome China's return to the region. To oppose China's return would be to fight the inevitable while making the negotiation of multilateral settlements of the region's problems more difficult. But to welcome China's return will equally require a different way of thinking. Europe and the United States share similar heritages and this has made settlements easier to reach. But even so, conflicts between France and the United States, for instance, are not uncommon. The potential for such conflicts between China and the United States will be all the greater.

China's rise also offers an opportunity for the Gulf to rebalance its relationship with the United States. The region has long chafed at the United States' perceived economic and military hegemony. The Gulf's leadership is likely to use China's rise as a way to break this hegemony. But it is unlikely they will abandon the United States entirely. The United States still clearly plays an important role in the region's security, either through its arm sales or military bases in the region. Long-standing personal and political relationships between the Gulf and the United States also help to secure the relationship. China, by contrast, will take time to build similar relationships with the Gulf. Still, the Gulf's leadership is more likely to use China's rise as a way to signal that the United States is no longer their only partner, and to force the United States to take more heed of the region's interests.

Chapter 1. The Portuguese Presence in the Persian Gulf

1. I use the term Persian Gulf unapologetically, not to please the Iranians, who insist on it, but because they are right, since this is the term for the waterway that has been in use since antiquity.

2. A conference held in Paris in 2007 resulted in the publication of: Dejanirah Couto and Rui Manuel Loureiro, eds., *Revisiting Hormuz: Portuguese Interactions in the Persian Gulf Region in the Early Modern Period* (Wiesbaden: Harrassowitz Verlag, 2008). The meeting convened at the Smithsonian Institution in Washington in the same year produced Rudi Matthee and Jorge Flores, eds., *Portugal, the Persian Gulf, and Safavid Persia* (Leuven, Belgium: Peeters, 2011).

3. Sanjay Subrahmanyam, "Written on Water: Designs and Dynamics in the Portuguese Estado da Índia," in *Empires: Perspectives from Archaeology and History*, ed. Susan E. Alcock et al. (Cambridge, UK: Cambridge University Press, 2001), 42–69.

4. João Teles e Cunha, "The Portuguese Presence in the Persian Gulf," in *The Persian Gulf in History*, ed. Lawrence G. Potter (New York: Palgrave Macmillan, 2009), 208.

5. Ibid.

6. See Willem Floor, *The Persian Gulf: A Political and Economic History of Five Port Cities, 1500–1730* (Washington, DC: Mage Publishers, 2006), 231.

7. For this, see James Onley, *The Arabian Frontier of the British Raj: Merchants, Rulers, and the British in the Nineteenth-Century Gulf* (Oxford: Oxford University Press, 2008).

8. For a recent study that makes a strong argument for a forward-looking, determined, and robust Ottoman Indian Ocean strategy, see Giancarlo Casale, *The Ottoman Age of Exploration* (Oxford: Oxford University Press, 2010). This remains contested. For an alternative view, see Svat Soucek, chap. 10 in *The Persian Gulf: Its Past and Present* (Costa Mesa, CA: Mazda Publishers, 2008).

9. On De Gouvea, see Carlos Alonso, O.S.A. [Ordo Sancti Augustini (Order of Saint Augustine)], *Antonio de Gouvea, O.S.A., Diplomatico y visitador apostolico en Persia (†1628)* (Valladolid, Spain: Estudio Agustiniano, 2000).

10. See Rudi Matthee, "The Politics of Protection: European Missionaries in Iran during the Reign of Shah Abbas I (1587–1629)," in *Contacts and Controversies between Muslims, Jews, and Christians in the Ottoman Empire and Pre-Modern Iran*, ed. Sabine Schmidtke and Camille Adang (Würzburg, Germany: Ergon Verlag, 2010), 245–271.

11. For this, see Rudolph Matthee, *The Politics of Trade in Safavid Iran: Silk for Silver, 1600–1730* (Cambridge, UK: Cambridge University Press, 1999).

12. Niels Steensgaard, *The Asian Trade Revolution of the Seventeenth Century: The East India Companies and the Decline of the Caravan Trade* (Chicago and London: The University of Chicago Press, 1973).

13. See Glenn J. Ames, *Renascent Empire? The House of Braganza and the Quest for Stability in Portuguese Monsoon Asia, ca. 1640–1683* (Amsterdam: Amsterdam University Press, 2000), 12–14, for the standard reasons scholars have advanced to explain the decline of the Portuguese in Asia.

14. Floor, *The Persian Gulf*, 467.

Chapter 2. The Dutch in the Persian Gulf

1. Lawrence G. Potter, introduction to *The Persian Gulf in History*, ed. Lawrence G. Potter (New York: Palgrave Macmillan, 2009), 7.

2. For a thoughtful discussion on the historiography of the Persian Gulf, as well as its historic regional identity and people, see Potter, *The Persian Gulf in History*, 1–24.

3. Willem Floor, "Dutch Relations with the Persian Gulf," in *The Persian Gulf in History*, ed. Lawrence G. Potter (New York: Palgrave Macmillan, 2009), 233.

4. Jonathan I. Israel, *Dutch Primacy in World Trade, 1585–1740* (Oxford: Clarendon Press, 1989), 12.

5. Immanuel Wallerstein, *The Modern World-System I: Capitalist Agriculture and the Origins of the European World-Economy in the Sixteenth Century* (New York: Academic Press, 1974), 196–197.

6. Immanuel Wallerstein, *The Modern World-System II: Mercantilism and the Consolidation of the European World Economy, 1600–1750* (New York: Academic Press, 1980).

7. Israel, *Dutch Primacy*, 6; Wallerstein, *The Modern World System II*, 38–39. Wallerstein defines "hegemony" as "a situation wherein the products of a given core state are produced so efficiently that they are by and large competitive even in other core states, and therefore the given core state will be the primary beneficiary of a maximally free world market." In other words, "there is a . . . moment in time when a given core power can manifest *simultaneously* productive,

commercial, and financial superiority *over all other core powers*. This momentary summit is what we call hegemony."

8. Israel, *Dutch Primacy*, 2–3.

9. Ibid., 13.

10. Wallerstein, *The Modern World-System II*, 38–39; Israel, *Dutch Primacy*, vii.

11. Israel, *Dutch Primacy*, 38–79.

12. C. R. Boxer, *The Dutch Seaborne Empire, 1600–1800* (London: Hutchinson, 1965; New York: Alfred A. Knopf, 1965; London: Penguin Books, 1990), 29. Citation refers to the Penguin edition.

13. For discussions, see, for example, Israel, *Dutch Primacy*, especially 7–37; and J. de Vries and A. van der Woude, *The First Modern Economy: Success, Failure, and Perseverance of the Dutch Economy, 1500–1815* (Cambridge: Cambridge University Press, 1997).

14. Israel, *Dutch Primacy*, 16–17, 415.

15. Holden Furber, *Rival Empires of Trade in the Orient, 1600–1800* (Minneapolis: University of Minnesota Press, 1976), 7–8.

16. Femme S. Gaastra, "The Dutch East India Company in National and International Perspective," in *Les Flottes des Compagnie des Indes, 1600–1857*, ed. Philippe Haudrère (Vincennes, France: Service Historique de la Marine, 1996), 299.

17. Glenn J. Ames, *The Globe Encompassed: The Age of European Discovery, 1500–1700* (Upper Saddle River, NJ: Pearson Prentice Hall, 2008), 102–103; M. A. P. Meilink-Roelofsz, "Aspects of Dutch Colonial Development in Asia in the Seventeenth Century," in *Britain and the Netherlands in Europe and Asia*, ed. J. S. Bromley and E. H. Kossman (New York: St. Martin's Press, 1968), 61–62.

18. Kerry Ward, *Networks of Empire: Forced Migration in the Dutch East India Company* (Cambridge: Cambridge University Press, 2009), 59.

19. Om Prakash, *The Dutch East India Company and the Economy of Bengal, 1630–1720* (Princeton, NJ: Princeton University Press, 1985), 7.

20. Ames, *The Globe Encompassed*, 115; Meilink-Roelofsz, "Aspects of Dutch Colonial Development," 78.

21. Leonard Blussé and George Winius, "The Origin and Rhythm of Dutch Aggression against the Estado da Índia, 1601–1661," in *Indo-Portuguese History: Old Issues, New Questions*, ed. T. R. de Souza (Delhi: Concept, 1984), 73–83.

22. De Vries and Van der Woude, *The First Modern Economy*, 386.

23. Meilink-Roelofsz, "Aspects of Dutch Colonial Development," 64; Gaastra, "The Dutch East India Company in National and International Perspective," 315.

24. Meilink-Roelofsz, "Aspects of Dutch Colonial Development," 63.

25. Potter, *The Persian Gulf in History*, 1; Prakash, *The Dutch East India Company and the Economy of Bengal*, 5.

26. D. W. Davies, A *Primer of Dutch Seventeenth Century Overseas Trade* (The Hague: Martinus Nijhoff, 1961), 94–95; Femme Gaastra, *The Dutch East India Company: Expansion and Decline* (Zutphen, the Netherlands: Walburg Pers., 2003), 50–52; Ward, *Networks of Empire*, 60; Furber, *Rival Empires of Trade*, 9.

27. Floor, "Dutch Relations with the Persian Gulf," 236. For more on France's efforts in the Persian Gulf, see Israel, *Dutch Primacy*, 288; and Anna Kroell, *Louis XIV, la Perse et Mascate* (Paris: Société d'Histoire de l'Orient, 1977).

28. Rudi Matthee, "Boom and Bust: The Port of Basra in the Sixteenth and Seventeenth Centuries," in *The Persian Gulf in History*, ed. Lawrence G. Potter (New York: Palgrave Macmillan, 2009), 113; Davies, *A Primer*, 96.

29. Matthee, "Boom and Bust," 111.

30. Floor, "Dutch Relations with the Persian Gulf," 254.

31. Furber, *Rival Empires of Trade*, 46. Spain/Portugal had not delivered military aid promised for use against the Turks.

32. Davies, *A Primer*, 97; and João Teles e Cunha, "The Portuguese Presence in the Persian Gulf," in *The Persian Gulf in History*, ed. Lawrence G. Potter (New York: Palgrave Macmillan, 2009), 208, 216.

33. Michael Howard, *War in European History* (Oxford: Oxford University Press, 1979), chap. 3.

34. For an overview of VOC military power and weaponry, see Tristan Mostert, "Chain of Command: The Military System of the Dutch East India Company, 1655–1663" (master's thesis, Leiden University, 2007), chap. 2, esp. 17–37; and D. de Iongh, *Het Krijgswezen onder de Oostindische Compagnie* (The Hague: WP van Stockum en Zn., 1950).

35. Gaastra, "The Dutch East India Company in National and International Perspective," 311; and Mostert,"Chain of Command," 22–25. For a table documenting the number of sailors and soldiers who worked for the VOC and the Dutch Republic, 1630–1770, see Gaastra, "The Dutch East India Company in National and International Perspective," 307.

36. Mostert, "Chain of Command," 25–27.

37. Victor Enthoven, "Van Steunpilaar tot Blok aan het Been: De VOC en de Unie," in *De Verenigde Oost-Indische Compagnie: Tussen Oorlog en Diplomatie*, ed. Gerrit Knaap and Ger Teitler (Leiden, the Netherlands: KITLV Uitgeverij, 2002), 35–58. For more on Dutch trade companies and privateering, see Virginia Lunsford, *Piracy and Privateering in the Golden Age Netherlands* (New York: Palgrave Macmillan, 2005), 9–34.

38. Niels Steensgaard, "The Dutch East India Company as an Institutional Innovation," in *Dutch Capitalism and World Capitalism*, ed. Maurice Aymard (Cambridge: Cambridge University Press, 1977), 235–258. For case studies of particular VOC land/sea campaigns undertaken, see Mostert, "Chain of Command," chap. 4, 76–123; and C. R. Boxer, "The Siege of Fort Zeelandia and the Capture of Formosa from the Dutch, 1661–1662," in *Dutch Merchants*

and Mariners in Asia, 1602–1795, ed. C. R. Boxer (London: Variorum Reprints, 1988), 16–47.

39. Mostert, "Chain of Command," 10–11.

40. Jan Glete, "Warfare at Sea," in *War in the Early Modern World, 1450–1815*, ed. Jeremy Black (London: Routledge, 1998), 25–52; Geoffrey Parker, *The Military Revolution: Military Innovation and the Rise of the West, 1500–1800* (Cambridge: Cambridge University Press, 2000), chap. 3; Carlo M. Cipolla, *Guns, Sails, and Empire: Innovation and the Early Phases of European Expansion, 1400–1700* (Manhattan, KS: Sunflower University Press, 1985), chap. 2.

41. Jaap Bruijn, *The Dutch Navy of the Seventeenth and Eighteen Centuries* (Columbia: University of South Carolina Press, 1993). Naval historians generally view the Dutch as the supreme naval power up to about 1650, after which point England's Royal Navy became increasingly dominant.

42. Jaap R. Bruijn, "Facing a New World: The Dutch Navy Goes Overseas (ca. 1750–ca. 1850)," in *Colonial Empires Compared: Britain and the Netherlands, 1750–1850. Papers Delivered to the Fourteenth Anglo-Dutch Historical Conference, 2000*, ed. Bob Moore and Henk van Nierop (Aldershot, Hampshire, UK: Ashgate, 2003), 113–115.

43. Mostert, "Chain of Command," 18.

44. Furber, *Rival Empires of Trade*, 45; Mostert, "Chain of Command," 40–45 and 52–54; and J. R. Bruijn, F. Gaastra, and I. Schöffer, *Dutch Asiatic Shipping in the 17th and 18th Centuries* (The Hague: Nijhoff, 1979–87), 1:23–27, 40.

45. Anthony Reid, *Europe and Southeast Asia: The Military Balance* (Townsville, Queensland, Australia: James Cook University of North Queensland Press, 1982), 6–7; and Mostert, "Chain of Command," 18.

46. All of the company's operations in Asia were organized according to regional "directorates."

47. On Basra, see Rudi Matthee, "Boom and Bust," 110, 114–120; and Floor, "Dutch Relations with the Persian Gulf," 243.

48. Floor, "Dutch Relations with the Persian Gulf," 240.

49. Prakash, *The Dutch East India Company and the Economy of Bengal*, 172; and Floor, "Dutch Relations with the Persian Gulf," 240–248. See these sources for the contracts' specific details over time.

50. Davies, *A Primer*, 99.

51. All earnings assessments and data in this paragraph come from Prakash, *The Dutch East India Company and the Economy of Bengal*, 172–173; Davies, *A Primer*, 99–100; and Floor, "Dutch Relations with the Persian Gulf," 254–255. For details about the value of the silk trade over the years, see Floor, "Dutch Relations with the Persian Gulf," 251–252. For a detailed profile of profits during the eighteenth century, see Floor, "Dutch Relations with the Persian Gulf," 255, table 12.4.

52. J. E. Peterson, "Britain and the Gulf: At the Periphery of Empire," in *The Persian Gulf in History*, ed. Lawrence G. Potter (New York: Palgrave Macmillan, 2009), 278.

53. Israel, *Dutch Primacy*, 212.

54. Davies, *A Primer*, 98.

55. Floor, "Dutch Relations with the Persian Gulf," 240.

56. Prakash, *The Dutch East India Company and the Economy of Bengal*, 27.

57. Ward, *Networks of Empire*, 60.

58. Om Prakash, "Asian Trade and European Impact: A Study of the Trade from Bengal, 1630–1720," in *Precious Metals and Commerce: The Dutch East India Company in the Indian Ocean Trade* (Aldershot, Hampshire, UK: Variorum, 1994), chap. IV, 48.

59. Prakash, "Asian Trade and European Impact," 46–47.

60. Israel, *Dutch Primacy*, 180.

61. All import data comes from Prakash, *The Dutch East India Company and the Economy of Bengal*, 172–173, 176–177; Israel, *Dutch Primacy*, 179; and Davies, *A Primer*, 100.

62. Floor, "Dutch Relations with the Persian Gulf," 253.

63. Om Prakash, "Precious Metal Flows in Asia and World Economic Integration in the Seventeenth Century," in *Precious Metals and Commerce: The Dutch East India Company in the Indian Ocean Trade*, chap. IX, 88. See also F. S. Gaastra, "The Export of Precious Metals from Europe to Asia by the Dutch East India Company, 1602–1795," in *Precious Metals in the Later Medieval and Early Modern World*, ed. J. F. Richards (Durham, NC: Carolina Academic Press, 1983), 465–467.

64. All export data comes from Prakash, *The Dutch East India Company and the Economy of Bengal*, 172; Floor, "Dutch Relations with the Persian Gulf," 252; and Davies, *A Primer*, 100.

65. Davies, *A Primer*, 98–99.

66. Israel, *Dutch Primacy*, 152–153.

67. Meilink-Roelofsz, "Aspects of Dutch Colonial Development," 66.

68. Floor, "Dutch Relations with the Persian Gulf," 238–239.

69. Meilink-Roelofsz, "Aspects of Dutch Colonial Development," 64. Also see B. H. M. Vlekke, *Geschiedenis van den Indischen Archipel van het Begin der Beschaving tot het Doorbreken der Nationale Revolutie* (Roermond, the Netherlands: Romen & Zonon, 1947), 171; and M. A. P. Meilink-Roelofsz, *Asian Trade and European Influence in the Indonesian Archipelago between 1500 and about 1630* (The Hague: Nijhoff, 1962), 211–213, 215.

70. Floor, "Dutch Relations with the Persian Gulf," 257.

71. Ibid., 240.

72. Ibid., 239, 242–248. For more on VOC military operations against the Iranians, see Willem M. Floor and Mohammad Hassan Faghfoory, *The First Dutch-Persian Commercial Conflict: The Attack on Qeshm Island, 1645* (Costa Mesa, CA: Mazda, 2004); and Willem M. Floor, *Commercial Conflict between Persia and the Netherlands, 1712–1718* (Durham, UK: Centre for Middle Eastern and Islamic Studies, University of Durham Press, 1988).

73. Floor, "Dutch Relations with the Persian Gulf," 244.

74. Ibid., 243 and 254.

75. Ibid., 239.

76. Ward, *Networks of Empire*, 60.

77. Furber, *Rival Empires of Trade*, 143.

78. Floor, "Dutch Relations with the Persian Gulf," 248–249. See also Willem Floor, *The Afghan Occupation of Persia, 1722–1730* (Zutphen, the Netherlands: Walburg Pers., 2003).

79. Floor, "Dutch Relations with the Persian Gulf," 249–250. See also Willem Floor, "Dutch Trade in Afsharid Persia (1730–1753)," *Studia Iranica* 34 (2005): 43–94; Willem Floor, "The Iranian Navy in the Gulf during the Eighteenth Century," *Iranian Studies* 20 (1987): 31–53.

80. Floor, "Dutch Relations with the Persian Gulf," 250–251. See also Willem Floor, "The Decline of the Dutch East India Company in Bandar Abbas (1747–1759)," *Moyen Orient & Ocean Indien* 6 (1989): 45–80.

81. Floor, "Dutch Relations with the Persian Gulf," 255; Prakash, "Precious Metal Flows in Asia," 88. See also Gaastra, "The Exports of Precious Metals," 465–467.

82. Floor, "Dutch Relations with the Persian Gulf," 251.

83. De Vries and Van der Woude, *The First Modern Economy*, 449–455.

84. Peterson, "Britain and the Gulf," 278–279.

85. Furber, *Rival Empires of Trade*, 282–284; Peterson, "Britain and the Gulf," 278–279.

86. Israel, *Dutch Primacy*, 399–400.

87. Ibid., 377–404.

88. Floor, "Dutch Relations with the Persian Gulf," 256.

Chapter 3. The Great Game and Power Projection

1. See Robert Johnson, *Spying for Empire: The Great Game in Central and South Asia, 1757–1947* (London: Greenhill, 2006).

2. Cited in "The Persian Empire: England and Russia in the East," *The Westminster Review* (1881), art. IV, 442.

3. After the defeat of Persia in the Caucasus and the Treaty of Turkmenchay in 1828, Russian influence in Persia had increased. Russian officers trained the

Persian army and more Russian officials made their way to Tehran, which explains their presence in the Persian forces at Herat.

4. H. Pottinger, *Account of the Defence of Herat*, L/MIL/17/14/22, India Office Records (IOR), British Library, London; George Pottinger, *The Afghan Connection* (Edinburgh: Scottish Academic Press, 1983), 44.

5. G. J. Alder, "The Key to India? Britain and the Herat Problem, 1830–63," *Middle East Studies* 10 (1974): 306.

6. [G. R. Elsmie], *Epitome of Correspondence Regarding our Relations with Afghanistan and Herat* (Lahore: Government Press, 1863), 50.

7. Charles John, 1st Earl Canning, to Vernon Smith, 7 December 1856, Can/32 no. 44, Mss Eur B 324, IOR. Disraeli later put it even more succinctly, telling the House of Lords that the "key of India is not Herat and Candahar [sic]. The key of India is London," suggesting diplomacy between the capitals was the best form of defense. ("The Persian Empire," 414.)

8. Edward Ingram, *The Beginning of the Great Game in Asia, 1828–34* (Oxford: Oxford University Press, 1979), 50–84; C. J. Barlett, *Defence and Diplomacy: Britain and the Great Powers, 1815–1914* (Manchester: Manchester University Press, 1993), 27.

9. David Gillard, *The Struggle for Asia: A Study in British and Russian Imperialism* (London: Methuen, 1977), 30–33.

10. Shah Nasr ud-Din had spent two years suppressing a rebellion in Khorasan following his accession in 1848, but a new round of repression began in 1852 when the Babis of Meshed tried to assassinate him. The governor of Herat had allowed Persian troops into the city to help quell disorders that had spilled over the border, but an agreement was concluded with the British envoy that Persian forces would not enter the city unless it was occupied by a foreign power. However, the withdrawal of the British mission in 1854, increasing Russian pressure, and the rebellion of the Afghan Mohammed Yusuf Sadozai in Herat had prompted the shah to act.

11. Captain G. H. Hunt and George Townsend, *Outram and Havelock's Persian Campaign, to which is prefixed a Summary of Persian History, an Account of the Various Differences between England and Persia, and an Inquiry into the Origin of the Late War* (London: Routledge, 1858).

12. The papers of Sir James Outram (1803–63), including his handwritten reports from the campaign, are held at The National Army Museum (NAM), London, 6308–44, NRA 35498.

13. Sir James Outram, *Lieutenant General Sir James Outram's Persian Campaign in 1857: Comprising Orders and Despatches relating to the Military Operations in Persia* (London: printed for private circulation only by Smith, Elder, 1860); Lionel J. Trotter, *The Bayard of India: A Life of General Sir James Outram, Bart., G.C.B., etc.* (Edinburgh: Blackwood and Sons, 1903), British Library, London, W485855.

14. *Papers of General John Jacob relative to the Persian War*, IOR/H/552, 1840–1872, Secret Committee to Lieutenant-General Sir James Outram, 195–201, 6 March 1857, with copy of letter from Lord Clarendon (secretary of state for foreign affairs) relative to conclusion of peace with Persia, 233–54, 11 and 15 May 1857, and Russian troops on the Persian Frontier and the Persian Treaty, IOR.

15. R. F. Thomson to Salisbury, 26 April 1876, no. 16, Secret, FO 65, The National Archives (TNA), London.

16. Report of the War Minister to the Tsar, 8/20 April 1878, A. Iliasov, ed., *Prisoedinenie Turkmenii k Rossii* (Ashkhabad, 1960), no. 177, 332–336, cited in Firuz Kazemzadeh, *Russia and Britain in Persia, 1864–1914* (New Haven, CT: Yale University Press, 1968), 46.

17. M. A. Terentiev, *Istoriia zavoevaniia Srednei Azii*, 2:428–430, cited in Kazemzadeh, *Russia and Britain in Persia*, 47.

18. R. Thomson to Lord Salisbury, 6 July 1878, no. 84, Secret, Letters from India, L/PS/7/20, 1878; see also telegrams from Ronald Thomson to viceroy, Letters from India, L/PS/7 /19, 1878. See also FO 65/1028-34, TNA, London.

19. R. Thomson to Lord Salisbury, 14 August 1878, no. 123, Secret, Letters from India, 1878, L/PS/7/20, IOR, and FO 65/1028-34, TNA, London.

20. R. L. Greaves, *Persia and the Defence of India, 1884–1892* (London: University of London Press, 1959), 50.

21. Sir A. Alison, Memorandum, 16 April 1880, FO 65/1100, TNA.

22. Military Parliamentary Papers, C-2811, Memorandum on our future policy in Afghanistan, 16 August 1880, no. 7, 43–44, IOR, London.

23. Lord Hartington to Lord Ripon, 11 November 1880, no. 45, Secret, Political and Secret Dispatches to India, L/PS//7/6 (1880), 379–86.

24. See Edmond O'Donovan, *The Merv Oasis: Travels and Adventures East of the Caspian, 1879–80–81*, vol. 1 (London: G. P. Putnam's and Sons, 1882).

25. Baba Khan, Native Agent at Meshed, 6, 9, and 18 July 1885, Dufferin Papers, D1071H/M12/13, Public Record Office of Northern Ireland.

26. Major J. S. Rothwell, "England's Means of Offence against Russia," 7 July 1884, L/PS/20, IOR.

27. Wolfe Murray, "Military Operations in the Event of War with Russia," 17 April 1885, L/PS/20, IOR.

28. In 1887, one such skirmish between the Afghans and Russians resulted in a boundary revision; see Salisbury to George Frederick Charles, Baron de Staal, 7 July 1892, FO 65/1439, 887, TNA.

29. M. S. Bell, "British Commercial Enterprise in Persia and Communications Required to Develop It" (pamphlet), 30 November 1887, 2.

30. Wolff to Salisbury, 14 November 1888, FO 539/40, TNA.

31. Mr. E. Law [commercial attaché to Tehran] to White, 13 December 1888, FO 539/40, TNA .

32. Brackenbury to Foreign Office, 9 February 1889, FO 65/1377, TNA.

33. Wolff to Salisbury, 19 February 1889, FO 65/1377, TNA. See also Jennifer Siegel, *Endgame: Britain, Russia, and the Final Struggle for Central Asia* (London: I. B. Tauris, 2003).

34. Major H. A. Sawyer, "Summary of Events for the Year 1888," 4 January 1889, FO 65/1377, TNA.

35. Major Wolfe Murray [Intelligence Division], "Memorandum by Intelligence Department on a projected line of Railway from the Caspian through Tehran to the Persian Gulf," 15 March 1889, FO 539/41, TNA.

36. Brackenbury to Currie, 28 March 1889, FO 78/1378, TNA.

37. Salisbury to Wolff, 9 January 1890, FO 539/44, TNA.

38. Morier to Salisbury, 12 November 1890, FO 539/50, TNA.

39. Kazemzadeh, *Russia and Britain in Persia*, 314–315.

40. J. Rabino to Colonel Picot, 14 May 1898, confidential, FO 60/601, TNA.

41. H. M. Durand to Lord Salisbury, 31 March 1899, FO 60/630, TNA.

42. *Novoe Vremya*, 9/21 May 1899, FO 65/1593, TNA.

43. Kazemzadeh, *Russia and Britain in Persia*, 326–327.

44. Ibid., 334.

45. "Dnevnik A. N. Kuropatkina," *Krasnyi Arkhiv*, 2 (1922): 31, cited in Kazemzadeh, *Russia and Britain in Persia*, 339.

46. Andrew Roberts, *Salisbury: Victorian Titan* (London: Weidenfeld and Nicolson, 1999), 769.

47. G. N. Curzon to Mrs. Cragie, cited in Earl of Ronaldshay, *The Life of Lord Curzon*, (London: Ernest Benn Ltd., 1928), 2:100–101.

48. Curzon papers, III/159/59/204, F1/12, Mss Eur F 11, IOR, cited in Roberts, *Salisbury*, 768.

49. David Holden, "Britain's Arabian Oil Empire, 1901–1971," in *The British Empire* (London: Orbis, 1980), 285.

50. Curzon to Lord Selbourne, Admiralty, 29 May 1901, Selbourne Papers, Bodleian Library, Oxford.

51. David Gilmour, *Curzon* (London: John Murray, 1994), 203.

52. Ibid., 269.

53. Ronaldshay, *The Life of Lord Curzon*, 2:316; see also Lord Curzon, *Lord Curzon in India: Being a Selection from his Speeches as Viceroy and Governor-General of India, 1898–1905* (New York: Macmillan, 1905), 500–507.

54. G. P. Gooch and Harold Temperley, *British Documents on the Origins of the War, 1898–1914*, vol. 4 (London: His Majesty's Stationery Office, 1927).

Chapter 4. The Gamekeeper versus the Mercenary Spirit

1. J. B. Kelly, *Britain and the Persian Gulf, 1795–1880* (Oxford: Clarendon Press, 1968, reissue 1991), 1.

2. Ibid.

3. Ibid.

4. The best account of the EIC's activities in the Gulf in the seventeenth and eighteenth centuries is in J. G. Lorimer, *Gazetteer of the Persian Gulf, Oman, and Central Arabia* (Calcutta: Government of India, 1908–15), 1:10–168.

5. See Kelly, *Britain and the Persian Gulf*, 62–98.

6. Ibid., 354–410.

7. See James Onley, "The Politics of Protection in the Gulf: The Arab Rulers and the British Resident in the Nineteenth Century," *New Arabian Studies* 6 (2004): 30–92.

8. Kelly, *Britain and the Persian Gulf*, 500–530.

9. J. B. Kelly, *Arabia, the Gulf, and the West*, (London: Weidenfeld and Nicolson, 1980), 186–187.

10. J. B. Kelly, "The Legal and Historical Basis of the British Position in the Persian Gulf," *Middle Eastern Affairs*, no. 1, St. Antony's Papers, no. 4 (London: Chatto & Windus, 1958).

11. J. B. Kelly, "The Future in Arabia," *International Affairs* 42, no. 4 (October 1966): 632–633.

12. Ian Spellar, "Naval Diplomacy: Operation *Vantage*, in *The Royal Navy and Maritime Power in the Twentieth Century*, ed. Ian Spellar (London: Frank Cass, 2005), 164–180.

13. Staff Report to the Committee on Foreign Relations, United States Senate, November 1987, "War in the Persian Gulf: The U.S. Takes Sides" (Washington, DC: U.S. Government Printing Office, 1987); Andrew Rathmell, "Threats to the Gulf—Part 1," *Jane's Intelligence Review*, March 1995, 129–132.

14. Kelly, *Arabia, the Gulf, and the West*, 274–289.

15. Ibid., 310–313.

16. H. St. J. B. Philby, *Arabia* (London: C. Scribner's & Sons, 1930), 181.

17. Kelly, *Arabia, the Gulf, and the West*, 69–78; see also J. B. Kelly, *Eastern Arabian Frontiers* (London: Faber & Faber, 1964).

18. Kelly, *Arabia, the Gulf, and the West*, 50–51.

Chapter 5. Why Didn't America Replace the British in the Persian Gulf?

1. Letter from U.S. Secretary of State Dean Rusk to British Secretary of State for Foreign Affairs George Brown, 6 January 1968, FCO 8, Box 36, File No. B 3/7, File Name: "Persian Gulf: Political Affairs (Ext): Bilateral: U.S. Interest In," The National Archives, Kew, England (hereafter cited as TNA).

2. Briefing Memorandum from the Assistant Secretary of State for Near Eastern and South Asian Affairs (Battle) to Secretary of State Rusk, Washington, D.C., 9 January 1968, Subject: British Plans to Accelerate Withdrawal of Military Presence from Persian Gulf: Your Meeting with Foreign Secretary Brown, 11 January 1968, in *Foreign Relations of the United States, 1964–1968*, vol. XXI, *Near East Region; Arabian Peninsula* (hereafter cited as *FRUS XXI*), ed. Nina Davis Howland (Washington, DC: U.S. Government Printing Office, 2000), Document 122, 256.

3. Ibid., 258.

4. Ibid.

5. Information Memorandum from the Assistant Secretary of State for Near Eastern and South Asian Affairs (Battle) to Secretary of State Rusk, Washington, D.C., 22 February 1968, Subject: Outlook in the Persian Gulf States, Source: National Archives and Records Administration, RG 59, Central Files 1967–69, POL 33 PERSIAN GULF, Secret, drafted by Brewer (Secretary of State Rusk's initials on the memorandum indicate that he read it), in *FRUS XXI*, 282.

6. Memorandum from the Deputy Assistant Secretary of Defense for International Security Affairs (Schwartz) to the Assistant Secretary of Defense for International Security Affairs (Warnke), I-22215/68, Washington, D.C., 22 April 1968. Subject "U.S. Arms Sales in the Persian Gulf," Source: Washington National Records Center, RG 330, OASD/ISA (Office of Assistant Secretary of Defense, International Security Affairs), Files: FRC 72 A 1498, Persian Gulf 000.1–1968, Secret, in *FRUS XXI*, 292.

7. Carl E. Bartch, U.S. State Department, Washington, D.C., 16 January 1968, in "U.S. Won't Fill Vacuum," *New York Times*, 17 January 1968.

8. Ibid.

9. Record of Meeting, IRG/NEA (Interdepartmental Regional Group/Office of Near Eastern Affairs), Washington, D.C., 1 February 1968, Interdepartmental Regional Group for Near East and South Asia, Record of IRG Meeting, 1 February 1968, Source: Central Intelligence Agency, DDO/NE (Critchfield) Files: Job 80–00105A, Box 2, IRG/NEA Working File, Communist Presence—Arabian Peninsula, Persian Gulf, Secret, in *FRUS XXI*, 272.

10. Memorandum from Secretary of Defense McNamara to the Secretary of the Air Force (Zuckert), I-23,914/64, Washington, D.C., 14 June 1965, Subject: Request for Approval of Facilities to Support Contingency Planning, Source: Washington National Records Center, RG 330 OASD/ISA Files: FRC 70 A 3717, 680.1, Indian Ocean Islands, Secret, Drafted by Lang, in *FRUS XXI*.

11. Memorandum from the Assistant Secretary of Defense for International Security Affairs (Warnke) to Secretary of Defense McNamara, I-23190/68, Washington, D.C., 12 June 1968, Subject: The Soviets and the Persian Gulf, Source: Washington National Records Center, RG 330, OSD Files: FRC 73 A 1250, Persian Gulf 800, Persian Gulf 1968, Secret, in *FRUS XXI*, 297.

12. Memorandum from the Deputy Secretary of Defense (Nitze) to the Chairman of the Joint Chiefs of Staff (Wheeler), Washington, D.C., 2 August 1968, Subject: Persian Gulf Study, Source: Washington National Records Center, RG 330, OSD Files: FRC 73 A 1250, Persian Gulf 092, 2 August 1968, Secret, in *FRUS* XXI, 304.

13. Memorandum from the Deputy Assistant Secretary of Defense for International Security Affairs (Schwartz) to the Assistant Secretary of Defense for International Security Affairs (Warnke), I-22215/68, Washington, D.C., 22 April 1968, Subject "U.S. Arms Sales in the Persian Gulf," Source: Washington National Records Center, RG 330, OASD/ISA Files: FRC 72 A 1498, Persian Gulf 000.1—1968, Secret, in *FRUS* XXI, 292.

14. Hedrick Smith, "U.S. Putting Hope in New Asia Blocs: Rostow Thinks Void Left by British Will Be Filled," *New York Times*, 20 January 1968, 3.

15. Sir Patrick Henry Dean, British Ambassador to the United States, British Embassy Washington, Telegram No. 725, titled "The Persian Gulf."

16. Sir Dennis Wright, "Discussions with United States Officials at the Foreign Office, Wednesday, 27 March 1968," 106, TNA.

17. Ibid.

18. Memorandum from the Assistant Secretary of Defense for International Security Affairs (Warnke) to Secretary of Defense McNamara, I-23190/68, Washington, D.C., 12 June 1968, Subject: The Soviets and the Persian Gulf, Source: Washington National Records Center, RG 330, OSD Files: FRC 73 A 1250, Persian Gulf 800, Persian Gulf 1968, Secret, in FRUS XXI, 297.

19. Ibid.

20. "USS Valcour (AVP-55, later AGF-1), 1946–1977--Views of the ship taken in 1946–1960," U.S. Navy Historical Center, cited 9 October 2006, http://www.history.navy.mil/photos/sh-usn/usnsh-v/avp55.htm.

21. A. B. Urwick, letter from British Embassy to British Foreign Office, Arabian Desk Officer, entitled "The Persian Gulf," 9 March 1968, FCO 8, Box 36, File No. B 3/7, File Name: "Persian Gulf: Political Affairs (Ext): Bilateral: U.S. Interest In," TNA.

22. A. B. Urwick, letter from A. B. Urwick (British Embassy Washington) to A. A. Acland (Arabian Department, London), entitled "The Future of Comideastfor," 12 February 1969, FCO 8, Box 935, File No. BN 3/304/2, File Name: "Persian Gulf: Political Affairs (Ext): Bilateral: U.S. Interest In: COMIDEASTFOR," TNA.

23. Ibid.

24. "U.S. Future Role in Persian Gulf," Times (London), 23 April 1970.

25. D. F. Murray, letter to Mr. Breeze, House of Commons, titled "Mideastfor," 12 December 1970, FCO 8, Box 1304, File Name: "United States Interest in Persian Gulf," TNA.

26. Sir Denis Allen, British Foreign Office, Memorandum of Record: Anglo-American Talks on the Middle East in the [U.S.] State Department, 13 September 1968, FCO 8, Number 37, Section B3/7, TNA.

27. R. A. Jones, Note for the Record, 31 December 1970, FCO 8, Box 1304, File Name: "United States Interest in Persian Gulf," TNA.

28. Ambassador John Patrick Walsh, telegram from Amembassy Kuwait to Secstate Washington Dc, Subject: "Future Arrangements for Mideastfor," 18 November 1970, 1105Z, RG 218: Records of the Chairman of the Joint Chiefs of Staff, Admiral Moorer, Box 106, File Name: "B-7: Middle East--General," Accession 92–0028, U.S. National Archives II, College Park, Maryland (hereafter cited as USNA2).

29. Thacher, telegram from Amembassy Jidda to Secstate Washington Dc, Subject: "Future Arrangements for Comideastfor," 18 November 1970, 1235Z, RG 218: Records of the Chairman of the Joint Chiefs of Staff, Admiral Moorer, Box 106, File Name: "B-7: Middle East--General," Accession 92–0028, USNA2.

30. Ibid.

31. D. F. Murray, letter to Mr. Breeze, House of Commons, titled "Mideastfor," FCO 8, 1304, 12 December 1970, TNA.

32. Ibid.

33. See Spencer Mawby, *British Policy in Aden and the Protectorates 1955–67* (London: Routledge, 2005).

34. "Soviet Experts' Plans in Iraq: Dams, Reservoirs, and 310-mile Canal," *Times* (London), 11 February 1960.

35. "Parties Reappear in Iraq: Communists One of First Three," *Times* (London), 10 February 1960.

36. Nicholas Herbert, "Visit to Gulf by Soviet Navy," *Times* (London), 13 May 1968.

37. Ibid.

38. Salvatore R. Mercogliano, "Military Sealift Command: Ships that Wait," in "American Merchant Marine at War," http://www.usmm.org/msts/wait.html (accessed 16 December 2011).

Chapter 6. Richard Nixon, Great Britain, and the Anglo-American Strategy of Turning the Persian Gulf into an Allied Lake

1. Lyndon Johnson to British prime minister Harold Wilson, 11 January 1968, National Security File, Special Head of State Correspondence, United Kingdom, Folder 2 of 4, Lyndon Baines Johnson Library (hereafter cited as LBJL), Austin, Texas.

2. Anthony Sampson, *The Arms Bazaar: The Companies, The Dealers, The Bribes: From Vickers to Lockheed* (London: Hodder and Stoughton, 1977), 259.

3. This argument is developed in Tore T. Petersen, *Richard Nixon, Great Britain, and the Anglo-American Alignment in the Persian Gulf and Arabian Peninsula* (Brighton, England and Portland, ME: Sussex Academic Press, 2009).

4. One notable exception is Simon Smith, "Power Transferred? Britain, the United States, and the Gulf, 1956–71," *Contemporary British History* 21, no. 1 (March 2007): 1–23; and Simon Smith, *Britain's Revival and Fall in the Gulf: Kuwait, Bahrain, Qatar, and the Trucial States, 1950–1971* (London: RoutledgeCurzon, 2004). Unfortunately, Smith confines himself largely to the transition between Johnson and Nixon in the Persian Gulf.

5. Stephen E. Ambrose, *Nixon: Ruin and Recovery, 1973–1990* (New York: Simon & Schuster, 1991), 168.

6. William B. Quandt, *American Diplomacy and the Arab–Israeli Conflict since 1967* (Berkeley, CA: University of California Press, 1993), 132; Robert Dallek, *Nixon and Kissinger: Partners in Power* (London: Allen Lane, 2007), 169–171; Burton I. Kaufman, *The Arab Middle East and the United States: Inter-Arab Rivalry and Superpower Diplomacy* (New York: Twayne Publishers, 1996), whose chapter on Nixon's Middle East policy deals with the Yom Kippur War.

7. Nixon to Legislative Leadership Meeting, 17 February 1970, in *Foreign Relations of the United States (FRUS), 1969–1976*, vol. 1, *Foundations of Foreign Policy, 1969–1972* (Washington, DC: Government Printing Office, 2003), 192.

8. See for instance John Freeman, UK ambassador to Washington, to Foreign and Commonwealth Office (hereafter cited as FCO with appropriate filing designations), 20 January 1970, FCO 7/1803/ALUS 1/2, The National Archives (TNA), Kew, England; Nixon "has repeatedly made it clear to me in terms which I can no longer doubt that he regards his Administration as having (and needing) more intimate relations with Britain than with any other foreign country."

9. FCO brief, 23 September 1970, FCO 7/1810/ NV (70) C1, TNA.

10. Henry Kissinger, *Years of Upheaval* (London: Weidenfeld and Nicolson, 1982), 141, 708 (for quote).

11. This argument is developed in Tore T. Petersen, "Post-Suez Consequences: Anglo-American Relations in the Middle East from Eisenhower to Nixon," in *Reassessing Suez 1956: New Perspectives on the Crisis and its Aftermath*, ed. Simon C. Smith (Aldershot, Hampshire, UK: Ashgate Publishing, 2008), 215–26.

12. Alan P. Dobson, *Anglo-American Relations in the Twentieth Century: Of Friendship, Conflict, and the Rise and Decline of Superpowers* (London: Routledge, 1995), 140; David Reynolds, *Britannia Overruled: British Policy and World Power in the 20th Century* (London: Longman, 1996), 241.

13. Memorandum of conversation (hereafter cited as MC), Nixon and Heath, 3 October 1970, FCO 7/1815/ALUS 2/5, TNA.

14. Uzi Rabi, *The Emergence of States in a Tribal Society: Oman under Sa'id bin Taymur, 1932–1970* (Brighton, England and Portland, ME: Sussex Academic Press, 2007), is one of the few studies based on the recently declassified archives.

15. Sisco to Rogers, 29 July 1970, United States Department of State Central File (Subject Numeric File), Political Affairs & Relations (hereafter cited as POL) 15–1 Oman, National Archives, College Park.

16. Wm. Roger Louis, "The British Withdrawal from the Gulf, 1967–71," *The Journal of Imperial and Commonwealth History* 231, no. 1 (January 2003): 83–108.

17. D. F. Hawley, "Oman: Annual Review for 1971," 3 January 1972, FCO 8/1848/ NBM 1/4, TNA.

18. For the importance of al-Buraimi, see Tore T. Petersen, "Anglo-American Rivalry in the Middle East: The Struggle for the Buraimi Oasis, 1952–1957, *The International History Review* 14, no. 1 (February 1992): 71–91.

19. MC, Rogers and Home, 11 July 1970, FCO 7/1828/ALUSJ/548/12, TNA.

20. MC, Heath, Home, Luce, et al., 22 July 1970, PREM 15/538/ 172/2, TNA.

21. John Lewis Gaddis, *Strategies of Containment: A Critical Appraisal of Postwar American National Security Policy* (New York: Oxford University Press, 1982), 298–299.

22. Nixon to Kissinger, 10 February 1970, "The President's Annual Review of U.S. Foreign Policy," 2/8/70, vol. 1, Folder 2 of 3, Richard Nixon Presidential Materials Staff, National Security File (hereafter cited as RNNSC), Box 325, National Archives, College Park, Maryland.

23. J. B. Kelly, *Arabia, the Gulf, and the West* (New York: Basic Books, 1980), 290. Kelly observes that the shah in 1967 invented the title Aryamehr (light of the Aryans) for himself.

24. Asadollah Alam, *The Shah and I: The Confidential Diary of Iran's Court, 1969–1977* (London: I. B. Tauris, 1991), 365. As late as April 1974, only 1 percent of Iranian villages were supplied with clean, piped drinking water, while only one of twenty-five villages had electricity.

25. Henry Kissinger, *White House Years* (Boston: Little, Brown and Company, 1979), 1261.

26. Tad Szulc, *New York Times*, 25 July 1971, 1. See for example: Douglas MacArthur, U.S. ambassador to Tehran, to Rogers, 25 January 1971; and MacArthur to Rogers, 2 February 1971; both in Iran, Jan–31 Aug 71, Folder 3, Box 602, RNNSC.

27. John J. Hess, *New York Times*, 3 October 1971, 84.

28. Ibid., 5 October 1971, 36.

29. Charlotte Curtis, *New York Times*, 13 October 1971, 3.

30. Loren Jenkins, *Newsweek*, 25 October 1971, 16.

31. "Iran: Let the World take Note," *Newsweek*, 11 October 1971, 19–20.

32. Saunders to Kissinger, 18 May 1972, Nixon Tehran briefing book, Folder 2 of 2, Box 479, RNNSC. This was, incidentally, the theme Nixon had also pursued in Moscow, observing to Kissinger while in the Soviet capital: "We would seek

to usher in a period of genuine power restraint." Kissinger, *White House Years*, 1209.

33. "Joint U.S.-Iranian Communiqué," 31 May 1972, *FRUS, 1969–1976*, vol. E-4, *Documents on Iran and Iraq, 1969–1972*, PDF version; Peter Ramsbothan, UK ambassador to Tehran, to Home, 1 June 1972, FCO 8/1884/NPB 3/304/1, TNA.

34. Ramsbothan to Home, "Iran: Annual Review for 1972," 22 December 1972, FCO 8/2049 NBP 1/2, TNA.

35. P. R. H. Wright, "PM dinner: suggested remarks," 23 June 1972, FCO 8/18888/NBP 3/548/5, TNA.

36. R. J. Andrew to the Lord Bridges, 24 July 1972, PREM 15/990, TNA.

37. *New York Times*, 10 September 1973.

38. Henry Kissinger, *Years of Renewal* (New York: Simon & Schuster, 1999), 396–397.

39. Sisco to Rogers, 18 May 1972, POL 7 Saud.

40. Morris to Home, 31 December 1970, FCO 8/1734/NBs1/2, TNA.

41. Parsons to Allen, 13 April 1972, FCO 8/1806/NB 25/1, TNA.

42. Anthony Royle, parliamentary undersecretary of state to General Basil Eugster, 10 April 1972, FCO 8/1914/NBS 10/3, TNA. For a discussion on the National Guard and Anglo-Saudi relations in the 1960s, see Tore T. Petersen, *The Decline of the Anglo-American Middle East, 1961–1969: A Willing Retreat* (Brighton, England and Portland, ME: Sussex Academic Press, 2006).

43. MC, Morriss and Saqqaf, 15 April 1972, FCO 8/1908/NBS 2/1, TNA.

44. Saunders to Scowcroft, 5 February 1973, Iran-Oil, HAK office files, Box 137, RNNSC.

45. See Akins to Davies, 20 November 1970, PET 6 Iran.

46. Julius Katz to Philip Trezise, 25 November 1970, PET 6 Iran.

47. Frank Brenchley, *Britain and the Middle East: An Economic History, 1945–87* (London: Lester Crook Academic Publishing, 1989), 205.

48. Daniel Yergin, *The Prize: The Epic Quest for Oil, Money, and Power* (New York: Simon & Schuster, 1992), 524, 555–558.

49. Melvin Small, *The Presidency of Richard Nixon* (Lawrence: University Press of Kansas, 1999), 138, 139. "OPEC's [Organization of the Petroleum Exporting Countries] supremacy over the oil companies meant that its Arab members could use the oil weapon in a crisis." See also F. Gregory Gause, "British and American Policies in the Persian Gulf, 1968–1973," *Review of International Studies* 2 (1985): 247–73.

50. Richard C. Thornton, *The Nixon Kissinger Years: The Reshaping of American Foreign Policy* (St. Paul, MN: Paragon House, 2001), 77–78, 83 (for last quote). Kissinger, *Years of Upheaval*, 863: Kissinger indirectly supports this conclusion in his memoirs by paraphrasing his aides' (Fred Bergsten and Harold Saunders) memorandum prior to the Tehran talks: "The rise in the price of energy would

affect primarily Europe and Japan and probably improve America's competitive position. To sustain a confrontation would require us to be prepared to ration oil at home to support the European economies." Franz Schurmann, *The Foreign Politics of Richard Nixon: The Grand Design* (Berkeley: Institute of International Studies, University of California, Berkeley, 1987), 273, 276, 277: Schurmann reaches a similar conclusion, noting the limited power of OPEC and wonders why "the camel sheikdoms and banana republics were turning the tables on the major oil companies—until then the most powerful cartel in the world."

51. Allen J. Matusow, *Nixon's Economy: Booms, Busts, Dollars, and Votes* (Lawrence: University Press of Kansas, 1998), 131.

52. Francisco Parra, *Oil Politics: A Modern History of Petroleum* (New York: I. B. Tauris, 2004), 114.

53. Bennett H. Wall, *Growth in a Changing Environment: A History of Standard Oil Company (New Jersey) Exxon Corporation, 1950–1975* (New York: McGraw-Hill Book Company, 1988), 765.

54. Kissinger, *Years of Renewal*, 667; Kelly, *Arabia*, 458: "The Arab oil producers are militarily insignificant—gazelles . . . in a world of lions," (quoting Senator William Fulbright); James E. Akins, "The Oil Crisis: This Time the Wolf is Here," *Foreign Affairs*, April 1973, 462–490: Akins, in charge of oil policy in the Nixon White House, makes a similar point; "There have been and still are countries which are richer than any country in OPEC, but there is none which is so small, so inherently weak, and which has gained so much for so little activity of its own."

55. MC, Nazir and William Porter, undersecretary of state for political affairs, 28 September 1973, PET 12 Saud.

56. MC, Love and Nazir, 28 September 1973, POL 7 Saud.

57. Akins, "The Oil Crisis." This was nothing new from Akins, having warned about the crisis in a *Newsweek* interview on 28 August 1972.

58. Anthony Sampson, *The Seven Sisters: The Great Oil Companies and The World They Shaped* (New York: Bantam Books, 1976), 288; Kelly, *Arabia*, 382: Kelly concurs: "The impression produced was that of the utter dependence of Western Europe and Japan upon Middle-Eastern oil, and of the impotence of the industrial countries in the face of OPEC's resolution and might."

59. A. K. Rothnie to Home, 22 January 1974, FCO 8/2332/NB1/2 SA -73, TNA.

60. MC, Nazir and Kissinger, et al., 15 December 1973, POL Saud-U.S.

61. Kissinger to American embassy Tehran, 1 August 1974, Iran, vol. VI—Jan 74—Box 603, RNNSC.

62. United States Senate, *U.S. Arms Policy, Hearings before the Committee on Foreign Relations and the Subcommittee on Foreign Assistance of the Committee on Foreign Relations*, 94th Cong. (1976) on "Proposed Sale of Arms to Iran and Saudi Arabia."

63. MC, Faisal and Lord Aldington, in British embassy Jeddah to Foreign Office, 13 December 1973, FCO 8/2108/NB 3/548/3, TNA.

64. Home to British embassy, Paris, 27 December 1973, FCO 8/2108/NBS/548/3, TNA.

65. Statement by Senator Frank Church, 18 March 1975, *Multinational Corporations and United States Foreign Policy, Hearings before the Subcommittee on Multinational Corporations of the Committee on Foreign Relations*, United States Senate, pt. 9 (Washington, DC: Government Printing Office, 1975), 259–260.

66. Sampson, *The Arms Bazaar*, 294; R. J. Andrews to the Lord Bridges, 24 July 1972, PREM 15/990, TNA.

Chapter 7. A Guiding Hand or Controlling Grasp?

1. Wm. Roger Louis, "Britain and the Middle East after 1945," in *Diplomacy in the Middle East: The International Relations of Regional and Outside Powers*, ed. L. Carl Brown (London: I. B. Tauris, 2004), 44.

2. Fred Halliday, *Arabia without Sultans*, 2nd ed. (London: Saqi Books, 2002), 540.

3. See J. E. Peterson, *Oman's Insurgencies: The Sultanate's Struggle for Supremacy* (London: Saqi Books, 2007); and Ian Gardiner, *In the Service of the Sultan* (London: Leo Cooper, 2006). See also John Akehurst, *We Won a War: The Campaign in Oman, 1965–1975* (Salisbury, UK: Michael Russell, 1982), and Walter C. Ladwig, "Supporting Allies in Counterinsurgency: Britain and the Dhofar Rebellion," *Small Wars and Insurgencies* 19, no. 1 (2008): 62–88.

4. See, for example, Thomas Mockaitis, *British Counterinsurgency in the Post-Imperial Era* (Manchester, UK: Manchester University Press, 1995), 72–95.

5. See Dale F. Eickelman and M. G. Dennison, "Arabizing the Omani Intelligence Services: Clash of Cultures?" *International Journal of Intelligence and Counterintelligence* 7, no. 1 (1994): 1–28.

6. Martin Thomas, *Empires of Intelligence: Security Services and Colonial Disorder after 1914* (London: University of California Press, 2008), 3–4.

7. See John Townsend, *Oman: The Making of a Modern State* (London: Croom Helm, 1974), and Eickelman and Dennison, "Arabizing the Omani Intelligence Services," 8–9. The failure of Sultan Said bin Taimur to redress the many socio-economic ills of his country was fully recognized by a senior British intelligence officer, working for G2Int, the Sultan's intelligence service. In a cable to his superiors just prior to the palace coup, this intelligence officer declared that, "He [bin Taimur] is fiddling while Rome burns and no one will change him."

8. For two conflicting studies of PFLOAG see Fred Halliday, *Arabia without Sultans* (Harmondsworth, UK: Penguin, 1974), and J. B. Kelly, *Arabia, the Gulf, and the West* (London: Harper Collins, 1980), 104–63.

9. "Report of tenure of Command of SAF by Col. D. de C. Smiley from April 1958 to March 1961," File GB165–0336, Middle East Archive, St. Anthony's College, Oxford.

10. Confidential: From J. M. Ides to P. H. H. Wright, "Oman State Office in Italy," 19 March 1970, FCO 8/1422, TNA. In this memo, it was stated clearly that "[the] Arabian peninsula and the Gulf are vital to Western Europe. Since much of our oil comes from there . . . [the] stability in Oman is essential to the area as a whole."

11. JIC Report on the Implications of Oil Supplies and British Oil interests in the Middle East, 9 September 1968, POWE/63/449 (JIC (68) 24), TNA.

12. Eickelman and Dennison, "Arabizing the Omani Intelligence Services," 6.

13. Dale Eickelman, interview notes with senior Omani Intelligence official, 17 August 1988.

14. Sultan bin Taimur had tried to remove Dennison altogether during Smiley's command of the SAF. As a result, Smiley re-employed Dennison as a "recruiting officer," perfect cover for his forays into the interior of Oman.

15. Letter from Philip de Zeutta to Prime Minister [Harold Macmillan], 26 June 1961, PREM 11/4923 338047, TNA. In this letter to Macmillan, de Zeutta noted that Smiley had stated that bin Taimur "was impossible to work with," and that Oman's hope lay in bin Taimur's son, Qaboos, being cultivated to take over the reins of power.

16. Quoted in Eickelman and Dennison, "Arabizing the Omani Intelligence Services," 9–10.

17. J. E. Peterson, *Oman in the Twentieth Century: Political Foundations of an Emerging State* (London: Croom Helm, 1978), 200–204.

18. See Stephen Dorril, *MI6: Fifty Years of Special Operations* (London: Fourth Estate, 2000), 729–34. On Landon, see Rob Sharp, "International Man of Mystery: The Extraordinary Life of the White Sultan," *The Independent, Extra Magazine*, 12 July 2007.

19. Secret: From British Consulate General, Muscat, to Sir Stewart Crawford, Bahrain, "Security Situation in Oman," 17 June 1970, FCO 8/1422, TNA.

20. Confidential: From D. G. Crawford, British Consulate General, Muscat, to M. S. Weir, Bahrain, "Security Situation in Oman," 13 July 1970, FCO 8/1422, TNA.

21. UK Eyes Only—Secret, "An outline plan to restore the situation in Dhofar using Special Air Service Regiment Troops," 7 April 1970, FCO 8/1437 (Doc 72), TNA.

22. Secret: From Commander, British Forces Gulf, to MoD, UK, Subject, "Situation in Musandam Peninsula," 14 November 1970, DEFE 25/186, TNA.

23. Confidential: From HQBF Gulf to Cabinet Office London, "Rebel Activities in Oman," 7 July 1970, FCO 8/1422, TNA.

24. Secret: From Chief of the Defence Staff to the Secretary of State for Defence, "Operation Intradon," 26 January 1971, DEFE 25/186, TNA.

25. Oman Intelligence Report No. 32, 14–27 January 1973, 4; Oman Intelligence Report No. 33, 28 January–10 February 1973, 7; both in DEFE 25/376 337937, TNA.

26. Secret: From D. F. Hawley, British Embassy, Muscat, to P. R. H. Wright, Middle East Department, FCO, "PFLOAG Plot," 15 January 1973, FCO 8/2018 338047, TNA.

27. Top Secret: From Major General Timothy Creasy to His Majesty Qaboos bin Said, Annex "C," "Organisation and Future Intentions of PFLOAG in Northern Oman," 4 January 1973, FCO 8/2018 338047, TNA.

28. Secret: Brief on Operation Jason for Distribution to Ministers and Embassies, FCO 8/2018 338047, TNA; Creasy to Qaboos, "Organisation and Future Intentions of PFLOAG in Northern Oman."

29. Hawley to Wright, "PFLOAG Plot."

30. Top Secret: From Major General Timothy Creasy to His Majesty Qaboos bin Said, Annex "A," "List of Detainees of PFLOAG in Northern Oman," 4 January 1973; Hawley to Wright, "PFLOAG Plot;" both in FCO 8/2018 338047, TNA. In total, some sixty-nine persons were arrested under Operation Jason. For a breakdown of their occupations, see Eickelman and Dennison, "Arabizing the Omani Intelligence Services," 13.

31. Confidential: Covert letter accompanying report of Defence attaché Col. Welch, from Donald Hawley to Alec Douglas-Home, 14 January 1973, DEFE 25/186, TNA.

32. Creasy to Qaboos, "Organisation and Future Intentions of PFLOAG in Northern Oman," 2.

33. Secret: From P. R. H. Wright to Mr. Le Quesne, Subject: Oman—Request for Interrogation Team, 4 January 1973, FCO 8/2018 338047, TNA.

34. Secret: From C. M. Le Quesne to Mr. Coles, 10 January 1973, FCO 8/2018 338047, TNA.

35. Secret: Telegram from Muscat to FCO, Subject: PFLOAG, 4 January 1973, FCO 8/2018 338047, TNA.

36. Secret: Telegram from Defence attaché Muscat to MODUK, 6 January 1973, FCO 8/2018 338047, TNA.

37. Secret: Telegram from FCO to Muscat, 16 January 1973, FCO 8/2018 338047, TNA.

38. Confidential: Telegram from British Embassy, Dubai, to FCO, Muscat, Doha, Bahrain, Kuwait, 24 January 1973, FCO 8/2018 338047, TNA.

39. Secret: Letter from Donald Hawley to Alec Douglas-Home, Defence attaché's Report, 20 January 1974, FCO 8/2233 337937, TNA.

40. Secret: From Colonel C. E. Welch, Defence attaché, Muscat, Annual Report, 29 November 1973, FCO 8/2233 337937, TNA.

41. Secret: SAS Assistance in the Sultanate of Oman, 17 August 1970, DEFE 25/186, TNA.

42. See Tony Geraghty, *Who Dares Wins: The Special Air Service, 1950 to the Gulf War* (London: Little and Brown, 1992), 203–204.

43. Confidential: From R. A. Kealy to Lt. Col. I. McKay, "Vertical Photography—Oman/PDRY Border," 7 March 1975, DEFE 25/186, TNA.

44. Concern over the effectiveness and reliability of *firqas* is a subject that has been rather underplayed in literature dealing with the Dhofar campaign. See, for example, Major General Tony Jeapes, *SAS Secret War* (London: Harper Collins, 1996). Jeapes, while noting their faults, regards the *firqas* as crucial to the counterinsurgency campaign. By contrast, see Secret: Oman Intelligence Report No. 52, 21 October–3 November 1973, FCO 8/2022, TNA. This report, written by the British military attaché to Muscat, Colonel C. E. Welch, paints a rather less benign view of their effectiveness.

45. Geraint Hughes, "A Model Campaign Reappraised: The Counter-Insurgency War in Dhofar, Oman, 1965–1975," *The Journal of Strategic Studies* 32, no. 2 (2009): 294.

46. Creasy to Qaboos, "List of Detainees of PFLOAG in Northern Oman."

47. For example, see Fred Halliday, *Mercenaries: Counter-Insurgency in the Gulf* (Nottingham, UK: Spokesman/Bertrand Russell Peace Foundation, 1977), 57.

Chapter 8. In Brzezinski's Forge

1. Jimmy Carter, Presidential Directive/NSC-63, Subject: Persian Gulf Security Framework, 15 January 1981, http://www.fas.org/irp/offdocs/pd/pd63.pdf (accessed 1 November 2008); "Carter Takes Charge," *Time*, 4 February 1980, http://www.time.com/magazine/article/0,9171,954497,00.html (accessed 29 November 2008); "Weather," *Washington Post*, 15 January 1981.

2. William E. Odom, "The Cold War Origins of the U.S. Central Command," *Journal of Cold War Studies* 8, no. 2 (Spring 2006): 54; Zbigniew Brzezinski, "Exit Interview," by Marie Allen, Washington, D.C., 20 February 1981, 4–5, http://www.jimmycarterlibrary.org/library/exitInt/exitBrzski.pdf (accessed 10 November 2008).

3. Jimmy Carter, Presidential Review Memorandum/NSC-10, Comprehensive Net Assessment and Military Force Posture Review, 18 February 1977, http://www.fas.org/irp/offdocs/prm/prm10.pdf (accessed 7 November 2008); Lawrence J. Korb, "National Security Organization and Process in the Carter Administration," in *Defense Policy and the Presidency: Carter's First Years*, ed. Sam C. Sarkesian (Boulder, CO: Westview Press, 1979), 124. At the time Korb wrote this chapter, he was a faculty member at the U.S. Naval War College and a consultant to the Department of Defense and the National Security Council staff. He interviewed NSC staff for the chapter.

4. Harold Brown, PRM/NSC-10, Military Strategy and Force Posture Review, Final Report, http://www.fas.org/irp/offdocs/prm/prm10.pdf (accessed 7 November 2008).

5. Jed C. Snyder, *Defending the Fringe: NATO, the Mediterranean, and the Persian Gulf*, SAIS Papers in International Affairs, No. 11 (Boulder, CO: Westview Press, 1987), 116; Brown, PRM/NSC-10, Military Strategy and Force Posture Review, Final Report.

6. Phil Williams, "Carter's Defence Policy," in *The Carter Years: The President and Policy Making*, ed. M. Glenn Abernathy, Dilys M. Hill, and Phil Williams (New York: St. Martin's Press, 1984), 91.

7. "Rapping for Carter's Ear," *Time*, 12 June 1978, http: //www.time.com/Magazine/ article/0,9171,948155,00.html (accessed 12 November 2008).

8. Zbigniew Brzezinski, *Power and Principle* (New York,: Farrar, Straus and Giroux, 1983), 177; Williams, "Carter's Defence Policy," 91; Zbigniew Brzezinski with Madeleine K. Albright, Leslie G. Denend, William Odom, interview by Inis Claude et al., 18 February 1982, Carter Presidency Project, Miller Center for Public Affairs, University of Virginia, 31, http:// webstorage3.mcpa.virginia.edu/ poh/transcripts/chp_1982_0218_brzezinski.pdf (accessed 5 December 2008). Hereinafter "Interview of Brzezinski et al."

9. Odom, "Cold War Origins," 57, n8.

10. Korb, "National Security Organization," 124; Interview of Brzezinski et al., 32.

11. Jimmy Carter, Presidential Directive/NSC-18, U.S. National Strategy, 26 August 1977, http://www.fas.org/irp/offdocs/pd/pd18.pdf (accessed 1 November 2008); Brzezinski, *Power and Principle*, 177–178; Odom, "Cold War Origins," 58–59.

12. Odom, "Cold War Origins," 59; Richard L. Kugler, *Commitment to Purpose: How Alliance Partnership Won the Cold War*, RAND Report MR-190-FF/RC (Santa Monica, CA: RAND Corporation, 1983), 311–314, http://www.rand.org/Pubs/ monograph_reports/MR190 (accessed 15 November 2008); Williams, "Carter's Defence Policy," 88–89; James McIntyre with Hubert Harris and Van Ooms, interviewed by Charles Jones et al., 28–29 October 1981, Carter Presidency Project, Miller Center for Public Affairs, University of Virginia, 9, http:// webstorage3.mcpa.virginia.edu/poh/transcripts/ohp_1981_1028_mcintyre .pdf (accessed 1 December 2008); Maxwell Orme Johnson, *The Military as an Instrument of U.S. Policy in Southwest Asia: The Rapid Deployment Joint Task Force, 1979–1982* (Boulder, CO: Westview Press, 1983), 61.

13. Kugler, *Commitment to Purpose*, 349–350; Lawrence J. Korb, "The Policy Impacts of the Carter Defense Program," in *Defense Policy and the Presidency: Carter's First Years*, ed. Sam C. Sarkesian (Boulder, CO: Westview Press, 1979), 169, 190, 194; Minton F. Goldman, "President Carter and the Soviet Union: The Influence of American Policy on the Kremlin's Decision to Intervene in Afghanistan," in *The Presidency and National Security*, ed. R. Gordon Hoxie (New York: Center for the Study of the Presidency, 1984), 226.

14. Richard Burt, "How U.S. Strategy toward Persian Gulf Region Evolved," *New York Times*, 25 January 1980.

15. "Diplomatic Dissonances," *Time*, 10 April 1978, http://www.time.com/time Magazine/article/0,9171,948051,00.html (accessed 10 November 2008); "Vance: Man on the Move," *Time*, 24 April 1978, http://www.time.com/time/Magazine/ article/0,9171,916105,00.html (accessed 10 November 2008).

16. Ambassador David Newsom, interview by the author, Charlottesville, Virginia, 30 May 2007.

17. Odom, "Cold War Origins," 56, 58.

18. Robert P. Haffa Jr., *The Half War: Planning U.S. Rapid Deployment Forces to Meet a Limited Contingency, 1960–1983* (Boulder, CO: Westview Press, 1984), 54–56.

19. Bernard Reich and Stephen H. Gotowicki, "The United States and the Persian Gulf in the Bush Administration," http://fmso.leavenworth.army.mil/docu ments/usgulf.htm; Burt, "U.S. Strategy toward Persian Gulf"; James H. Noyes, *The Clouded Lens: Persian Gulf Security and U.S. Policy*, 2nd ed. (Stanford, CA: Hoover Institution Press, 1982), 121, 136; Brzezinski, *Power and Principle*, 357.

20. Interview of Brzezinski et al., 35, 39; Odom, "Cold War Origins," 59.

21. Raymond L. Garthoff, *The Great Transition: American-Soviet Relations and the End of the Cold War* (Washington, DC: Brookings Institution, 1994), 21; "Iran: The Crescent of Crisis," *Time*, 15 January 1979, http://www.time.com/time-Magazine/article/0,9171,919995,00.html (accessed 13 November 2008); "The Khomeini Era: Iran Becomes a Theocracy," *Time*, 12 February 1979, http:// www.time.com/ time/magazine/article/0,9171,920102,00.html (accessed 29 November 2008); "Iran: A Government Collapses," *Time*, 19 February 1979, http://www.time.com/Time/magazine/article/0,9171,912363,00.html; Erwin C. Hargrove, *Jimmy Carter as President: Leadership and the Politics of the Public Good* (Baton Rouge: Louisiana State University Press, 1988), 149; Odom, "Cold War Origins," 60.

22. Goldman, "Carter and the Soviet Union," 230–231; Amitav Acharya, *U.S. Military Strategy in the Gulf: Origins and Evolution under the Carter and Reagan Administrations* (New York: Routledge, 1989), 50; Johnson, *Military as an Instrument*, 14.

23. Brig. Gen. Michael Sheridan, U.S. Marine Corps (Ret.), telephone interview by author, 17 April 2007; Olav Njølstad, "The Carter Legacy: Entering the Second Era of the Cold War," in *The Last Decade of the Cold War: From Conflict Escalation to Conflict Transformation* (Portland, OR: Frank Cass, 2004), 203.

24. Njølstad, "The Carter Legacy," 203; Don Oberdorfer, "The Evolution of a Decision," *Washington Post*, 24 January 1980; "Iran: The Crescent of Crisis."

25. "A Week of Tough Talk," *Time*, 12 June 1978, http://www.time.com/time/ Magazine/article/0,9171,948154,00.html (accessed 14 November 2008).

26. C. Paul Bradley, *Recent United States Policy in the Persian Gulf* (Grantham, NH: Thompson & Rutter, 1982), 85–86; Haffa, *The Half War*, 61; Johnson, *Military as an Instrument*, 13.

27. Brzezinski, *Power and Principle*, 446–47; Odom, "Cold War Origins," 61; Oberdorfer, "Evolution of a Decision."

28. Odom, "Cold War Origins," 61–62.

29. Ibid.

30. Ibid., 62–63.

31. Dale R. Herspring, *The Pentagon and the Presidency: Civil-Military Relations from FDR to George W. Bush* (Lawrence: University Press of Kansas, 2005), 237–38.

32. Haffa, *The Half War*, 62; Brzezinski, *Power and Principle*, 447.

33. Johnson, *Military as an Instrument*, 62–63.

34. Memorandum from Marshall Brement to Zbigniew Brzezinski and David Aaron, Subject: Possible Soviet Move into Afghanistan, 7 September 1979, Thomson Gale Declassified Documents Reference System, Document No. CK3100094430 (accessed 31 July 2007); Robert M. Gates, *From the Shadows: The Ultimate Insider's Story of Five Presidents and How They Won the Cold War* (New York: Simon & Schuster, 1996), 132–33; Brzezinski, *Power and Principle*, 427–28.

35. "World: Who Lost Iran?" *Time*, 4 December 1979, http://www.time.com/time/magazine/article/0,9171,912266,00.html (accessed 14 November 2008).

36. Johnson, *Military as an Instrument*, 9, 64; Brzezinski, *Power and Principle*, 446.

37. *Hearings on NATO After Afghanistan Before the Committee on Foreign Affairs, Subcommittee on Europe and the Middle East*, 96th Cong. 7 (1980).

38. Jimmy Carter, *Keeping Faith: Memoirs of a President* (New York: Bantam Books, 1982), 471–472; Dennis Ross, "Considering Soviet Threats to the Persian Gulf," *International Security* 6, no. 2 (Autumn 1981): 164. Ross was the assistant to the director of Net Assessment in the Office of the Secretary of Defense (OSD) when he wrote this essay. Previously, he had worked in OSD's Office of Program Analysis and Evaluation, where he focused on Middle East military issues. Both offices produced studies of U.S.-Soviet military capabilities during the 1970s.

39. Hargrove, *Jimmy Carter as President*, 155; Carter, *Keeping Faith*, 473; "My Opinion of the Russians Has Changed Most Dramatically . . ." *Time*, 14 January 1980, http://www.time.com/time/magazine/article/0,9171,921764,00.html (accessed 29 November 2008).

40. Brzezinski, *Power and Principle*, 430.

41. Melvyn P. Leffler, "From the Truman Doctrine to the Carter Doctrine: Lessons and Dilemmas of the Cold War," *Diplomatic History* 7, no. 4 (October 1983): 245–246; Brzezinski, *Power and Principle*, 444.

42. Oberdorfer, "Evolution of a Decision."

43. Jimmy Carter, "The State of the Union Address Delivered before a Joint Session of the Congress," 23 January 1980, in Public Papers of the Presidents of the United States, John T. Woolley and Gerhard Peters, The American Presidency Project [online], Santa Barbara: University of California (hosted), Gerhard Peters (database), http://www.presidency.ucsb.edu/ws/?pid=33079.

44. Hargrove, *Jimmy Carter as President*, 114, 153–54, 156; Leffler, "From the Truman Doctrine," 255.

45. Interview of Brzezinski et al., 40.

46. Kugler, *Commitment to Purpose*, 341–342, 345.

47. Harold Brown, *Department of Defense Annual Report, Fiscal Year 1981* (Washington, DC: Department of Defense, January 1980), 115.

48. Hargrove, *Jimmy Carter as President*, 149.

49. U.S. Congress, Senate, Committee on Foreign Relations, *U.S. Security Interests and Policies in Southwest Asia*, 6 February 1980, CIS No. 80-S381–39, Testimony No. 9, 297–302; Bradley, *Recent United States Policy*, 99–101; Noyes, *The Clouded Lens*, 126–27; Col. David A. Quinlan, *The Role of the Marine Corps in Rapid Deployment Forces* (Washington, DC: National Defense University Press, 1983), 4–5; Organization of the Joint Chiefs of Staff, *United States Military Posture for FY 1982* (Washington, DC: Department of Defense, January 1981), 50.

50. Kugler, *Commitment to Purpose*, 342.

51. Organization of the Joint Chiefs of Staff, *United States Military Posture*, 55–56; *A Discussion of the Rapid Deployment Force with Lieutenant General P. X. Kelley*, Special Analysis No. 80–4, American Enterprise Institute for Public Policy Research, 1980, 3–4; Bradley, *Recent United States Policy*, 98–99; E. Asa Bates, "The Rapid Deployment Force—Fact or Fiction," *RUSI: Journal of the Royal United Services Institute for Defence Studies* 126, no. 2 (June 1981): 24; Haffa, *The Half War*, 126.

52. Robert W. Komer, interview by the Office of the Secretary of Defense Historical Office, Arlington, VA, 25 March 1981, 49. Hereinafter, "OSD Interview."

53. Robert W. Komer, *Blowtorch*, USD(P) [Under Secretary of Defense for Policy] chapter, unpublished memoir, copy made available to the author by Douglas Komer; Bates, "The Rapid Deployment Force," 24.

54. *Hearings on S2294 Before the Committee on Armed Services*, 96th Cong. 1243–1244 (1980) (Washington, DC: U.S. Government Printing Office, 1980); Komer, OSD interview, 50; Paul K. Davis, "Observations on the Rapid Deployment Joint Task Force: Origins, Direction, and Mission," RAND Paper P-6751, June 1982, 8, 10, http://www.rand.org/pubs/papers/2005/P6751.pdf. Davis served in the Department of Defense between August 1977 and August 1981, as director of Regional Studies and as acting deputy assistant secretary of defense (Regional Programs). In this capacity, he directed studies and programs that contributed to the Department of Defense's establishment of what became the RDJTF.

55. Harold Brown, "What the Carter Doctrine Means to Me," *MERIP Reports*, no. 90 (September 1980), 22–23.

56. Memorandum for Zbigniew Brzezinski from William Odom, Subject: MILCON: M-B-B Luncheon Item, 30 July 1980. Reproduced in the Thomson Gale

Declassified Documents Reference System, Document No. CK3100487560 (accessed 31 July 2007).

57. Komer, OSD interview, 45–45, 48.

58. Davis, "Observations," 16; Sheridan interview.

59. Sheridan interview.

60. Davis, "Observations," 16–18.

61. Sheridan interview; Davis, "Observations," 16–18.

62. Komer, OSD interview, 82, 86–87; Snyder, Defending the Fringe, 117.

63. Komer, OSD interview, 88.

64. Ibid., 88–89.

65. Paul Jabber, "U.S. Interests and Regional Security in the Middle East," Daedalus 109 (Fall 1980): 80; Jeffrey Record, The Rapid Deployment Force and U.S. Military Intervention in the Persian Gulf (Cambridge, MA: Institute for Foreign Policy Analysis, 1981), 34–35, 54; James R. Schlesinger, "Rapid (?) Deployment (?) Force (?)," Washington Post, 24 September 1980.

66. Bradley, Recent United States Policy, 99.

67. Summary of a Special Coordinating Committee Meeting, Subject: Security Assistance for Southwest Asia, 28 October 1980, Thomson Gale Declassified Documents Reference System, Document Number: CK3100472777 (accessed 31 July 2007).

68. Interview of Brzezinski et al., 41.

69. Gordon Goldstein, Lessons in Disaster: McGeorge Bundy and the Path to War in Vietnam (New York: Times Books/Henry Holt & Company, 2008), 27.

70. Quoted in Johnson, Military as an Instrument, 61.

71. Kugler, Commitment to Purpose, 311–312.

72. Olav Njølstad, "Shifting Priorities: The Persian Gulf in U.S. Strategic Planning in the Carter Years," Cold War History 4, no. 3 (April 2004): 21.

73. Jimmy Carter, Presidential Directive PD/NSC-62, Modifications in U.S. National Strategy, 15 January 1981, http://www.fas.org/irp/offdocs/pd/pd62.pdf (accessed 22 December 2008).

74. Korb, "The Policy Impacts," 194.

75. Jeffrey Record, Revising U.S. Military Strategy: Tailoring Means to Ends (Washington, DC: Pergamon-Brassey's, 1984), 37.

76. Odom, "Cold War Origins," 70–71.

77. Hargrove, Jimmy Carter as President, 153.

78. Noyes, The Clouded Lens, 126.

79. Record, Revising U.S. Military Strategy, 38.

Chapter 9. The Ties That Bind

1. Joe Stork and Martha Wenger, "The U.S. in the Persian Gulf: From Rapid Deployment to Massive Deployment," *Middle East Report* (Middle East Research and Information Project), no. 168 (January–February 1991): 22.

2. Terry L. Deibel, "Hidden Commitments," *Foreign Policy*, no. 67 (Summer 1987): 51.

3. David Skidmore, "Carter and the Failure of Foreign Policy Reform," *Political Science Quarterly* (Winter 1993–94): 708.

4. I. M. Destler, Leslie Gelb, and Anthony Lake, *Our Own Worst Enemy: The Unmaking of American Foreign Policy* (New York: Simon & Schuster, 1984), 73.

5. James A. Phillips, "The AWACS Sale: Prospects for U.S. Policy," *The Heritage Foundation: Backgrounder #153* (October 1981): 2.

6. Anthony H. Cordesman, *The Gulf and the Search for Strategic Stability: Saudi Arabia, the Military Balance in the Gulf, and Trends in the Arab-Israeli Military Balance* (Boulder, CO: Westview Press, 1984), 212.

7. Deibel, "Hidden Commitments," 51.

8. Ibid., 52.

9. Stork and Wenger, "The U.S. in the Persian Gulf," 22.

10. Skidmore, "Carter and the Failure of Foreign Policy Reform," 723.

11. Destler, Gelb, and Lake, *Our Own Worst Enemy*, 73.

12. Stork and Wenger, "The U.S. in the Persian Gulf," 22.

13. Michael Klare, "Have RDF—Will Travel," *The Nation*, 8 March 1980.

14. Kenneth N. Waltz, "A Strategy for the Rapid Deployment Forces," *International Security* (Spring 1981): 71.

15. Joe Stork, "Carter Doctrine and U.S. Bases in the Middle East," *Middle East Report* (Middle East Research and Information Project), no. 90 (September 1980): 5.

16. Ibid., 6.

17. Joe Stork and Martha Wenger, "U.S. Ready to Intervene in Gulf War," *Middle East Report* (Middle East Research and Information Project), no. 125/126 (July–September 1984): 45.

18. Ibid.

19. Ibid.

20. Ibid.

21. M. S. El Azhary, "The Attitudes of the Superpowers towards the Gulf War," *International Affairs* (Autumn 1983): 610.

22. Staff Report, "The Proposed AWACS/F-15 Enhancement Sale to Saudi Arabia," United States Senate Committee on Foreign Relations (Washington, DC: U.S. Government Printing Office, September 1981), 4.

23. Scott Armstrong, "Saudis' AWACS Just the Beginning of New Strategy," *Washington Post*, 1 November 1981.

24. Ibid.

25. Joe Stork and Jim Paul, "Arms Sales and the Militarization of the Middle East," *Middle East Report* (Middle East Research and Information Project), no. 112 (February 1983): 8.

26. Armstrong, "Saudis' AWACS."

27. Staff Report, "The Proposed AWACS/F-15 Enhancement Sale to Saudi Arabia," 5.

28. George J. Church, "AWACS: He Does It Again," *Time*, 9 November 1981.

29. Jonathan Marshall, "Saudi Arabia and the Reagan Doctrine," *Middle East Report* (Middle East Research and Information Project), no. 155 (November–December 1988): 12.

30. Fred Lawson, "The Reagan Administration in the Middle East," *Middle East Report* (Middle East Research and Information Project), no. 128 (November–December 1984): 29.

31. Deibel, "Hidden Commitments," 53.

32. Rachel Bronson, *Thicker than Oil: America's Uneasy Partnership with Saudi Arabia*, (London: Oxford University Press, 1995), 160.

33. Michael A. Palmer, *Guardians of the Gulf: A History of America's Expanding Role in the Persian Gulf, 1833–1992* (New York: The Free Press, 1992), 113.

34. Deibel, "Hidden Commitments," 56.

35. Bernard Gwertzman, "President Says U.S. Should Not Waver in Backing Saudis," *New York Times*, 18 October 1981.

36. Marshall, "Saudi Arabia and the Reagan Doctrine," 13.

37. Phillips, "The AWACS Sale," 2.

38. Stork and Paul, "Arms Sales and the Militarization of the Middle East," 8.

39. Ibid., 3.

40. Staff Report, "The Proposed AWACS/F-15 Enhancement Sale to Saudi Arabia," 46.

41. Ibid., 46–47.

42. Ed Magnuson, "Will the AWACS Deal Fly?" *Time*, 7 September 1981.

43. Cordesman, *The Gulf and the Search for Strategic Stability*, 333.

44. Rex B. Wingerter, "AWACS and U.S. Strategy," *Journal of Palestine Studies* 11, no. 2 (Winter 1982): 190.

45. Stork and Paul, "Arms Sales and the Militarization of the Middle East," 8.

46. Wingerter, "AWACS and U.S. Strategy," 190.

47. Bronson, *Thicker than Oil*, 161. See also: Cordesman, *The Gulf and the Search for Strategic Stability* , 333.

48. Church, "AWACS: He Does It Again."

49. Thomas L. McNaugher, *Arms and Oil: U.S. Military Strategy and the Persian Gulf* (Washington, DC: Brookings Institution, 1985), 14.

50. Martha Wenger, "The Central Command: Getting to War on Time," *Middle East Reports* (Middle East Research and Information Project), no. 128 (November–December 1984): 20.

51. Ibid., 22.

52. Stork and Wenger, "The U.S. in the Persian Gulf," 25.

53. Armstrong, "Saudis' AWACS."

54. Stork and Wenger, "U.S. Ready to Intervene in Gulf War," 47.

55. Ibid.

56. Lawson, "The Reagan Administration in the Middle East," 34.

57. Dilip Hiro, *The Longest War: The Iran-Iraq Military Conflict* (New York: Routledge, 1991), 153.

58. Stork and Wenger, "U.S. Ready to Intervene in Gulf War," 46.

59. Bob Woodward, *Veil: The Secret Wars of the CIA, 1981–1987* (New York: Simon & Schuster, 1987), 354.

60. Lawson, "The Reagan Administration in the Middle East," 34.

61. Robert C. Johansen and Michael G. Renner, "Limiting Conflict in the Gulf," *Third World Quarterly* (October 1985): 815.

Chapter 10. India's "Monroe Doctrine" and the Gulf

1. C. Raja Mohan, "The Return of the Raj," *American Interest*, May/June 2010, http://www.the-american-interest.com/article.cfm?piece=803.

2. C. Raja Mohan, "What If Pakistan Fails? India Isn't Worried . . .Yet," *Washington Quarterly* 28, no. 1 (Winter 2004–5): 127. See also C. Raja Mohan, "Beyond India's Monroe Doctrine," *The Hindu*, 2 January 2003, http://mea.gov.in/opinion/2003/01/02o02.htm, and "SAARC Reality Check: China Just Tore Up India's Monroe Doctrine," *Indian Express*, 13 November 2005, LexisNexis Database, http://www.indianexpress.com/storyOld.php?storyId=81928.

3. Jawaharlal Nehru, *India's Foreign Policy: Selected Speeches, September 1946–April 1961* (Delhi: Government of India, 1961), 113–115.

4. Devin T. Hagerty, "India's Regional Security Doctrine," *Asian Survey* 31, no. 4 (1991): 352. Indian and foreign commentators use "Indira Doctrine" or "Rajiv Doctrine" interchangeably with "India's Monroe Doctrine."

5. Dilip Bobb, "Cautious Optimism," *India Today*, 31 August 1987, 69. See also Hagerty, "India's Regional Security Doctrine," 351–363.

6. Hagerty, "India's Regional Security Doctrine," 351–353. See also Bhabani Sen Gupta, "The Indian Doctrine," *India Today*, 31 August 1983, 20; Raju G. C.

Thomas, *India's Search for Power: Indira Gandhi's Foreign Policy, 1966–1982* (New Delhi: Sage, 1984), esp. 292.

7. Manish Dabhade and Harsh V. Pant, "Coping with Challenges to Sovereignty: Sino-Indian Rivalry and Nepal's Foreign Policy," *Contemporary South Asia* 13, no. 2 (2004): 160.

8. Dexter Perkins, *A History of the Monroe Doctrine*, rev. ed. (Boston: Little, Brown and Company, 1963), 186; Alfred Thayer Mahan, *The Influence of Sea Power upon History, 1660–1783* (Boston: Little, Brown and Company, 1890; repr. New York: Dover Publications, 1987), 346.

9. Stephen Philip Cohen, *India: Emerging Power* (Washington, DC: Brookings Institution Press, 2001), esp. 63–65. Stephen Cohen detects a certain "core" of principles uniting Indian thinkers. The conviction that India should be preeminent in the Indian Ocean region ranks first among these.

10. Ibid.

11. Rahul Roy-Chaudhury, "India's Maritime Forces: Oceanic and Coastal Security Imperatives," in *The Future of War and Peace in Asia*, ed. N. S. Sisodia and S. Kalyanaraman (New Delhi: Magnum, 2010).

12. Perkins, *History*, 29.

13. Government of India, INBR-8, *Indian Maritime Doctrine* (New Delhi: Integrated Headquarters, Ministry of Defense (Navy), 25 April 2004), 64.

14. Government of India, INBR-8, *Indian Maritime Doctrine* (New Delhi: Integrated Headquarters, Ministry of Defense (Navy), 2009), 3. (Hereafter *Indian Maritime Doctrine*, 2009.)

15. Sureesh Mehta, in *Freedom to Use the Seas: India's Maritime Military Strategy*, Government of India (New Delhi: Integrated Headquarters, Ministry of Defense (Navy), 28 May 2007), iii.

16. Ibid.; Arun Prakash, "Shaping India's Maritime Strategy—Opportunities & Challenges" (speech, National Defense College, New Delhi, November 2005), available on the Indian Navy Web site, http://indiannavy.nic.in/cns_add2 .htm. At the time, Admiral Prakash was superintending the development of the *Maritime Military Strategy*.

17. J. D. Richardson, ed., *Compilation of the Messages and Papers of the Presidents* (New York: Bureau of National Literature, 1917), 2:287.

18. Ibid.

19. Christopher P. Cavas, "U.S. Navy Heads to Port As Exercises Wind Down," *Defense News*, 28 July 2004, http://www.defensenews.com/story .php?F=3108048&C=asiapac. First tested in 2004, the U.S. Navy's "Fleet Response Plan" allows it to temporarily surge two-thirds of its forces overseas, rather than the customary one-third.

20. Perkins, *History*, 168–169.

21. Richard Olney to Thomas F. Bayard, 20 July 1895, in *The Record of American Diplomacy: Documents and Readings in the History of American Foreign Relations*, ed. Ruhl J. Bartlett, 4th ed. (New York: Knopf, 1964), 341–345.

22. Perkins, *History*, esp. 266–275.

23. Alfred Thayer Mahan, *Naval Strategy, Compared and Contrasted with the Principles and Practice of Military Operations on Land* (Boston: Little, Brown and Company, 1911), 111.

24. Henry Cabot Lodge to Theodore Roosevelt, 30 March 1901, in *Selections from the Correspondence of Theodore Roosevelt and Henry Cabot Lodge, 1884–1918*, ed. Henry Cabot Lodge and Charles F. Redmond (New York: Charles Scribner's Sons, 1925; repr., New York: Da Capo, 1971), 1:486–487.

25. Alfred Thayer Mahan, *The Interest of America in Sea Power, Present and Future* (Boston: Little, Brown and Company, 1897; repr., Freeport, NY: Books for Libraries Press, 1970), 198.

26. Theodore Roosevelt, "Message of the President to the Senate and the House of Representatives," 6 December 1904, in *Foreign Relations of the United States, 1904*, U.S. Department of State (Washington, DC: Government Printing Office, 1905), xli; Perkins, *History*, 228–275.

27. Theodore Roosevelt to Elihu Root, 7 June 1904, in *The Letters of Theodore Roosevelt*, ed. Elting Morison et al. (Cambridge, MA: Harvard University Press, 1951–54), 4:821–823.

28. Rahul Roy-Chaudhury, interview by chapter co-author James R. Holmes, International Institute of Strategic Studies, London, England, 27 September 2009.

29. Manmohan Singh, in *Maritime Military Strategy* (2007), iii.

30. *Indian Maritime Doctrine* (2009), 55.

31. K. M. Panikkar, *Geographical Factors in Indian History* (Bombay: Bharatiya Vidya Bhavan, 1955), 58–59.

32. Roy-Chaudhury interview.

33. *Maritime Military Strategy* (2007), 41, 45–46, 60.

34. Roy-Chaudhury interview.

35. Peter Lehr, "Asymmetric Warfare in the Indian Ocean: What Kind of Threat from What Kind of Actor?" in *Maritime Security in the Indian Ocean Region: Critical Issues in Debate*, ed. V. R. Raghavan and Lawrence S. Prabhakar (New Delhi: Tata McGraw-Hill, 2008), 165–185.

36. Roy-Chaudhury, "India's Maritime Forces."

37. Roy-Chaudhury interview.

38. *The Kautilīya Arthaśāstra*, trans. R. P. Kangle, 2nd ed., repr. (Delhi: Motilal Banarsidass, 1988), part 3, 248–249. While normally conceived of as a circular arrangement, R. P. Kangle maintains that the mandala can be linear rather than circular.

39. Roy-Chaudhury interview.

40. Nassim Nicholas Taleb, *The Black Swan: The Impact of the Highly Improbable* (New York: Random House, 2007).

41. Gurpreet Khurana, "China-India Maritime Rivalry," *Indian Defense Review* 23, no. 4 (2009), http://www.indiandefencereview.com/2009/04/china-india-maritime-rivalry.html.

42. Roy-Chaudhury, "India's Maritime Forces."

43. Edward Wong, "Chinese Navy Flexes Muscle in U.S. Strongholds," *Times of India*, 25 April 2010, http://timesofindia.indiatimes.com/world/china/Chinese-navy-flexes-muscle-in-US-strongholds/articleshow/5854578.cms.

Chapter 11. China's Historic Return to the Gulf

1. Mohamed bin Huwaidin, *China's Relations with Arabia and the Gulf, 1949–1999* (London: RoutledgeCurzon, 2002).

2. "Open Doors 2009: International Students in the United States," Institute of International Education, 19 November 2009, http://www.iie.org/en/Research-and-Publications/~/media/Files/Corporate/Open-Doors/Fast-Facts/Fast%20Facts%202010.ashx.

3. "The U.S. Is Behind the Xinjiang Riots," *Al Thawra*, 29 July 2009.

4. General Administration of Customs of China.

5. International Monetary Fund, "Direction of Trade Statistics" (June 2010), http://elibrary-data.imf.org/FindDataReports.aspx?d=33061&e=170921. The exception is a period between May 2003 and November 2005 when Germany overtook the United States.

6. General Administration of Customs of China.

7. Ibid.

8. Visa Wait Times, Bureau of Consular Affairs, U.S. State Department (March 2008), http://travel.state.gov/visa/temp/wait/wait_4638.html.

9. Author's conversations with consular officials at Chinese embassy in Cairo, and with Egyptian traders, 15 March 2008.

10. "Jingmao wanglai cucheng qijing: Zhongguo chuxian Zhongdong jie" [Trade brings about a wonderful view: China emerges as a Middle East street], *Yazhou Xinwentai*, 14 March 2008.

11. International Monetary Fund, *World Economic Outlook Database* (July 2010).

12. General Administration of Customs of China.

13. Ibid.

14. International Monetary Fund, "Direction of Trade Statistics" (June 2010).

15. General Administration of Customs of China.

16. "Chinese Railway Workers Deported for Higher Wages Strike," *Zawya* (Dubai), 26 October 2010.

17. "Algeria Imposes Strict Limits on the Movement of Foreign Workers," *Elaph* (UK), 27 September 2009.

18. Kenneth Pomeranz, *The Great Divergence: China, Europe, and the Making of the Modern World Economy* (Princeton, NJ: Princeton University Press, 2000), 173.

19. "Musa Kusa to *Al Sharq Al Awsat*: We Deny Chinese Colonization of Africa," *Al Sharq Al Awsat*, 22 November 2009.

20. The e-mail was forwarded to the author.

21. General Administration of Customs of China.

22. *World Energy Outlook* (Paris: International Energy Agency, 2009).

23. Author's e-mail conversation with Paul Gamble, senior economist, Jadwa Investment Bank, 10 March 2010.

24. "China starts work on Guangdong crude oil reserve, beginning second phase of emergency stockpile plan," *Oilgram Price Report*, Platts, http://www.platts.com/, 9 March 2010.

25. Greg Torode, "PLA's First Carrier 'Ready By 2010': Blue-Water Plans Advancing, Says U.S.," *South China Morning Post*, 1 April 2010.

26. After adjusting for China's re-exports through Hong Kong.

27. "Wai meiti cheng zhongguo zai miandian kekedao jianli hai shang qingbao jiancezhan" [Foreign media says China to establish monitoring stations in Myanmar's Coco Island], *Zhongguo Pinglun Xinwenti*, 4 January 2010.

28. Daniel Kostecka, "Hambantota, Chittagong, and the Maldives—Unlikely Pearls for the Chinese Navy," *China Brief*, Jamestown Foundation, 19 November 2010.

29. "Yemen weiji beihou: meiguo suohou zhongguo shiyou jinkou?" [Background to the Yemen crisis: America strangles China's oil imports?], China Energy Web, http:// www.china5e.com, 27 January 2010 (author's translation).

30. General Administration of Customs of China.

31. "U.S. Enlists Oil to Sway Beijing's Stance on Tehran," *Wall Street Journal*, 20 October 2009.

32. Yin Gang, "Yilang yiwwei qiangying, biding beiju shouchang" [A blindly tough Iran will result in tragedy], *Huanqiu*, 20 February 2010.

CONTRIBUTORS

JASON H. CAMPBELL is a project associate at the RAND Corporation, where he focuses on issues of international security, twenty-first-century warfare, and measuring progress in post-conflict reconstruction. In a previous position at the Brookings Institution, Mr. Campbell co-authored *The Iraq Index* and established *The Afghanistan Index* and *The Pakistan Index* projects. Mr. Campbell's work has been published in the *New York Times*, the *Wall Street Journal*, the *Harvard International Review*, and the *Journal of Military History*. Mr. Campbell, who is currently a PhD candidate in the Department of War Studies at King's College London, holds a master's degree in international affairs from Catholic University and a bachelor's degree from Amherst College in political science and German.

JAMES R. HOLMES is associate professor of strategy at the Naval War College and co-author, along with Toshi Yoshihara, of *Red Star over the Pacific: China's Rise and the Challenge to U.S. Maritime Strategy* (2010). Professor Holmes is a graduate of Vanderbilt University, Salve Regina University, the Naval War College, Providence College, and the Fletcher School of Law and Diplomacy at Tufts University.

ROBERT JOHNSON is the deputy director of the Oxford Changing Character of War Program, and lecturer in the history of war at the University of Oxford, UK. His primary research interests are conflicts of the Middle East, Iran, Afghanistan, and Pakistan, including conventional operations, war by proxy, insurgency and counterinsurgency, intelligence, and strategy. He teaches more broadly on the history of war and military history in the twentieth century, but has given papers on Britain's strategic approach to the Persian Gulf in the nineteenth century, the Western strategic responses to the Iran-Iraq War in the waters of the Gulf, and on the current problems of containing Iran in an era of asymmetrical warfare. He has published a number of books and articles and is the author of *The Iran-Iraq War* (2010), *Oil, Islam, and Conflict* (2008), *Spying for Empire: The Great Game in Central and South Asia, 1757–1947* (2006), and *The Afghan Way of War* (2011).

CLIVE JONES is Professor of Middle East Studies and International Politics at the University of Leeds, UK, where he specializes in the Arab–Israeli conflict and Gulf security. His publications include *Britain and the Yemen Civil War* (2004), *Soviet Jewish Aliyah, 1989–92* (1996) with Emma Murphy, *Israel: Challenges to Democracy, Identity, and the State* (2002), and is co-editor with Ami Pedahzur of *The al-Aqsa Intifada: Between Terrorism and Civil War* (2005) and with Sergio Catignani, *Israel and the Hizbollah: An Asymmetric Conflict in Historical and Comparative Perspective* (2010).

FRANK L. JONES is Professor of Security Studies at the U.S. Army War College in Carlisle, Pennsylvania, where he holds the General Dwight D. Eisenhower Chair in National Security. Previously, he was a career member of the Senior Executive Service in the Office of the Secretary of Defense where he served in a number of high-level positions, including Deputy Assistant Secretary of Defense for Special Operations Policy and Support, before retiring in 2006. At the War College, he teaches courses in the theory of war and strategy, for which he is the course director; U.S. national security policy and strategy; and homeland security. He is the author of several book chapters and articles on topics such as defense policy making, terrorism, counterinsurgency, and maritime security.

SAUL KELLY is a reader in international history in the Defence Studies Department of King's College, London, at the Joint Services Command and Staff College, Shrivenham, UK. He has published a number of books and articles on aspects of British policy in the Middle East. His latest book is *War and Politics in the Desert* (2010).

VIRGINIA LUNSFORD is an associate professor at the U.S. Naval Academy in Annapolis, Maryland. She is a specialist in maritime history, especially the history of piracy and privateering; the history of early-modern Europe; and the history of the Netherlands. Professor Lunsford holds a PhD and an MA in history from Harvard University. She is the author of *Piracy and Privateering in the Golden Age Netherlands* (2005).

JEFFREY R. MACRIS is a Permanent Military Professor in the History Department at the U.S. Naval Academy in Annapolis, Maryland. He holds an MA and a PhD in Middle East Studies from Johns Hopkins University's School of Advanced International Studies, as well as a linguist certificate in Arabic. A resident of the Persian Gulf for several years, he is the author of *The Politics and Security of the Gulf: Anglo-American Hegemony and the Shaping of a Region* (2010).

RUDI MATTHEE is a professor at the University of Delaware where he teaches Middle Eastern history with a research focus on early modern Iran and the Persian Gulf. He received his PhD from the University of California, Los Angeles. He has authored *The Politics of Trade in Safavid Iran: Silk for Silver, 1600–1730* (1999); *The Pursuit of Pleasure: Drugs and Stimulants in Iranian History, 1500–1900* (2005); and *Persia in Crisis: The Decline of the Safavids and the Fall of Isfahan* (2012). He co-edited, with Beth Baron, *Iran and Beyond: Essays in Honor of Nikki R. Keddie* (2000); with Nikki Keddie, *Iran and the Surrounding World, 1501–2001: Interactions in Culture and Cultural Politics* (2002); and with Jorge Flores, *Portugal, the Persian Gulf, and Safavid Persia* (2011). Professor Matthee has served as the president of the Association for the Study of Persianate Societies (2009–11), and has received the Albert Hourani Book Prize (2006) from the Middle East Studies Association of North America, and the Said Sirjani Book Prize (2004–5) from the International Society for Iranian Studies.

TORE T. PETERSEN is professor of international and American diplomatic history at the Norwegian University of Science and Technology. He is the author of *The Middle East between the Great Powers: Anglo-American Conflict and Cooperation, 1952–7* (2000); *The Decline of the Anglo-American Middle East, 1961–1969: A Willing Retreat* (2006); and *Richard Nixon, Great Britain, and the Anglo-American Alignment in the Persian Gulf and Arabian Peninsula: Making Allies out of Clients* (2009).

BEN SIMPFENDORFER is managing director of Silk Road Associates, an economic and political consultancy based in Hong Kong with a specific focus on trade and investment links between Asia and the Middle East. He is author of *The New Silk Road: How a Rising Arab World is Turning Away from the West and Rediscovering China* (2009). He was previously the chief China economist at the Royal Bank of Scotland and the senior China economist at J. P. Morgan. He has lived in Beijing, Beirut, and Damascus, and is currently based in Hong Kong. He speaks Arabic and Chinese, and holds an MSc degree from the School of Oriental and African Studies, London University.

TOSHI YOSHIHARA is a professor in the Strategy and Policy Department at the U.S. Naval War College in Newport, Rhode Island, where he holds the John A. van Beuren Chair of Asia-Pacific Studies. Previously, he was a visiting professor in the Strategy Department at the Air War College. He is co-author of *Red Star over the Pacific: China's Rise and the Challenge to U.S. Maritime Strategy* (2010), *Indian Naval Strategy in the Twenty-first Century* (2009), and *Chinese Naval Strategy in the Twenty-first Century: The Turn to Mahan* (2008). He is also co-editor of *Asia Looks Seaward: Power and Maritime Strategy* (2008). His articles on maritime issues and naval strategy have appeared in *Journal of Strategic Studies, Comparative Strategy, Orbis, Naval War College Review, American Interest,* and *Joint Forces Quarterly.*

INDEX

223